IMAGES
of America

NEW PALTZ REVISITED

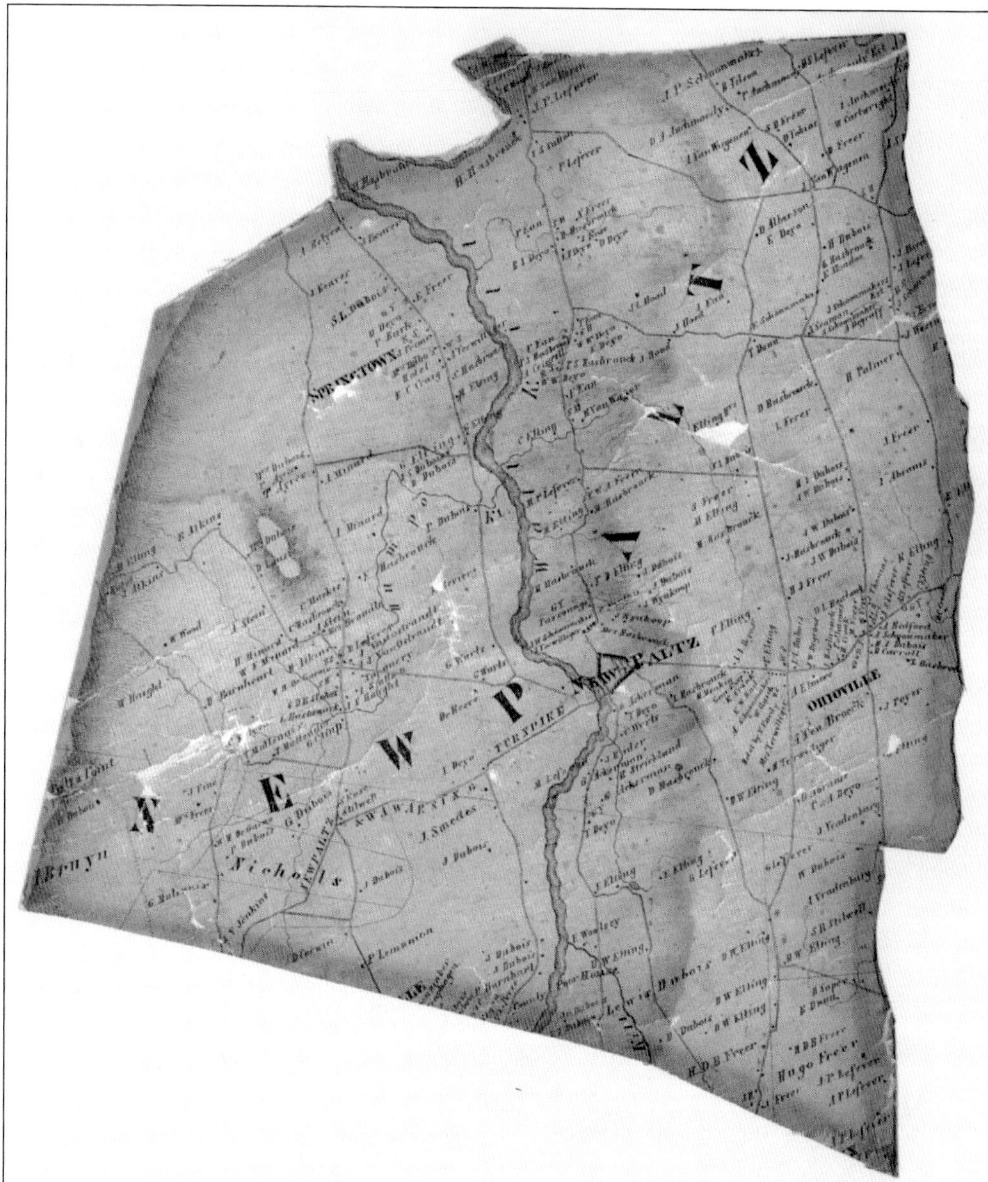

This map shows the town of New Paltz in 1858. (Courtesy Haviland-Heidgerd Historical Collection.)

ON THE COVER: Members of the New Paltz High School class of 1927 pose outside their soon-to-be alma mater on June 23, 1927. The class, 30 in number, was the largest in the history of New Paltz High School up to that year. (Courtesy of Elaine Kniffen.)

IMAGES of America

NEW PALTZ REVISITED

Carol A. Johnson

ARCADIA PUBLISHING

ISBN 978-0-7385-7318-2

Published by Arcadia Publishing
Charleston, South Carolina

Printed in the United States of America

Library of Congress Control Number: 2009943081

For all general information contact Arcadia Publishing at:
Telephone 843-853-2070
Fax 843-853-0044
E-mail sales@arcadiapublishing.com
For customer service and orders:
Toll-Free 1-888-313-2665

Visit us on the Internet at www.arcadiapublishing.com

This book is dedicated to my husband, Walter J. Tanczos.

Contents

Acknowledgments

Since the Haviland-Heidgerd Historical Collection was founded in 1965, the staff and volunteers have contributed many hours to preserve the history of New Paltz. It is impossible to thank all of them individually, but without their hard work and their love of local history this book would not have been possible. The Haviland-Heidgerd Historical Collection at Elting Memorial Library's archives, photograph collection, and research resources offer a treasure trove of fascinating stories and information about our community's history. Unless otherwise noted, all images appearing in this book were provided by the Haviland-Heidgerd Historical Collection.

I also wish to thank the board of trustees of Elting Memorial Library and John Giralico, the library's director. I thank Julie O'Connor for offering to edit my captions. I also need to thank my sisters, Linda Ackert and Donna Ziegler, and my friend Karen Skillman for keeping my feet on the ground; all the people who furnished images for this publication; Rosalie Nelson and Jason Capron for helping me at work; and especially Susan Stessin-Cohn, who is a computer genius. Finally, thanks to Marion Ryan, whose friendship and guidance I missed dearly.

INTRODUCTION

On May 26, 1677, men of Huguenot descent purchased nearly 40,000 acres of land that would become New Paltz from local Native Americans, referred to as Esopus Sachems. This agreement was confirmed by Gov. Edmund Andros four months later. The four corners of this patent were Moggonck (now Mohonk); Juffrou's Hook (the point by the Hudson River where the town line between Lloyd and Marlborough strikes the river); Rapoos (Pell's Island in the Hudson); and Tower-a-Toque (a point of white rocks in the Shawangunks behind the Tillson Estates development). The New Paltz patent consisted of all of the present town of Lloyd, about two-thirds of New Paltz, one-third of Esopus, and one-fourth of Rosendale.

The 12 men associated with the earliest settlement of New Paltz are called the patentees. They are Louis DuBois (1626–1696), Abraham DuBois (1657–1731), Isaac DuBois (1659–1690), Antoine Crispell (1635–1707), Christian Deyo (c. 1610–1676), Pierre Deyo (1646–1700), Hugo Freer (d. 1698), Abraham Hasbrouck (c. 1650–1717), Jean Hasbrouck (c. 1645–1714), Simon LeFevre (c. 1640–1690), Andries LeFevre (1636–c. 1703), and Louis Bevier (c. 1647–1720). Their families were a part of the group of French Protestants who fled to Die Pfalz during the religious persecutions of Louis XIV in the 17th century. New Paltz derives its name from their place of refuge, located in the Palatinate region of Germany along the Rhine River near Mannheim. Another man, Jan Eltinge, signed the treaty made by the New Paltz Huguenots and the natives as one of the witnesses. His son Roelif married Sarah DuBois, the daughter of Louis DuBois, the patentee, and settled here in 1720.

The legacy of these men continues in the daily lives of the residents of New Paltz today. Students attending the state university might live in Crispell or Deyo Hall, eat in Hasbrouck Dining Hall or work out in the Elting Gymnasium. Residents can live on Manheim Boulevard or DuBois Road, play ball at Hasbrouck Park, cheer on the "Hugies" at school, attend church on Huguenot Street, or borrow a book from the Elting Memorial Library.

The homes of the children and grandchildren of these men are the oldest in New Paltz. The site of seven original stone houses, Huguenot Street, is a National Historic Landmark. The founding of New Paltz was celebrated for generations with a pageant depicting the patentees and their families arriving in the spring of 1678 from Kingston. The Huguenots arrived in three carts on the west side of the Wallkill River. The site is now called "the Flats," but is historically referred to as "Tri-Cor," meaning "three carts." Stone House Day, now called the Colonial Street Festival, continues to honor the early settlers and their way of life.

The town of New Paltz was incorporated in 1785, more than a century after the original Huguenot families arrived. The community was governed by a corporation of 12 men called the Duzine, referring to the 12 men who acquired the patent (*douze* is French for 12). The land, augmented by other large land grants to the south, was eventually divided into large parcels and distributed among the 12 patentees, their relatives, and a few friends, with some pieces stretching from the Wallkill River to the Hudson River. The "Twelve Men" continued to be elected until about 1820. In 1820, there were fewer than 250 people living in what is now the village of New Paltz, but by 1887, the place was booming. About 300 people had moved to town since the 1880 census reported 493 village residents. There was a now a need for sidewalks, streetlights, and fire protection. The village of New Paltz was incorporated within the town in 1887, and there have been two separate forms of government ever since. Away from the village proper are the diverse hamlets of Ohioville, Springtown, Plutarch, and Butterville. Each hamlet had its own school district, church, post office, and unique individuals that all have a story of their own.

Education has always been one of the main concerns of the community. A Huguenot named Jean Cottin was hired as the first schoolmaster in 1689. Lessons were first taught in French, then Dutch, and finally English. Classes were first held in a church made of logs and then the 1717 stone church on Huguenot Street. The village schoolhouse was built on North Front Street in 1812. It was constructed with stones from a church that was torn down in 1773 and replaced with a larger edifice. This building served as the public school building to 1874. The Classical School occupied the upper story of this building from 1828 to 1833. For $25, students were given an introduction to Greek and Latin to prepare them for university.

In 1833, the community saw the establishment of the private New Paltz Academy, which served as a training ground for teachers. Located on the banks of the Wallkill, the school offered a two-year program that qualified graduates to teach in elementary schools and a three-year program that prepared them to teach high school. The academy also provided a high school education for the children of New Paltz and some students from surrounding communities. One-room schoolhouses dotted the countryside, and a bigger schoolhouse was built for the children of the village on Church Street in 1874. After the academy was destroyed by fire, a new building was constructed, and the New Paltz Normal School was established. The forerunner of the present State University of New York at New Paltz opened on February 15, 1886. Besides teachers in training, the student body included both elementary and secondary students.

The State University of New York at New Paltz today encompasses 257 acres in the village. It consists of the Schools of Education; Fine and Performing Arts; Business, Science, and Engineering; and the College of Liberal Arts and Sciences. From the 10 teachers and 89 students under the direction of Dr. Eugene Bouton, the college has grown to an enrollment of nearly 8,000, with 325 full-time faculty.

In 1906, the biggest fire in town history destroyed the normal school building along the river, and a new, larger building was opened in 1909. "Old Main" was home to the schoolchildren of New Paltz and teachers in training until a new high school was built on South Manheim Boulevard in 1931. A school of practice (now the van den Berg Learning Center) was built in 1932 to house the elementary students. A large addition to the high school in the 1950s enabled children attending rural one-room schoolhouses to attend school in a centralized location. In 1962 and 1972, elementary schools were added to the school district, and in 1968, a large high school was built on South Putt Corners Road.

Farmers sent their produce to market first by horse and wagon on the New Paltz Turnpike, later by rail on the Wallkill Valley Railroad, and now by truck on the New York State Thruway. The New Paltz area is a true four-season recreational paradise. In addition to natural beauty and a creative intellectual climate stimulated by the college, the town's proximity to New York City contributes to making it an enduring place to live.

One

The Huguenots and Huguenot Street

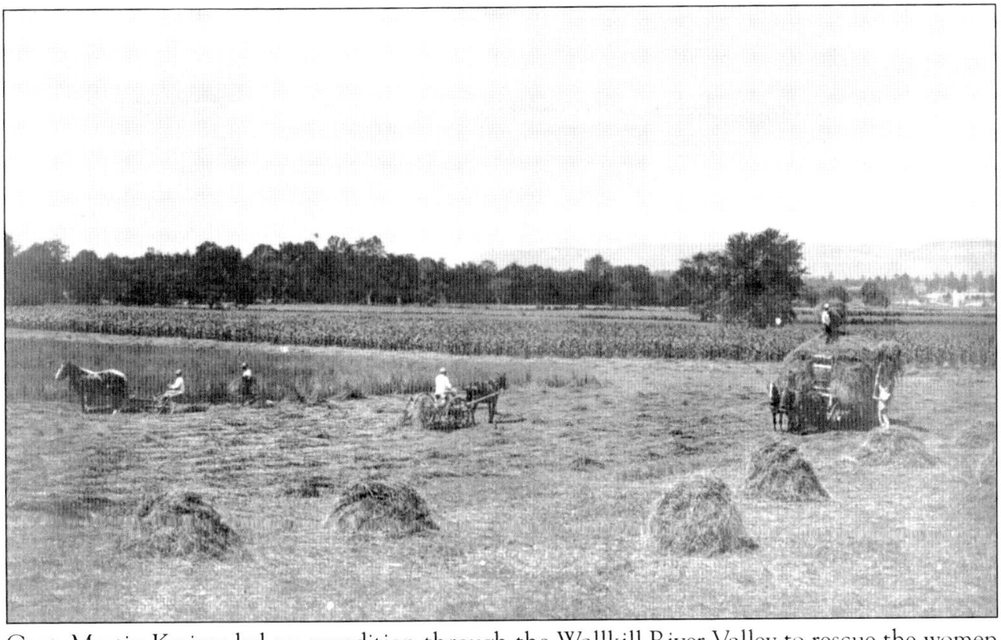

Capt. Martin Kreiger led an expedition through the Wallkill River Valley to rescue the women and children captured by the Esopus tribe in 1663. Louis DuBois was a part of this expedition. The recollections that DuBois had of these fertile lowlands led him to purchase the land in 1677, along with his sons Abraham and Isaac, Christian Deyo and his son Pierre, brothers Jean and Abraham Hasbrouck, brothers Simon and Andries LeFevre, Antoine Crispell, Louis Bevier, and Hugo Freer.

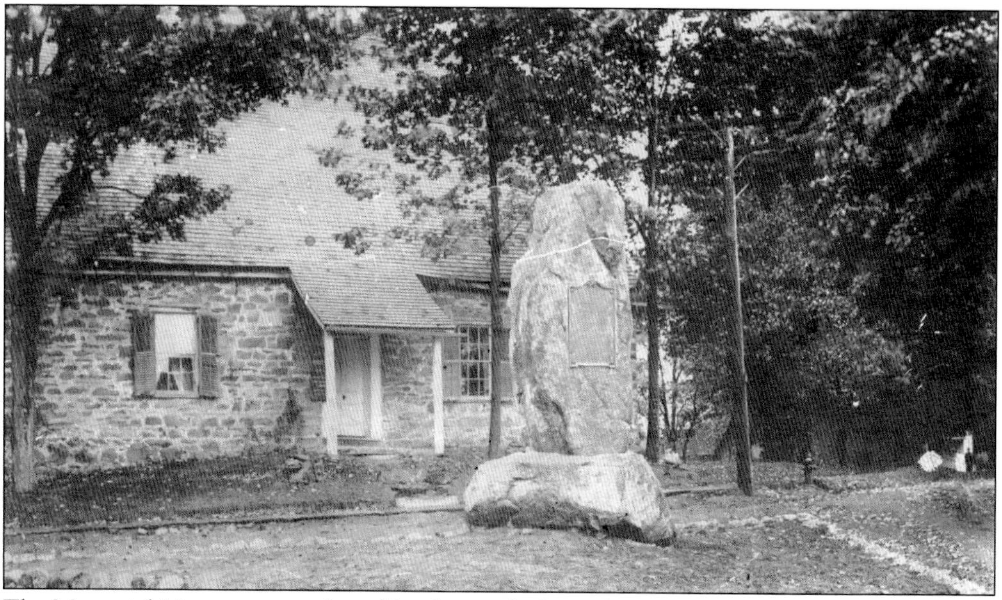

The Memorial House was purchased by the newly formed Huguenot, Patriotic, Historical, and Monumental Society of New Paltz in 1898. It was to serve as a place to house the documents, papers, and relics concerning the early settlers of New Paltz. A monument was erected in front of the house to honor the patentees in 1908. The monument's 12-ton shaft stands 11 feet tall, measuring 4 feet wide and 3 feet deep. (Photograph by H. L. Schultz.)

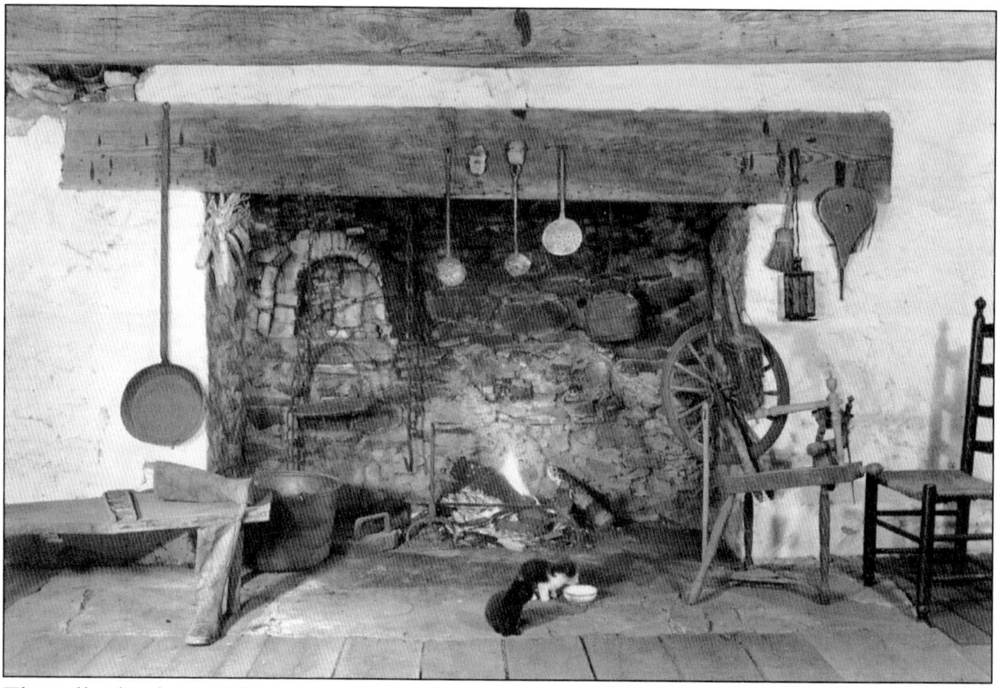

The cellar kitchen of the Bevier-Elting House and its subcellar have been the subject of great speculation. One long-told tale was that the subcellar provided access to a tunnel leading under the street to the Old Fort. Another rumor was that it was used to hide slaves as a part of the Underground Railroad. (Photograph by Erma DeWitt.)

Lanetta Elting DuBois owned the Bevier-Elting House in the summer of 1943, when she received some surprise visitors. Her cousin, Bob Lasher, had been asked to show U.S. president Franklin Roosevelt, Crown Princess Märtha of Norway, and others the old houses. When Lasher told DuBois who was outside, she said, "Oh, yes, Bobby—Stalin and Churchill too, I suppose." (Photograph by Erma DeWitt.)

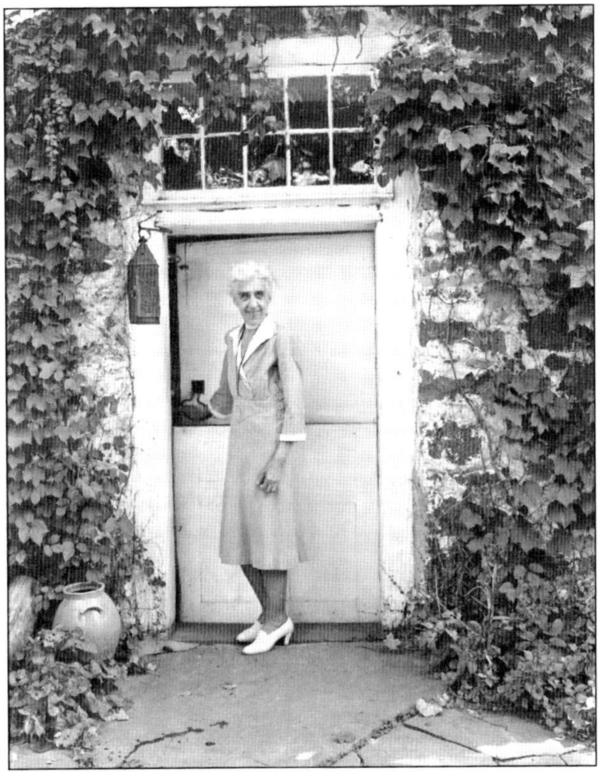

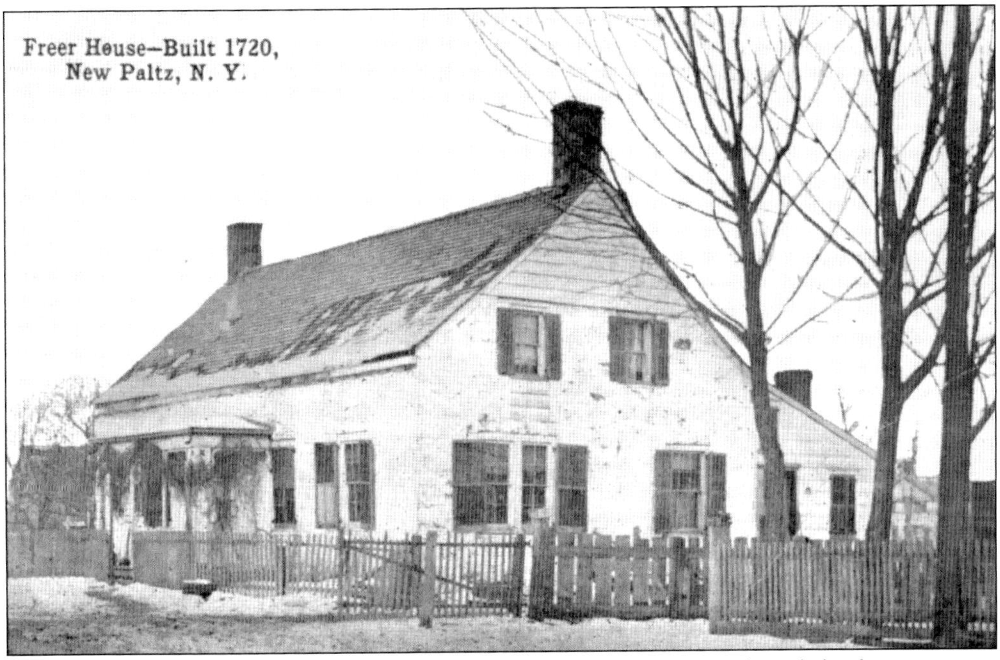

Moses Freer, a blacksmith, lived in the Freer House in the 1830s. He forged the first axes ever made in Ulster County. He also invented an easy-riding wagon spring, which earned him a large sum of money. He sold his house and went to Ohio to live for a few years but came back and settled in the little hamlet that he later named Ohioville.

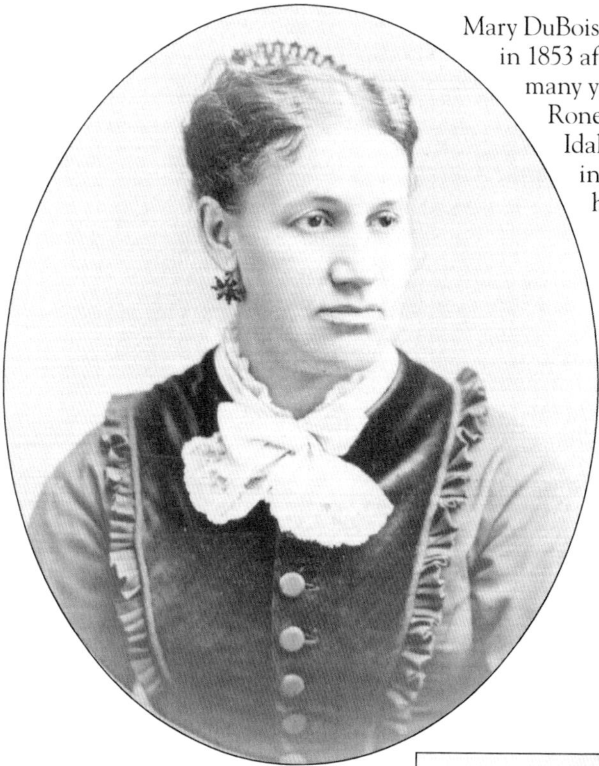

Mary DuBois (1838–1902) inherited the DuBois Fort in 1853 after her father, Daniel, died. Mary spent many years away from New Paltz. She married Ronello William Berry and lived in Boise, Idaho. After the death of her son, Arthur, in 1883, she returned to New Paltz with her two daughters, Marie and Louise. Ronello brought divorce proceedings against Mary for desertion in 1891. Mary died in her ancestral home on January 14, 1902.

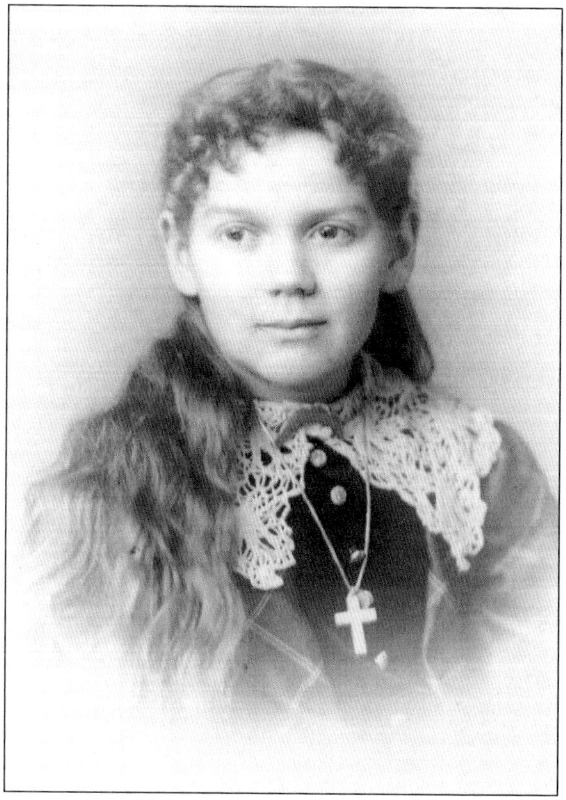

Mary's daughter Louise DuBois Berry (1879–1966) was the last of the DuBois line to own the home. Louise attended the New Paltz Normal School and married Dr. J. Clarence Dingman in 1908. After her marriage, she never lived in the home again. She rented the fort to various tenants, and in the 1930s, it became first a tearoom and then a restaurant.

Although married in Gardiner in April 1951, Rita Murphy and Paul Donahue chose to hold their wedding reception at the Old Fort Restaurant. Wedding receptions, engagement parties, and anniversaries were celebrated inside the restaurant or on the lawn from 1938 to 1990. Elsie Oates was the proprietor until her death in 1981. Alice Crans, best known for her home-style cooking, then took over the business. (Courtesy of Rita Donahue.)

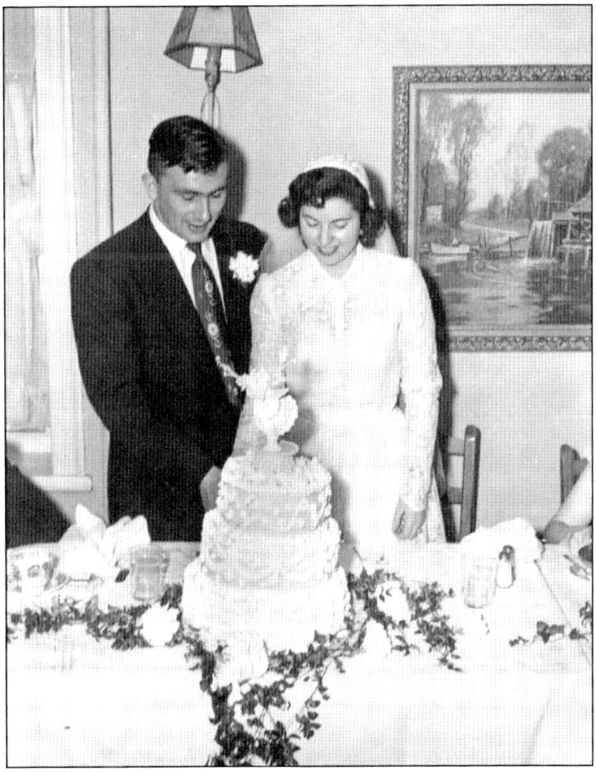

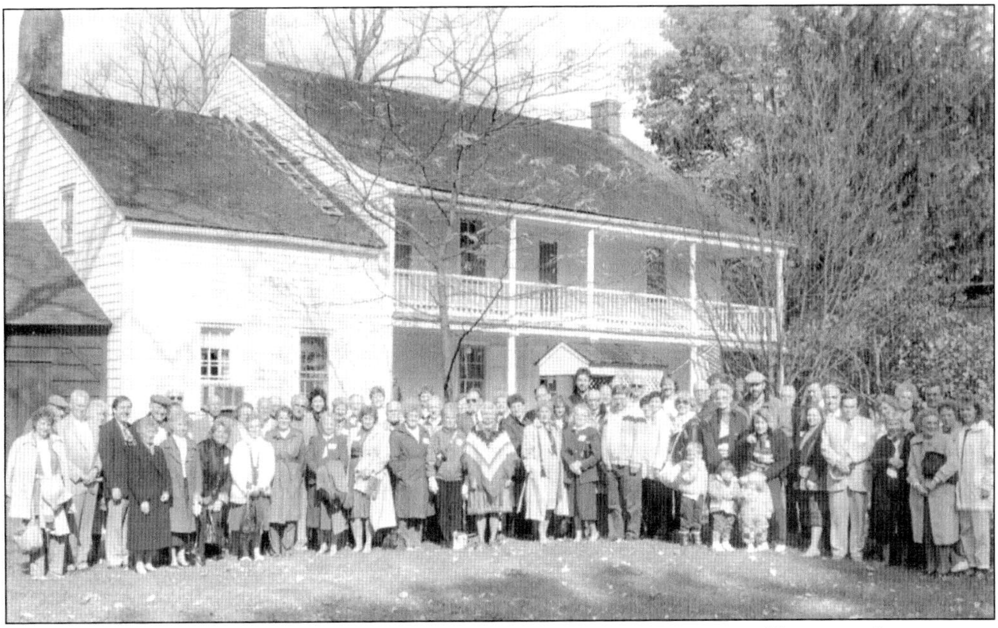

Descendants of the patentee families have formed family associations and have yearly reunions. The DuBois Family Association was formed in 1966 to purchase and preserve the DuBois Fort. The fort was purchased with funds raised by the family association and was given to the Huguenot Historical Society in 1968. Members of the DuBois family congregated in front of their ancestral home for this picture, taken on October 21, 1989.

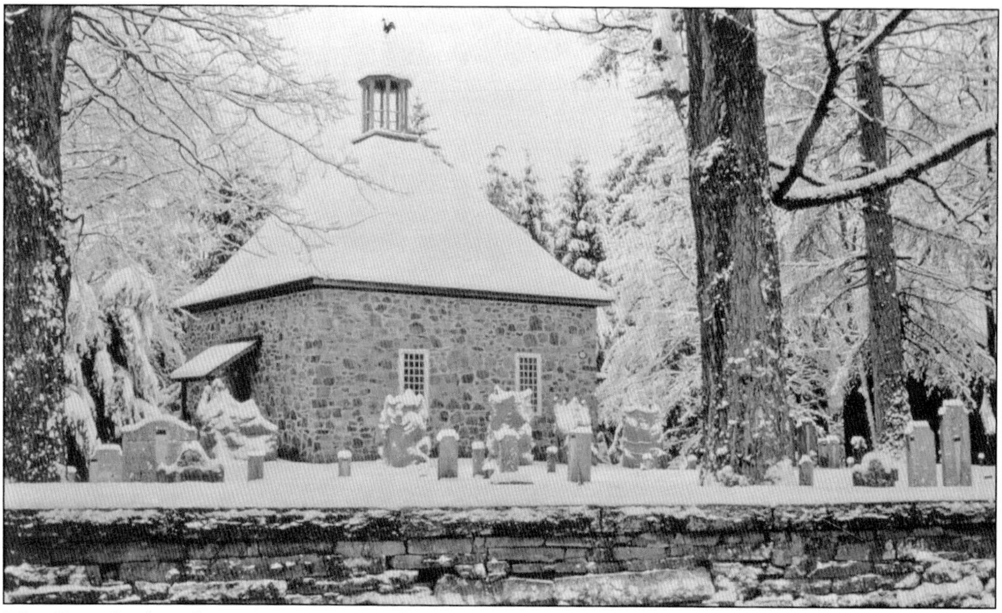

The French church was reconstructed in 1972 near the site of an earlier church built in 1717. The church is located in the old Huguenot cemetery where all the patentees are buried except Antoine Crispell and Louis DuBois. The earliest tombstone is that of patentee Andries LeFevre, who died in 1714. The last burial in the cemetery was Elizabeth Westbrook, the widow of Isaiah Hasbrouck, who died in 1864. (Photograph by Dennis O'Keefe.)

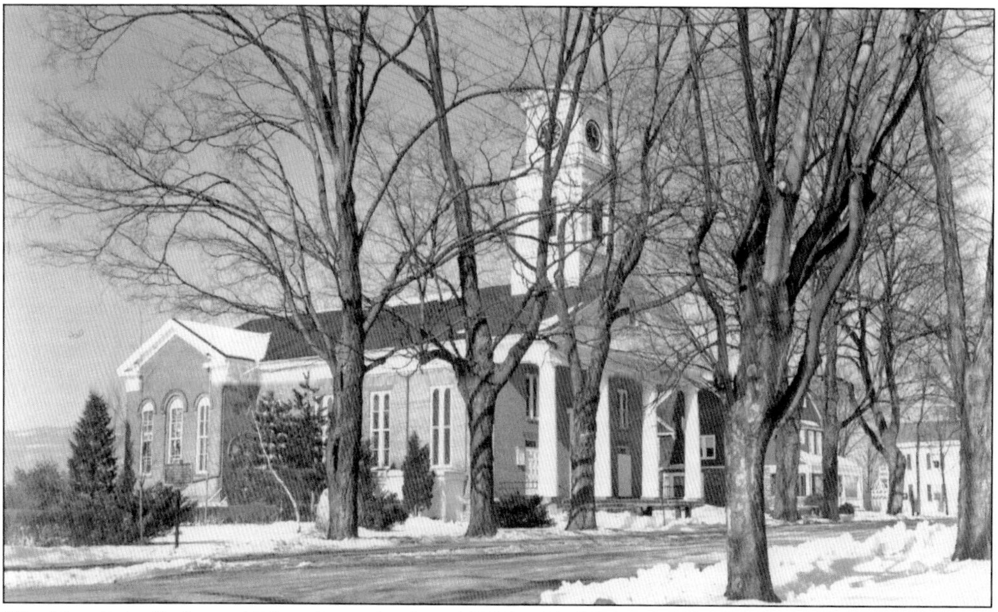

The New Paltz Reformed Church was built in 1839 by Abel Saxton. The congregation of the church had worshipped in three earlier structures, including a 1717 church that has been reconstructed on Huguenot Street. The first church was made of logs and was replaced by the 1717 stone church. The 1717 church served the congregation until being dismantled in 1772. A boulder now stands near where the 1772 church was located, immediately to the south of the present church. (Photograph by Erma DeWitt.)

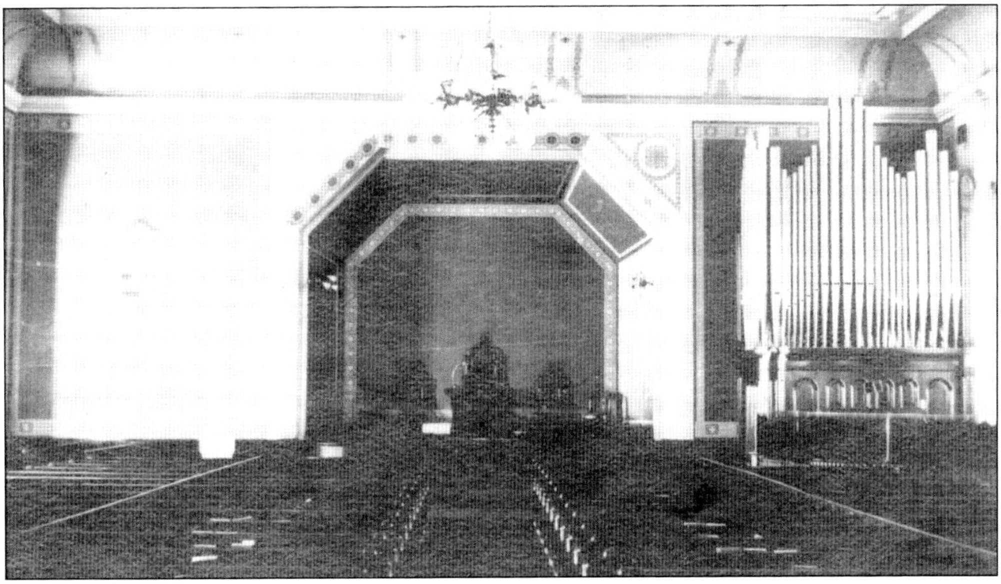

The 11,000-pound, 24-foot-tall pipe organ (pictured here on the right side of the church) was installed in 1892. It was relocated to St. Paul Evangelical Lutheran Church on Hasbrouck Avenue in Kingston, New York, in 1928. The Kern Memorial United Methodist Church in Oak Ridge, Tennessee, had the organ moved from Kingston and fully restored in 2006.

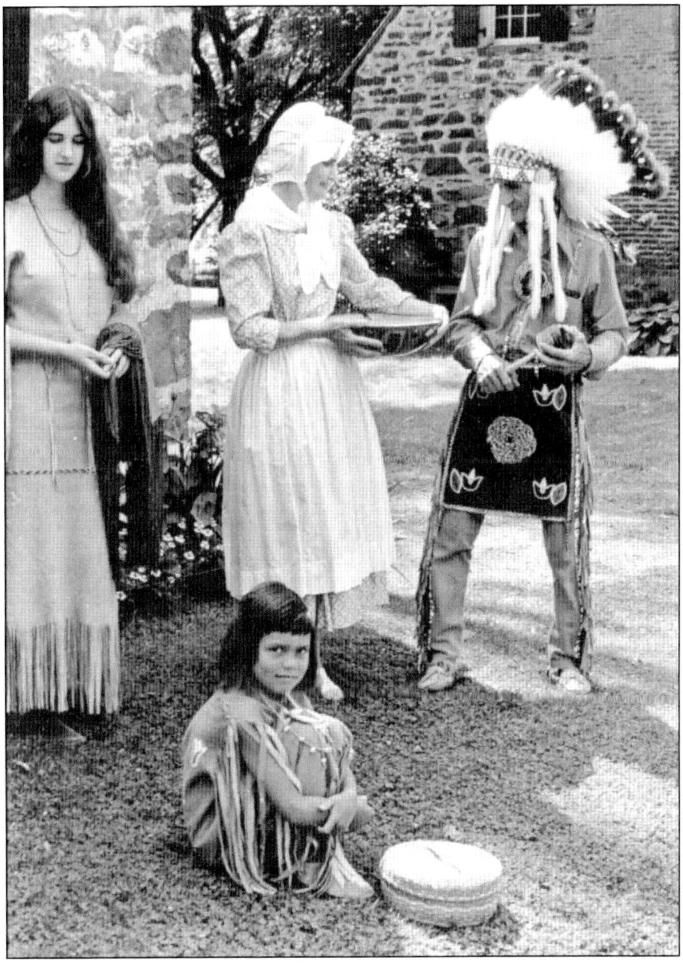

The first Stone House Day was held on August 5, 1950. Sponsored by the Reformed church, visitors would find themselves in the 18th century as they were guided through the old stone houses by villagers dressed in treasured period heirlooms. In 1975, the Association of Native Americans cosponsored the event, and the theme was "Two Cultures in Harmony." (Courtesy of the New Paltz Reformed Church.)

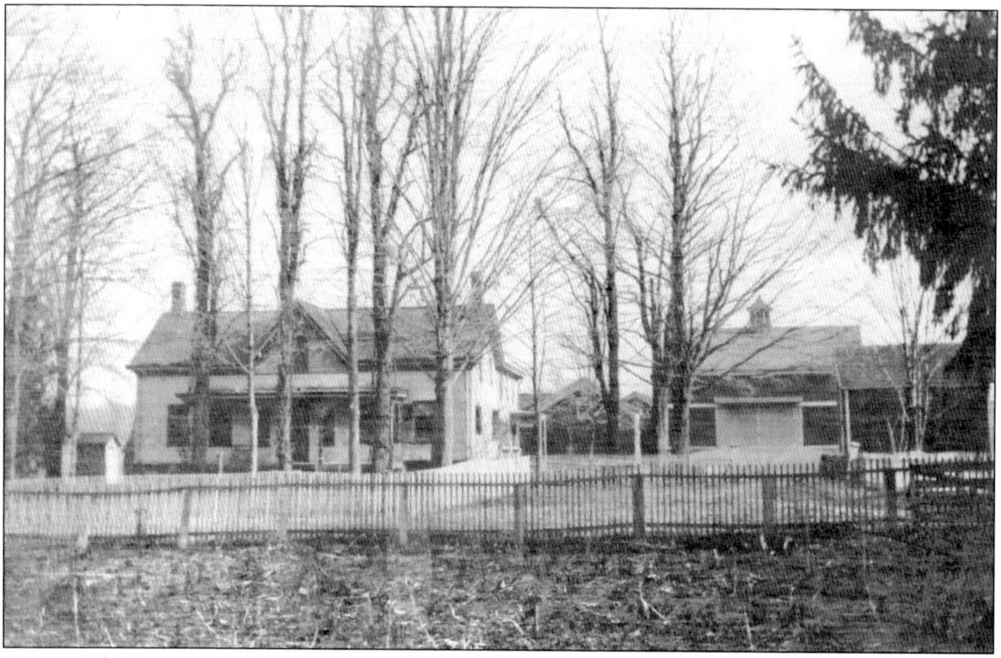

Rev. Stephen Goetschius was the minister of the Reformed church from 1775 to 1796. It was during his pastorate that his sermons switched from Dutch to English. His wife was Elizabeth DuBois. He built this home at 162 Huguenot Street in 1791. In 1796, the home was purchased by the Elting family, and it remained in their possession until 1961.

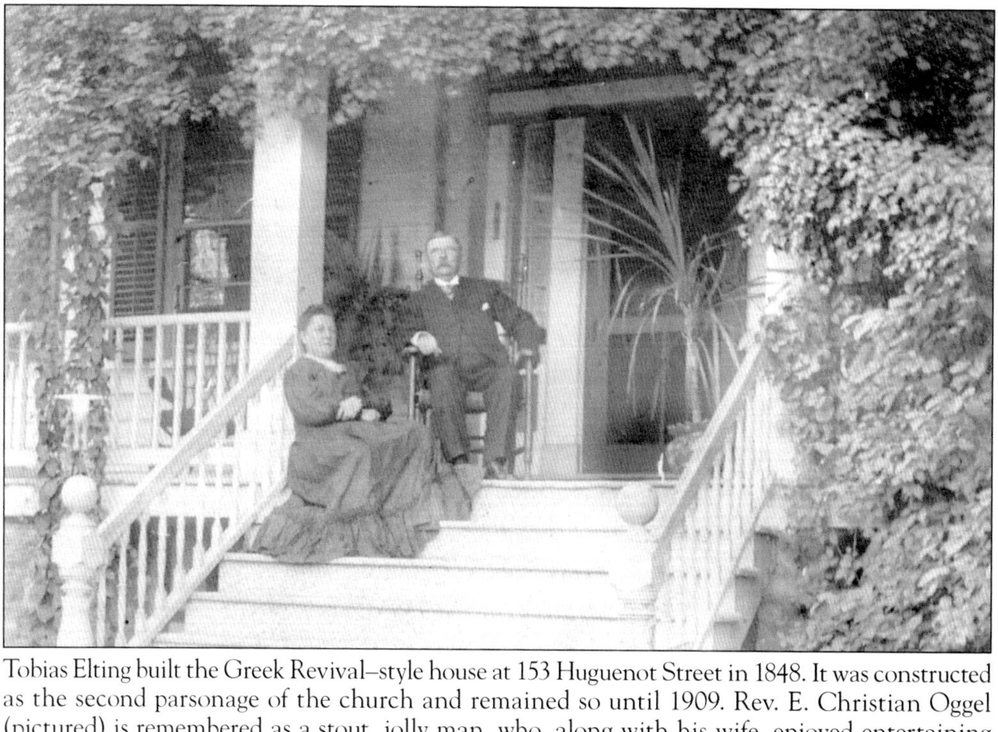

Tobias Elting built the Greek Revival–style house at 153 Huguenot Street in 1848. It was constructed as the second parsonage of the church and remained so until 1909. Rev. E. Christian Oggel (pictured) is remembered as a stout, jolly man, who, along with his wife, enjoyed entertaining church members at their home.

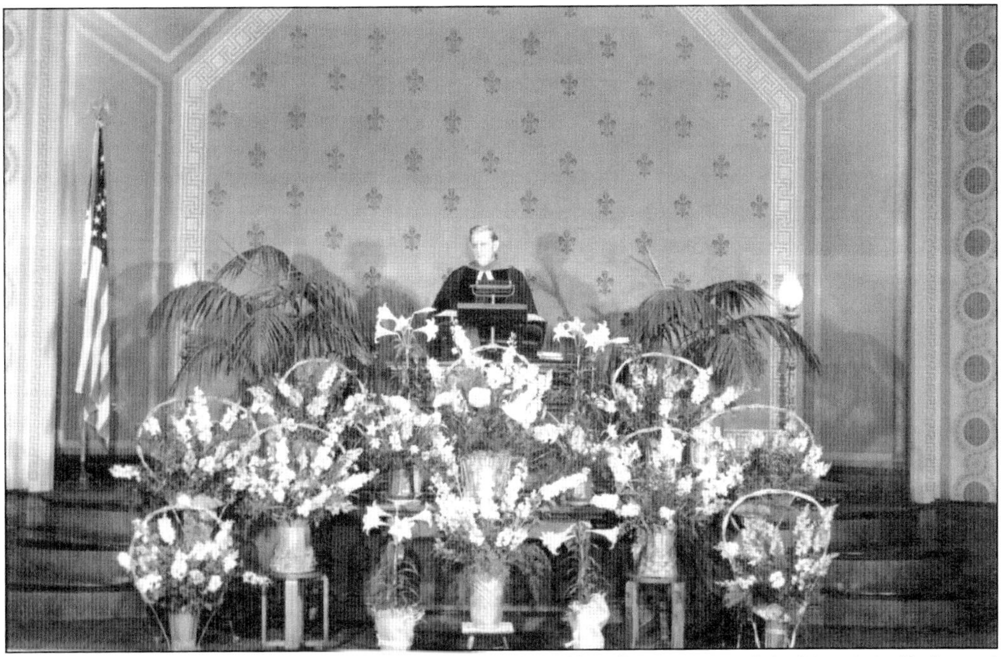

Rev. Gerret John Wullschleger (1903–1988) accepted a call to the ministry of the New Paltz Reformed Church and arrived in New Paltz in February 1931 with his wife and daughter, who were both named Nancy. Here he is giving an Easter Sunday sermon from the altar of the church. The dominie served for 38 years, retiring on January 1, 1969. (Courtesy of the New Paltz Reformed Church.)

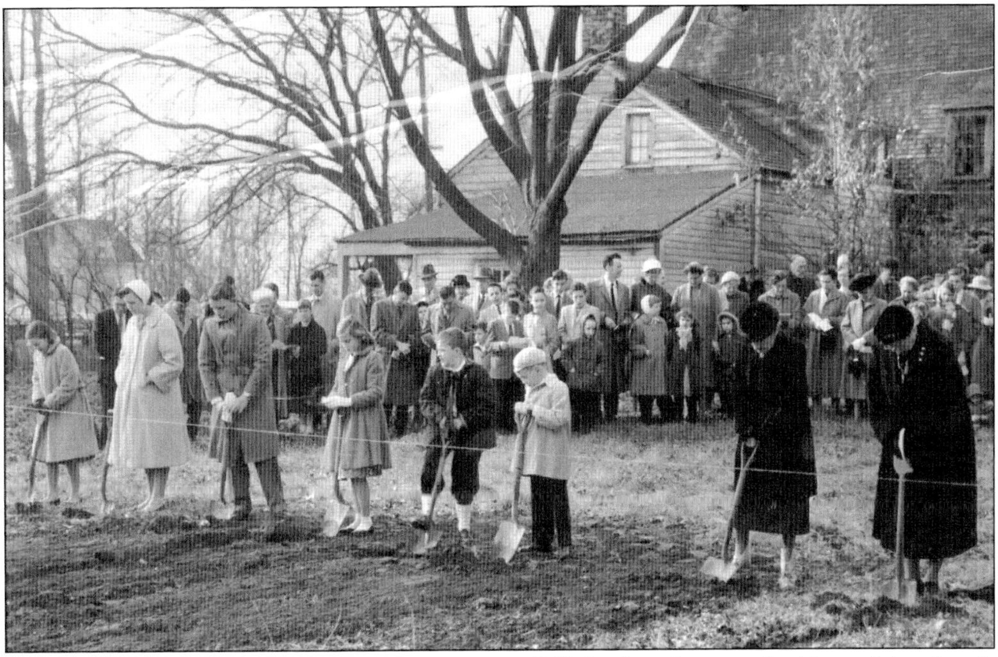

Ground was broken on Thanksgiving morning in 1957 for the education building of the church on land east of the Abraham Hasbrouck House. Named for Rev. Gerret Wullschleger, the building has housed the Huguenot Nursery School since February 1959. Today it is also the home of Twice Blessed, a thrift shop run by members of the church.

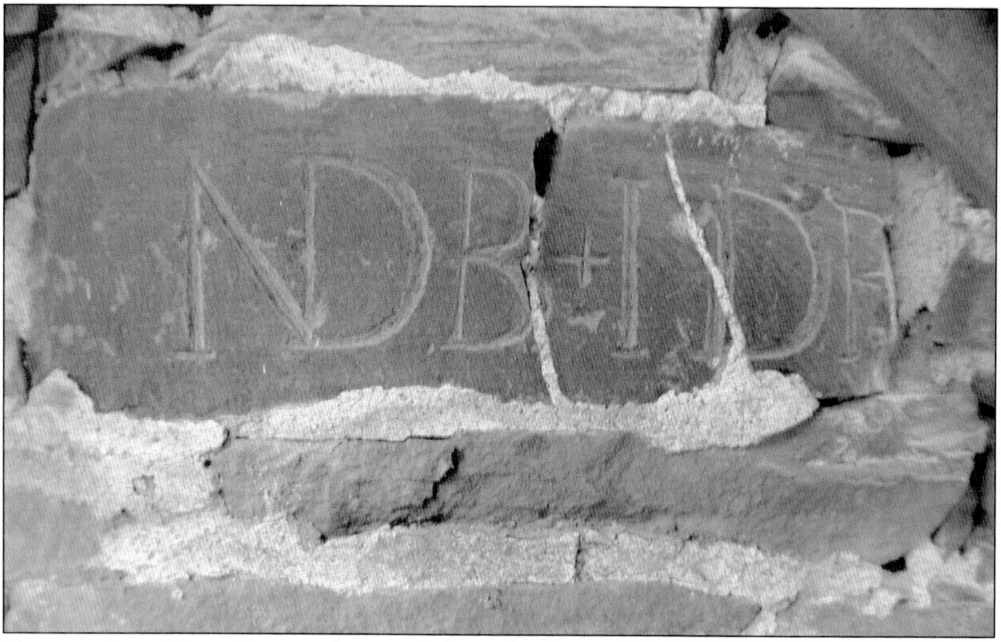

Huguenot Jean Cottin became the town's first schoolmaster in 1689. Lessons were taught in the settlement's early churches. New York passed an "Act for the Establishment of Common Schools" in 1812. Using stones from the 1717 church that was torn down in 1773, the first schoolhouse was constructed at 15 North Front Street. Pictured is an engraved stone in the exterior wall of the old schoolhouse. (Photograph by Julie O'Connor.)

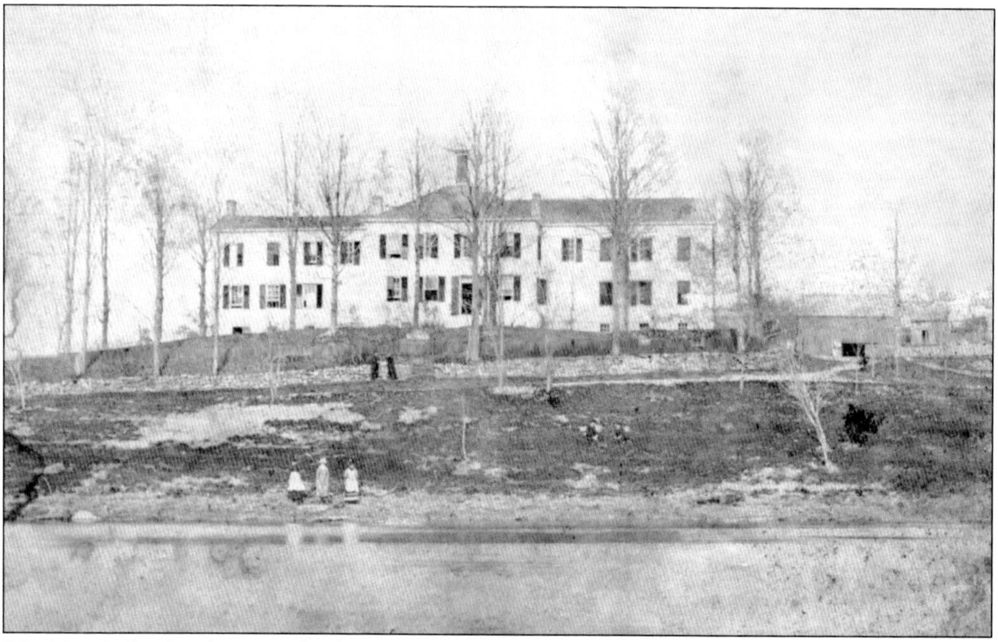

The New Paltz Academy was built on the banks of the Wallkill in 1833. It offered more advanced courses than what was taught in the common schools. For those who wanted to further their education at a university, it also offered Greek and Latin studies. The New Paltz Academy went up in flames on February 29, 1884.

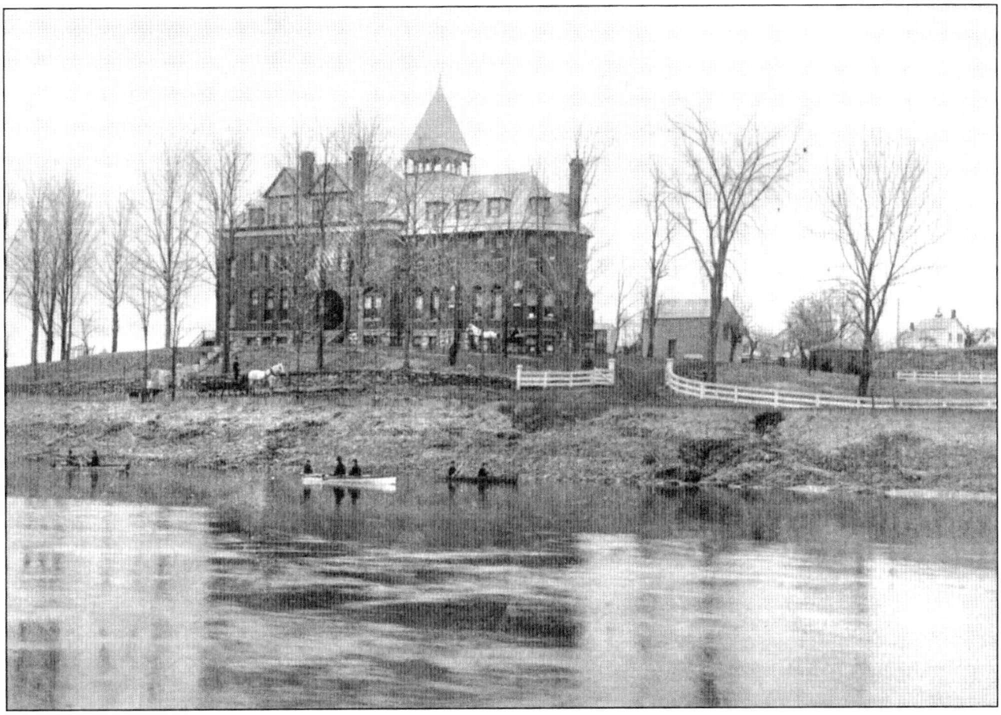

As early as 1866, local officials and community supporters wanted the New Paltz Academy to become a normal school for "the proper preparation of teachers." Ironically the state regents granted this request on March 20, 1885, after it had burned to the ground. The New Paltz Normal School, built on the site of the razed academy, opened on February 15, 1886.

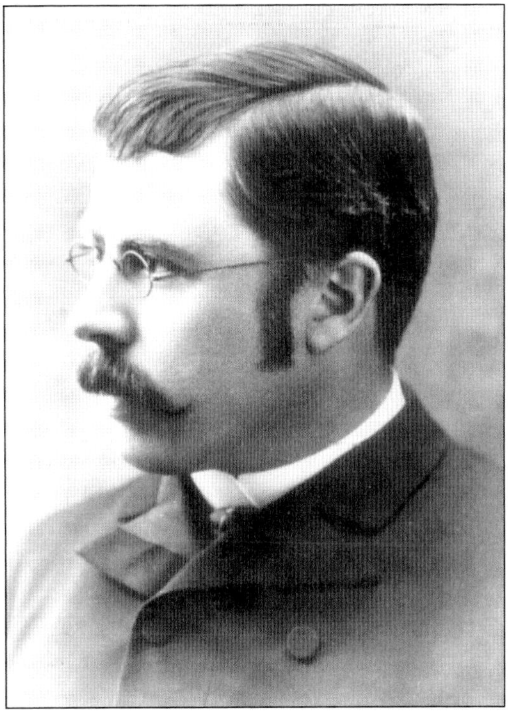

Dr. Eugene Bouton (pictured at right) was the first principal of the New Paltz Normal School. He held the post for two years, from 1886 to 1888. Frank S. Capen was the next principal, serving from 1888 to 1899. Myron T. Scudder was third, serving from 1899 to 1908. John C. Bliss was principal from 1908 to 1923. All of these men now have dormitories named in their honor on the State University of New York (SUNY)–New Paltz campus.

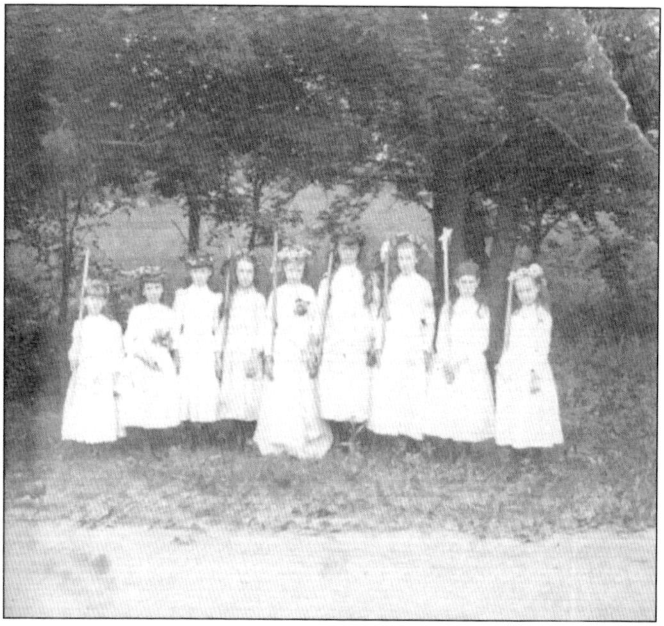

The New Paltz Normal School became the schoolhouse for the children of the village in 1889. Their teachers were students in the senior class, who were learning how to be teachers. Queen May Coe is shown here celebrating May Day with her attendants. Pictured from left to right are Susan Barlow, Bess Johnston, Ida Elmore, Emma Elting, May Coe, Lee Woolsey, Edna Moshier, Louise Capen, and Ida Kaiser.

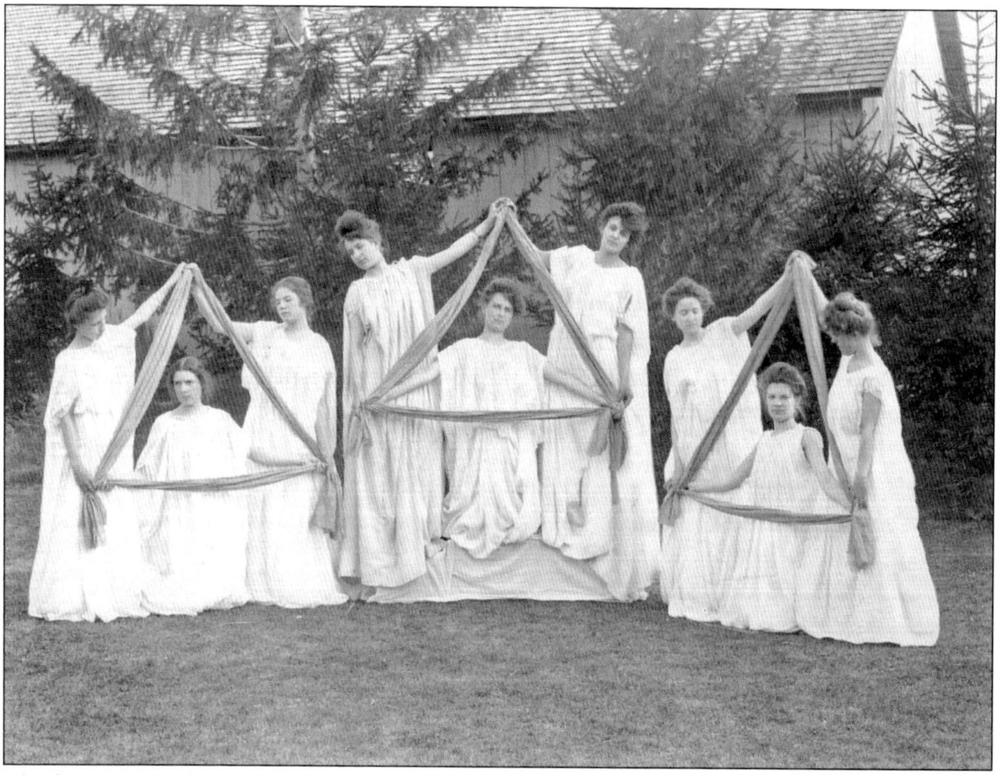

The first women's literary society at the school was founded as Phi Kappa Pi in 1888. In November 1896, the Thalia Literary Society was formed. In 1899, Phi Kappa Pi became Clio Sorority. Thalia had elected to "drink from the fountain of Arethusa" and became Arethusa Sorority. In this image, Mollie Irish (center) and her sisters from Arethusa are rehearsing for an upcoming theatrical event.

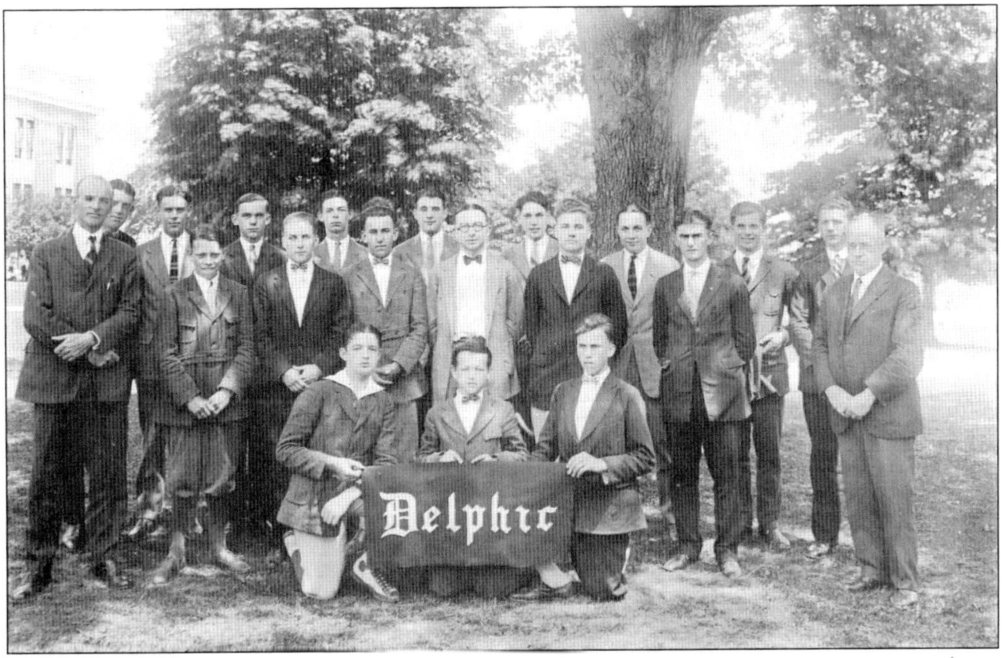

An early male student admitted, "We realize that the time of our cheering has sometimes been late, often we do not adjourn until the ghostly hour of ten; also we admit that the noise has been hideous." Two early men's groups met in the old normal school, and the meetings closed with yells and screams that woke up the village as the students made their way home. The two societies joined together and formed Delphic in 1899.

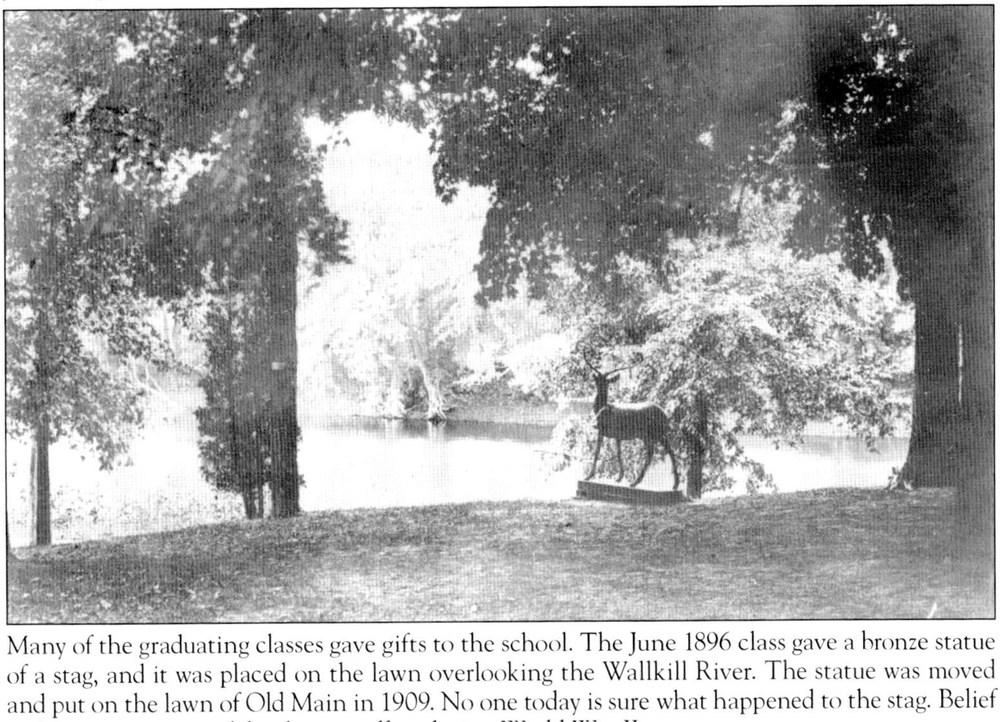

Many of the graduating classes gave gifts to the school. The June 1896 class gave a bronze statue of a stag, and it was placed on the lawn overlooking the Wallkill River. The statue was moved and put on the lawn of Old Main in 1909. No one today is sure what happened to the stag. Belief is that it was scrapped for the war effort during World War II.

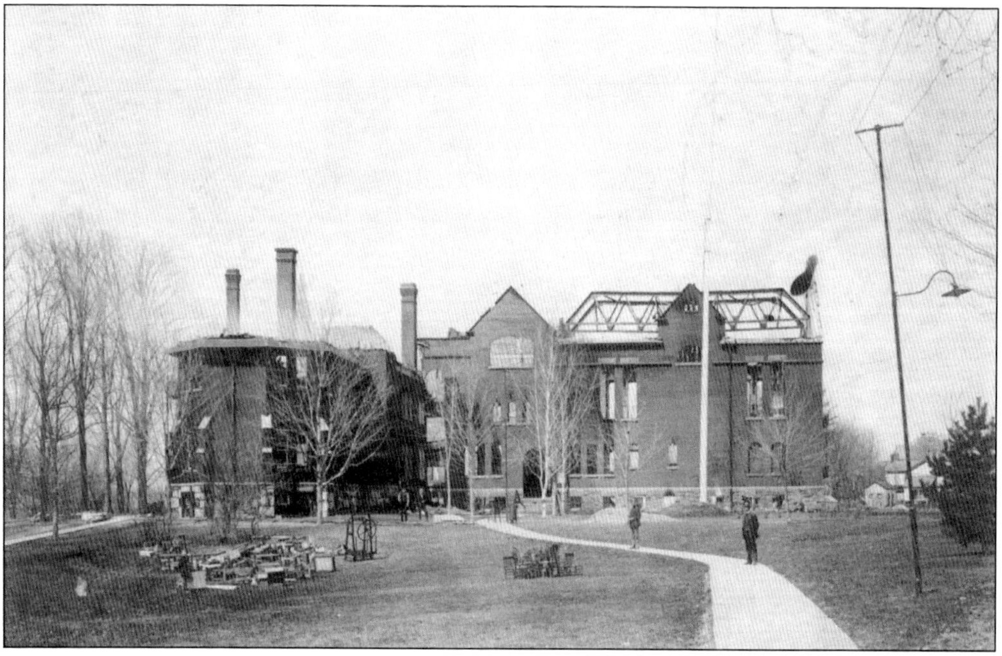

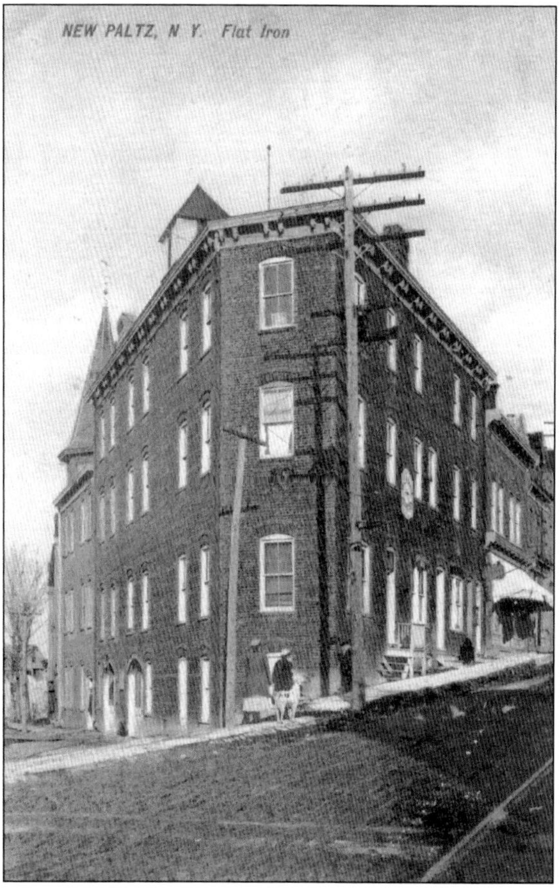

The biggest fire in the history of New Paltz occurred on the night of April 17, 1906. The school was closed for Easter, and necessary repairs were being made to the leaking water tank in the attic of the school. A lamp that a repairman was using exploded, and burning oil was sent flying in every direction. The building and most of its contents were totally destroyed.

Before the fire was even extinguished, principal Myron T. Scudder began to make arrangements to reopen the school. The students attended classes the next day in makeshift classrooms all over town. Many of the classes were held in Fireman's Hall. Built in 1893, the fire trucks were kept on the west side (Church Street side) of the building until 1950.

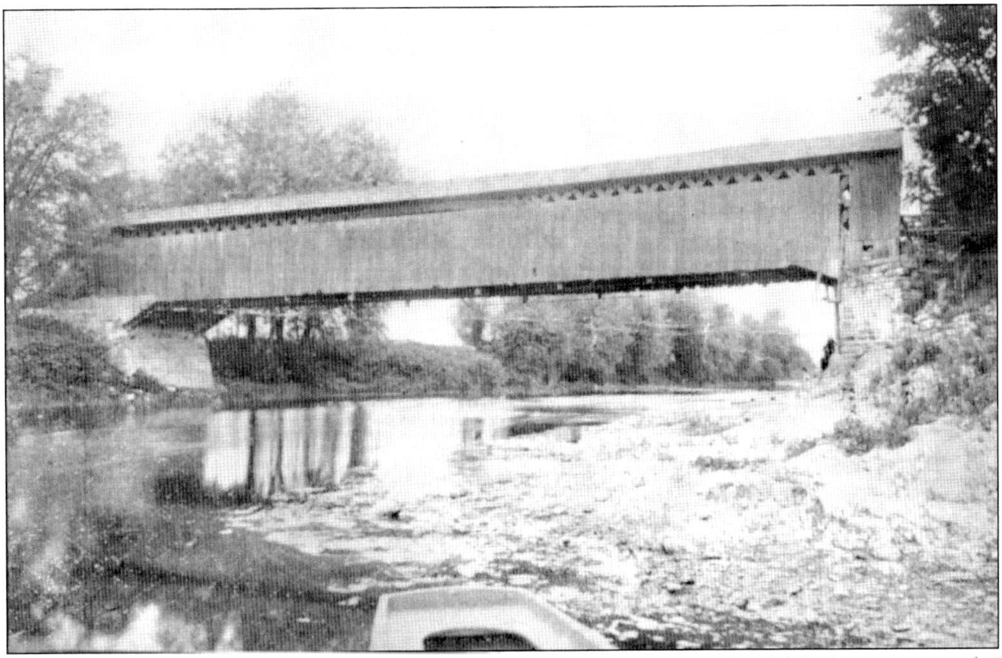

At first a scow was used to cross the Wallkill River. It was located at the old fording place to the south of the Memorial House. A covered bridge was built in 1845 to the south of the present bridge. A large number of people witnessed the burning of the bridge and its collapse into the river in August 1891. It was soon replaced by an iron bridge. (Photograph by H. L. Schultz.)

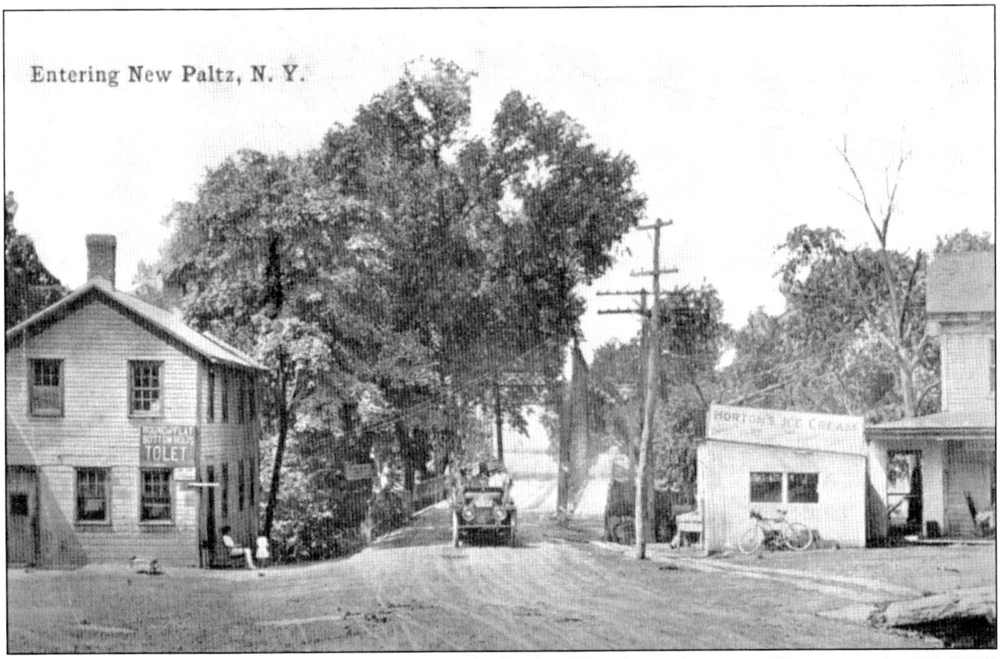

To the left of the old iron bridge is the home of Charles Bleecker, who rented boats on the Wallkill River. On the right is Horton's Ice Cream Stand and the home of James Patrick. To make room for the new bridge in 1939, the Pallus family moved the former Patrick home across Main Street and connected it to their residence on the left. (Courtesy of Vivian Wadlin.)

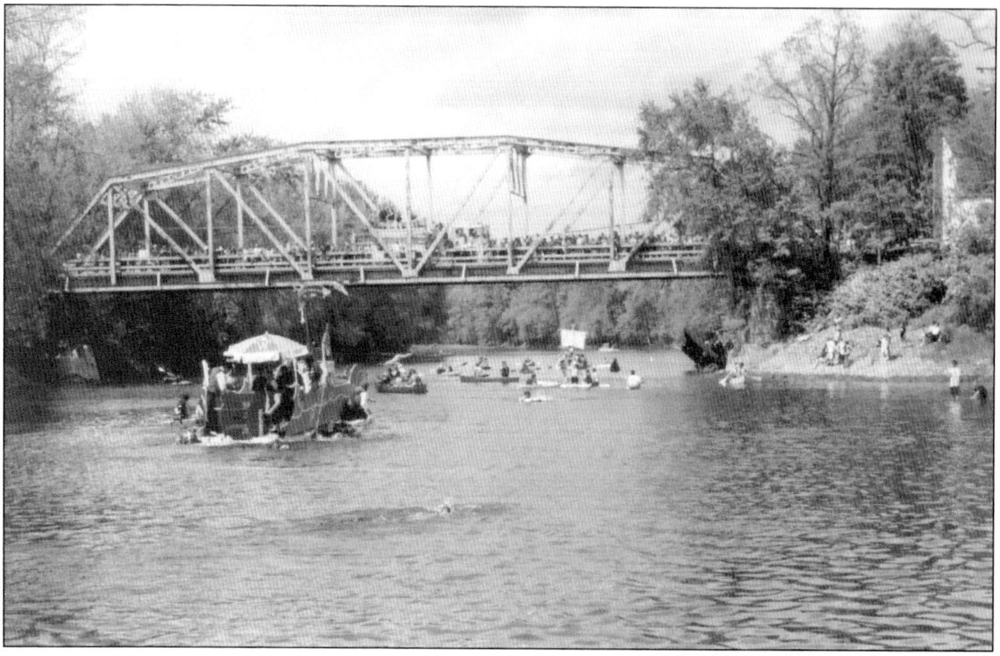

The present bridge was built just north of the old bridge in 1941, causing the curve in lower Main Street. The old bridge had been condemned five years earlier and traffic detoured. The old bridge's abutments can still be seen today to the south of the present bridge. Pictured are spectators on the bridge watching the regatta below in 2005. (Photograph by John Giralico.)

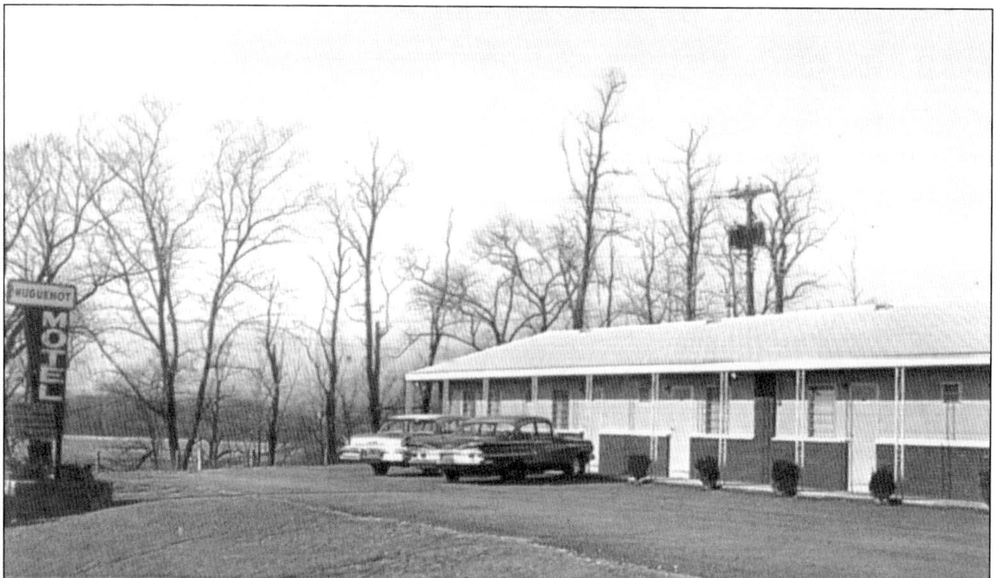

When the Huguenot Motel opened in 1960, it attracted widespread attention. The motel was the first structure in the Northeast in which unique, pre-engineered building procedures were used in its construction. After the motel was gutted by fire in 1988, the Gilded Otter brew pub opened on the site 10 years later. The *Gilded Otter* was the ship that Antoine Crispell, the first of the patentees to come to America, arrived on in 1660.

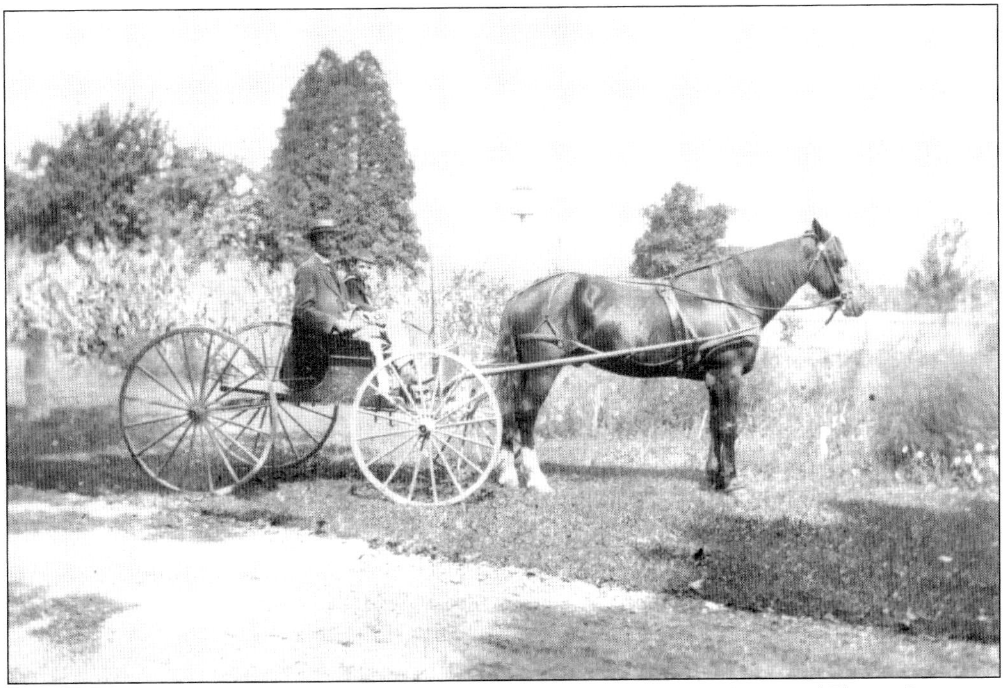

Philip LeFevre Elting partnered with William Adams to form the Adams and Elting Company of Chicago in the 1880s. This company became a leader in paint manufacturing and became a subsidiary of Glidden Paint. Their gunmetal grey paint is still used on battleships today. Born and raised on Huguenot Street, Elting's love of his boyhood home never subsided. His gift of $4,000 made possible the founding of the Elting Memorial Library, which stands today as a monument to his devotion to this community. Elting his shown above with one of his sons and a horse named Old Billie near his summer home at 169 Huguenot Street. Although spread throughout the country, members of the Elting family (below) came home to New Paltz every summer until 1943, when the house was sold.

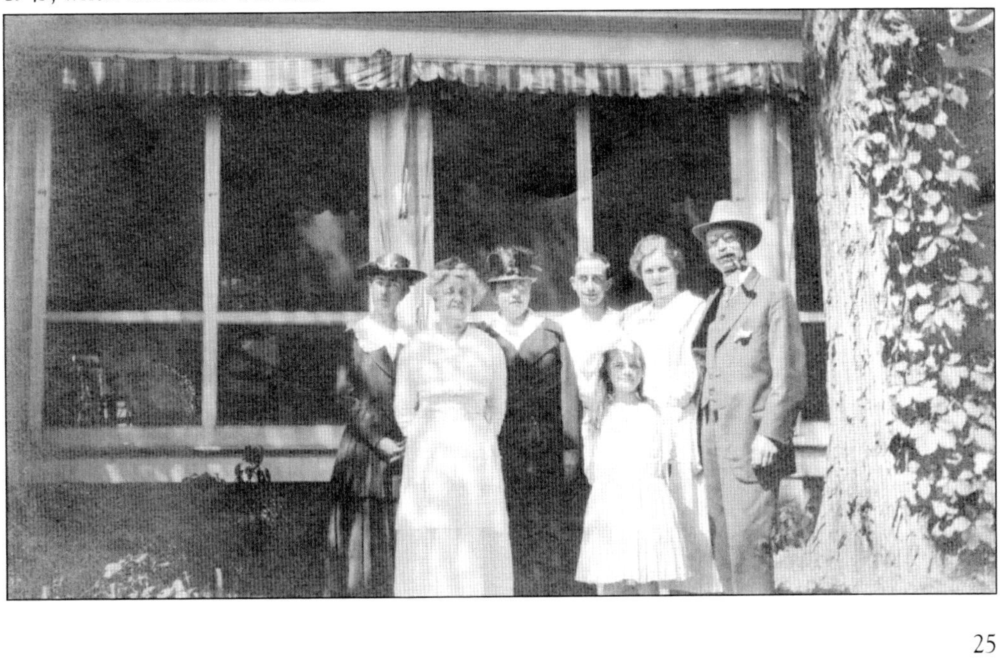

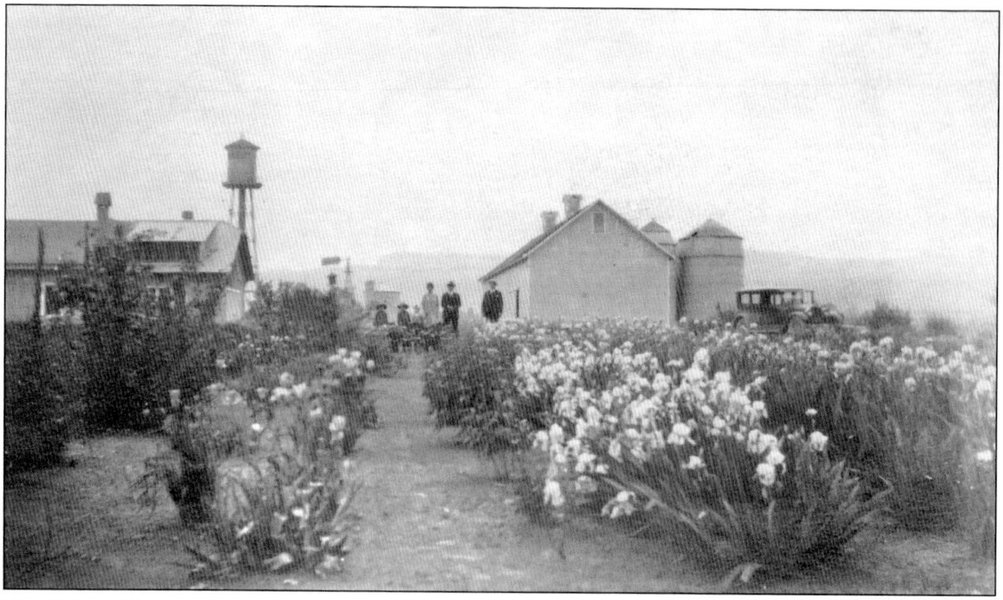

The Wallkill Valley Land Trust and the Open Space Institute successfully protected the last two farms in the village of New Paltz in 2007. The Meadow Valley Stock Farm has been owned by the Jewett family since 1919. The Huguenot Street Farm, owned by the Khosla family, is a thriving community-supported agriculture farm. Pictured above from left to right on Memorial Day 1927 are twins Jack McKenna and Bill McKenna, Dave Jewett Jr., Dorothy Jewett, David F. Jewett, and Warren McKenna. The group stands between some of the farm's outbuildings, including the creamery, the water tower, the barn, and silos. The Jewetts started with 20 head of blooded Holstein stock cows, which soon multiplied to nearly 300. Blue Bell (below) was an offshoot of the Holstein breed. She calved many times, lived a long life, and was a good milk producer. She is pictured with Dave Jewett Sr. (Both courtesy of the Jewett family.)

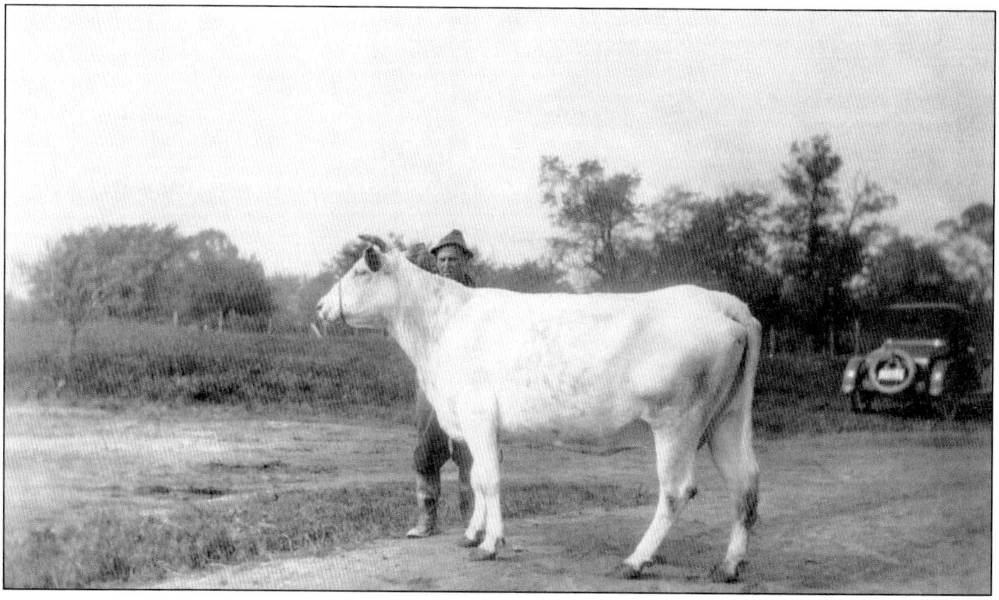

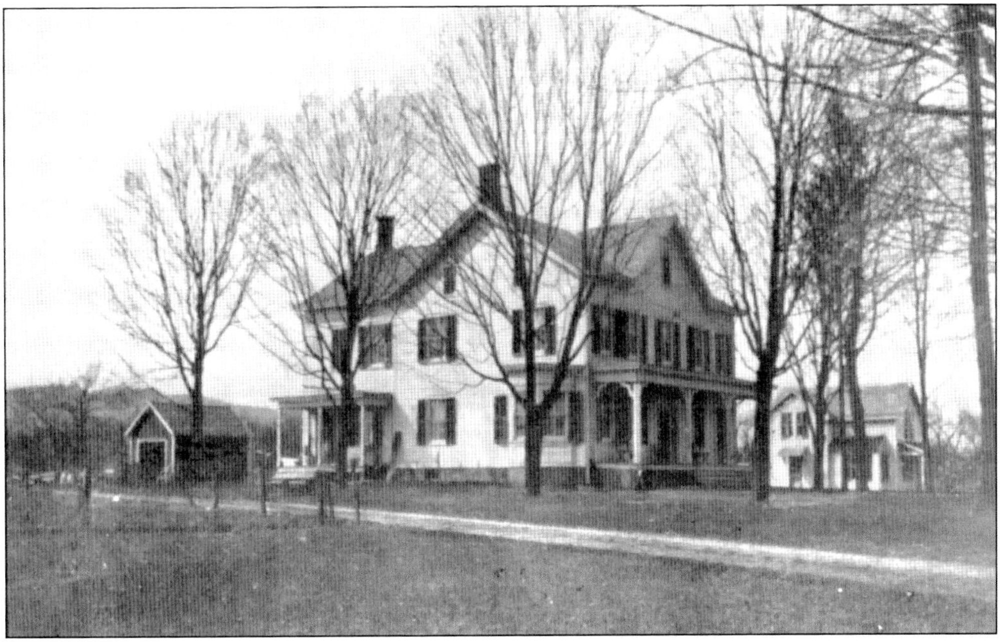

After the death of her husband, Mrs. Simon Hasbrouck turned her spacious home into a boardinghouse. She called it Maple Shade, due to the number of maple trees on the front lawn. She could accommodate 30 boarders, and her house was always one of the first in town to fill up. In 1901, she turned a part of her farm into golf links as an attraction for her summer boarders.

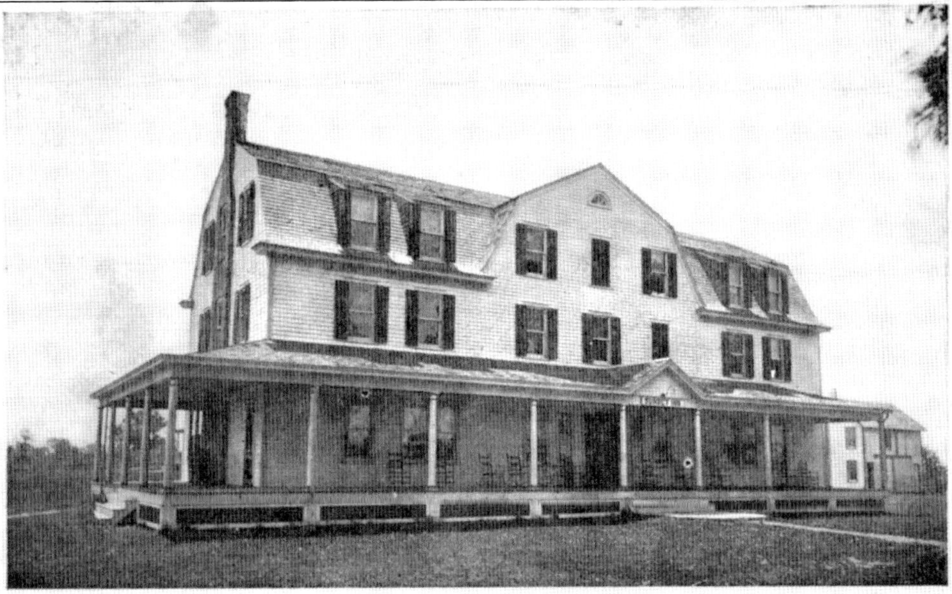

SUNSET INN, New Paltz, N. Y.

For two years, Maple Shade was owned and operated by Edgar and Ida Rider, but the Riders wanted something bigger. They built and operated the Sunset Inn, located on upper Main Street where Dedrick's Pharmacy and Convenient Deli are today. It had 28 bedrooms, two large living rooms, a dining room, and a kitchen. Astronaut Scott Carpenter stayed here as a child several times while traveling with his father.

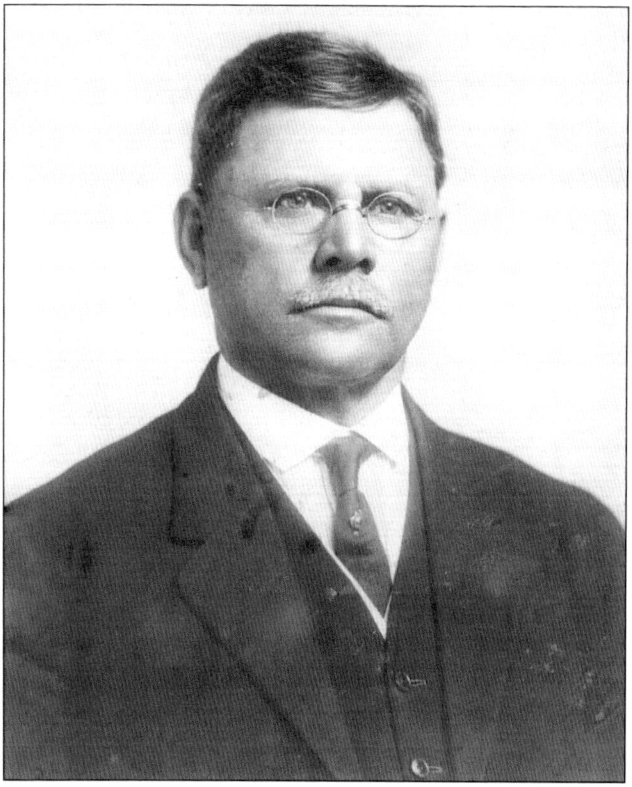

Joseph Walker, a well-known pioneer road builder, constructed hundreds of miles of roads across New York. He built several roads in Ulster County, including State Route 32. He purchased the farm and used it as a home and seasonal headquarters, where he wintered 100 horses, wagons, and other road-building equipment. He also mined a gravel bed on the property during the construction of Route 32. (Courtesy of Pat Walker.)

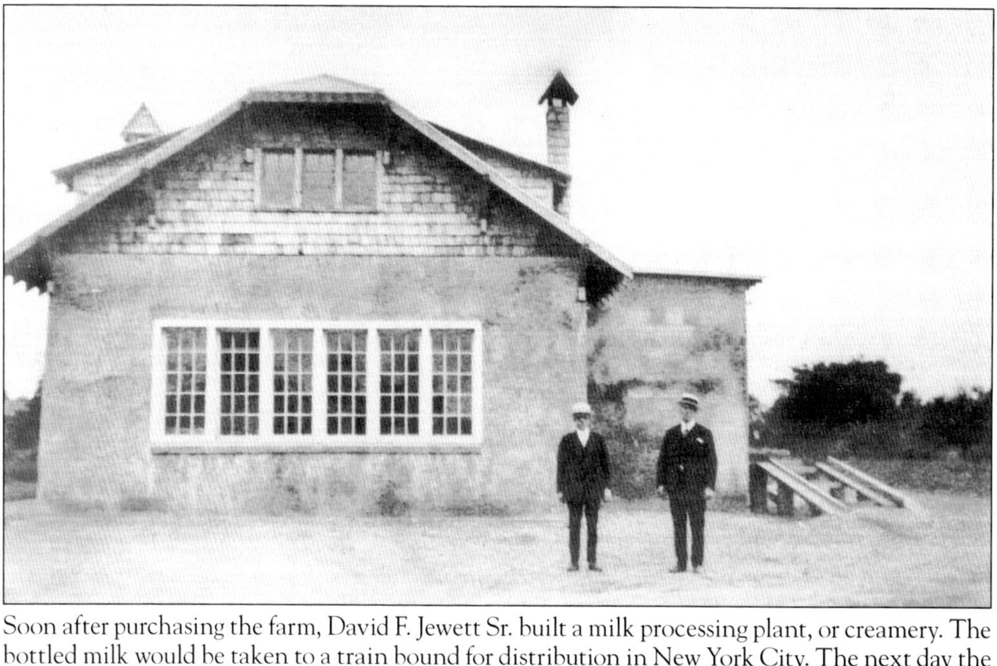

Soon after purchasing the farm, David F. Jewett Sr. built a milk processing plant, or creamery. The bottled milk would be taken to a train bound for distribution in New York City. The next day the empty milk bottles would return by train and would be trucked back to the creamery, where they were washed, sanitized, and refilled. In front of the bottling room are Joseph Fitzpatrick (left) and Warren McKenna. (Courtesy of the Jewett family.)

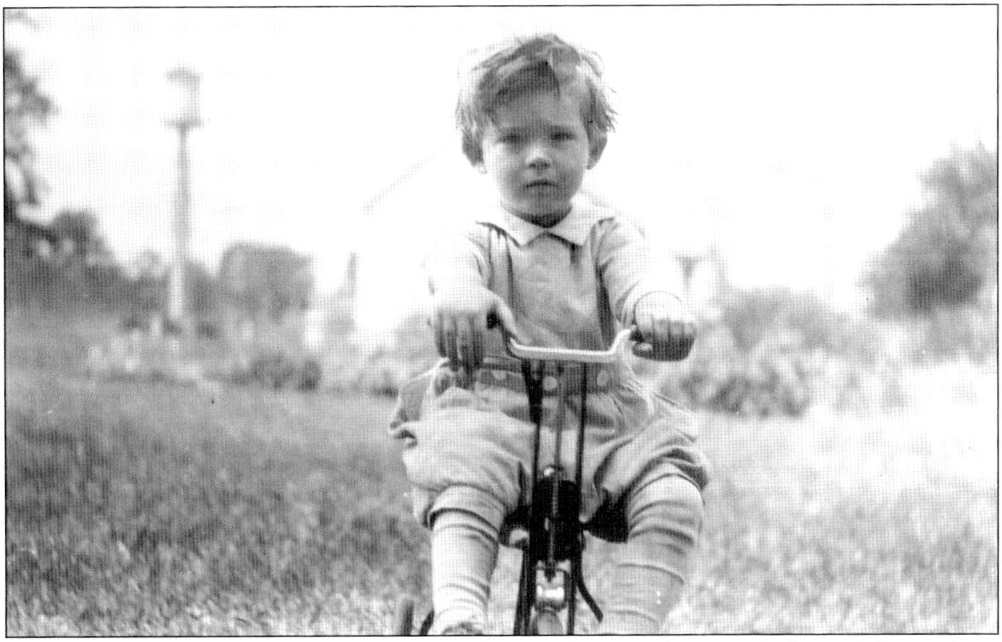

Young Dave Jewett rides his kiddie car on the farm in the 1927 photograph above. After working on the farm for many years and delivering milk throughout the village and town, Jewett opened his own business in 1953. The ice cream cone atop J. D.'s Dairy Bar on North Chestnut Street fast became a landmark in the village, becoming as well known as the van den Berg clock tower. The cone was bigger than the one that is perched on the roof of what is now Village Pizza. The original cone weighed 600 pounds. The ice cream part of the cone was concrete over a wire mesh frame, and the base came from a barrel-making firm. Dave and his wife, Mac, are pictured below at the opening of the dairy bar on August 15, 1953. (Both courtesy of the Jewett family.)

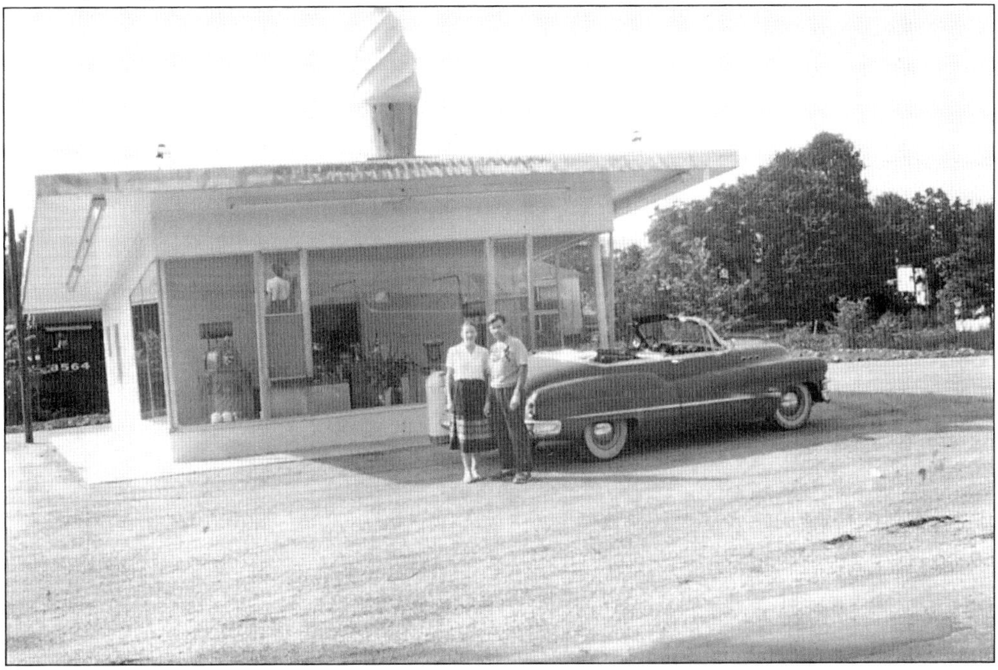

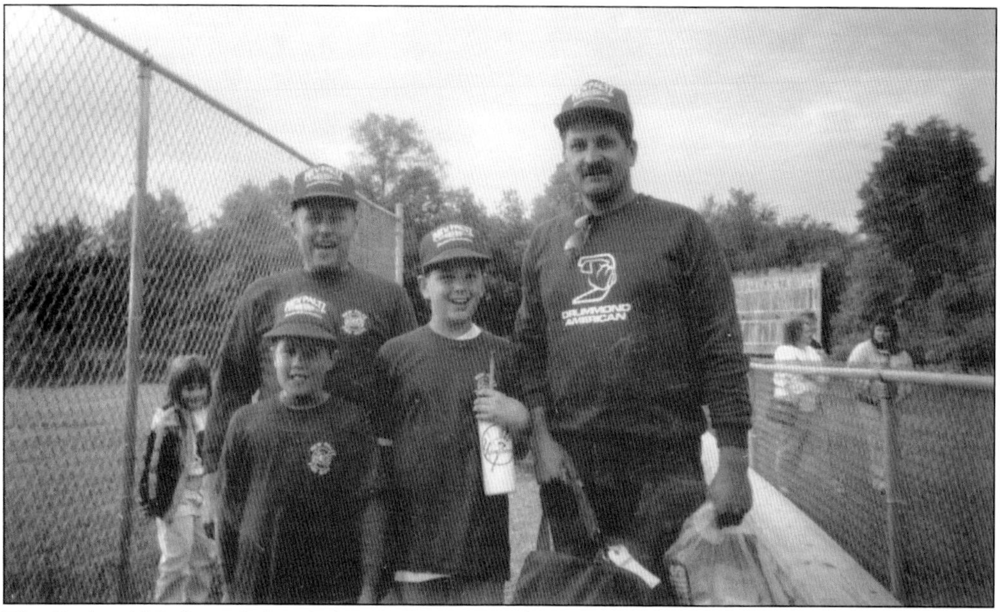

The Richard Hasbrouck family let a generation of New Paltz children play ball on their "Field of Dreams," a homemade baseball diamond near their home. The painted scoreboard read, "Welcome to Hasbrouck Field, Home of the Little Hugies." Coaches Lee John Fisher (left) and Ralph Scandariato (right) celebrate a victory with their sons Nicholas Fisher (left) and R. J. Scandariato after a game. (Courtesy of the Scandariato family.)

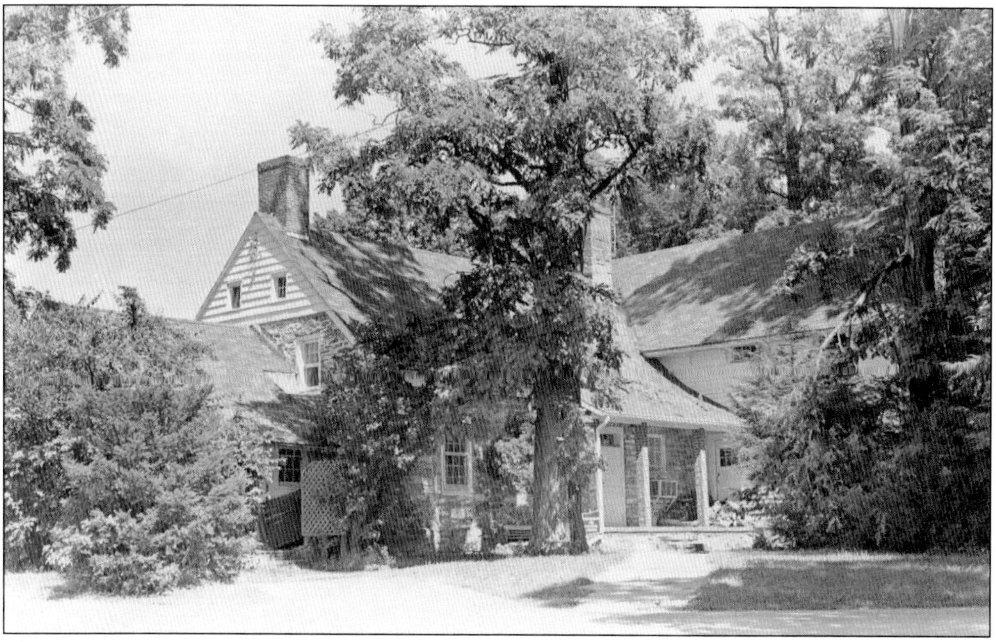

Abraham Elting's Locust Tree Farm stayed in the family for almost 200 years. Built in 1759, it was sold to settle the estate of Howard Elting in 1949. The farm became the Saddlewick School of Horsemanship and Briarwood Riding Academy. In the 1970s, it became a private country club. Gordon and Joanne Kreth purchased the property in 1979 and made the farmhouse into one of the finest restaurants in the Hudson Valley.

Two

The Town of New Paltz

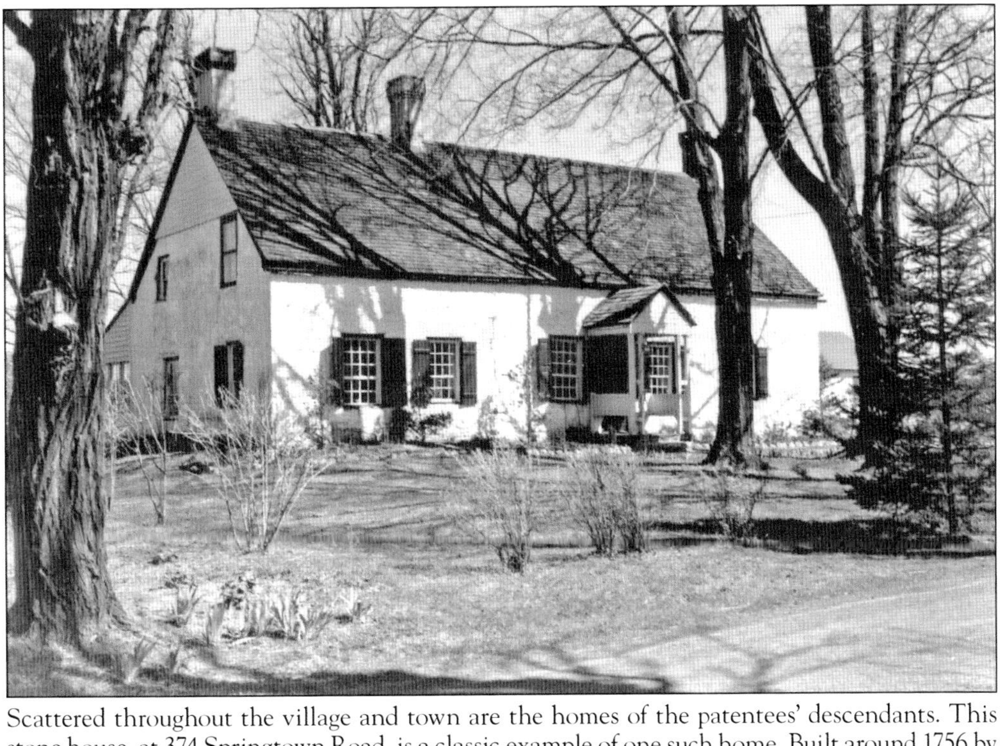

Scattered throughout the village and town are the homes of the patentees' descendants. This stone house, at 374 Springtown Road, is a classic example of one such home. Built around 1756 by Christoffel Deyo, a great-grandson of patentee Pierre Deyo, the house is similar to those on Huguenot Street. The home stayed within the Deyo family until 1862. (Photograph by Erma DeWitt.)

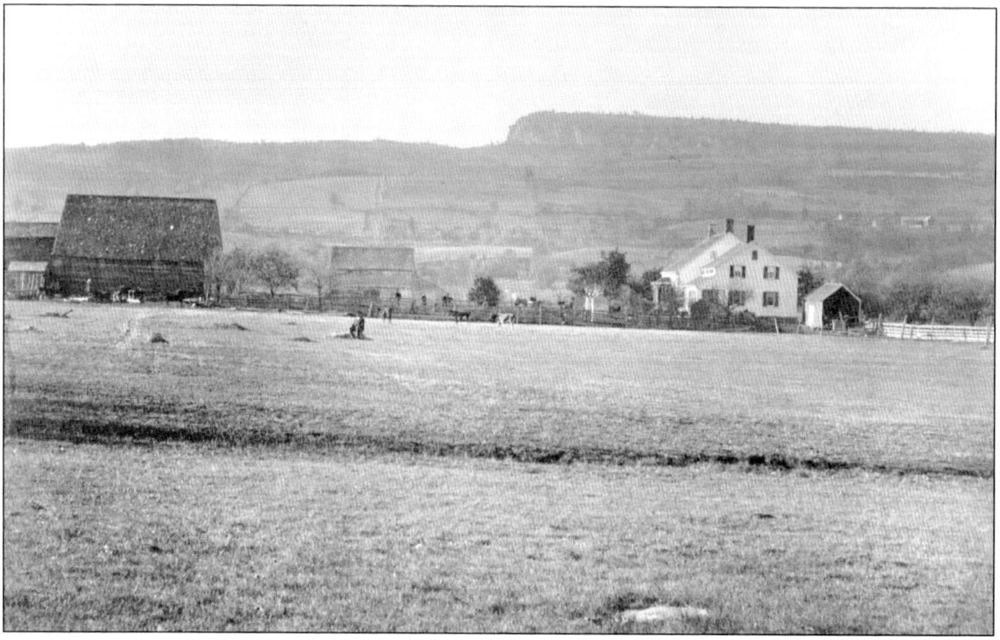

David and Maritje Hasbrouck located their stone house (above) in 1797 on Butterville Road, with a beautiful view of Paltz Point to the west. In 1869, John Stokes sold his property on the top of the mountain to the Smiley family. At that time, the Smiley family began calling Paltz Point Sky Top, and Alfred Smiley built the first observation tower there. These images were probably taken in 1877 or 1878, between the loss of the second observation tower to fire and the building of the third tower. Below is the Hiram Deyo family, who owned the farm from 1865 to 1907. The frame addition was added to the stone house in 1871. The addition was separated from the stone portion in 1985 and was moved to a nearby hay field, where it is now a separate residence. (Photographs by H. L. Schultz.)

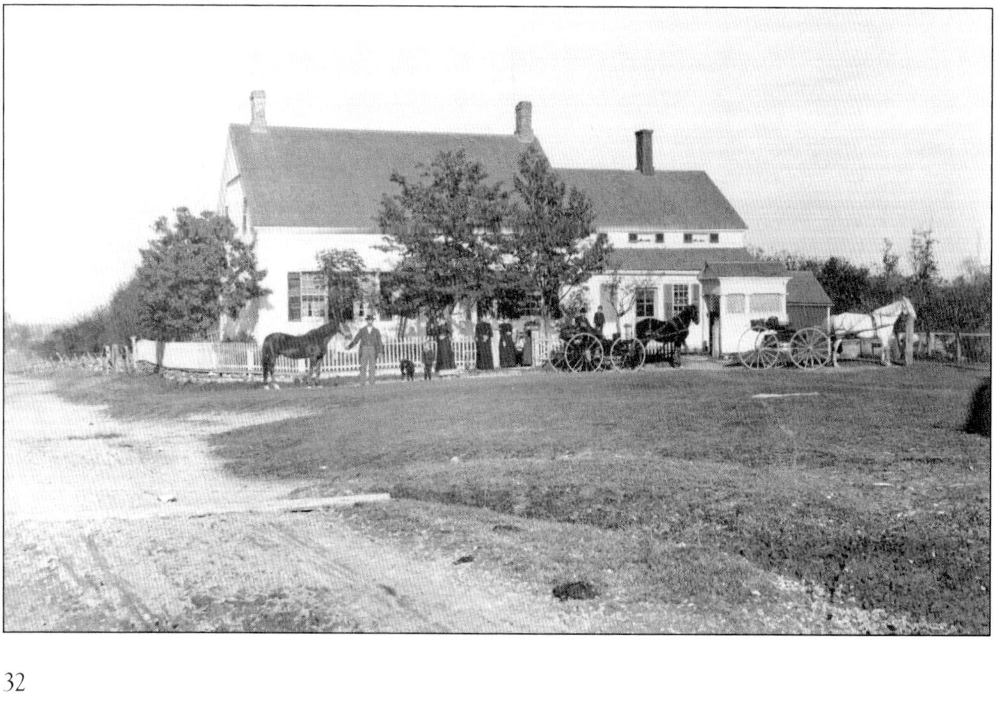

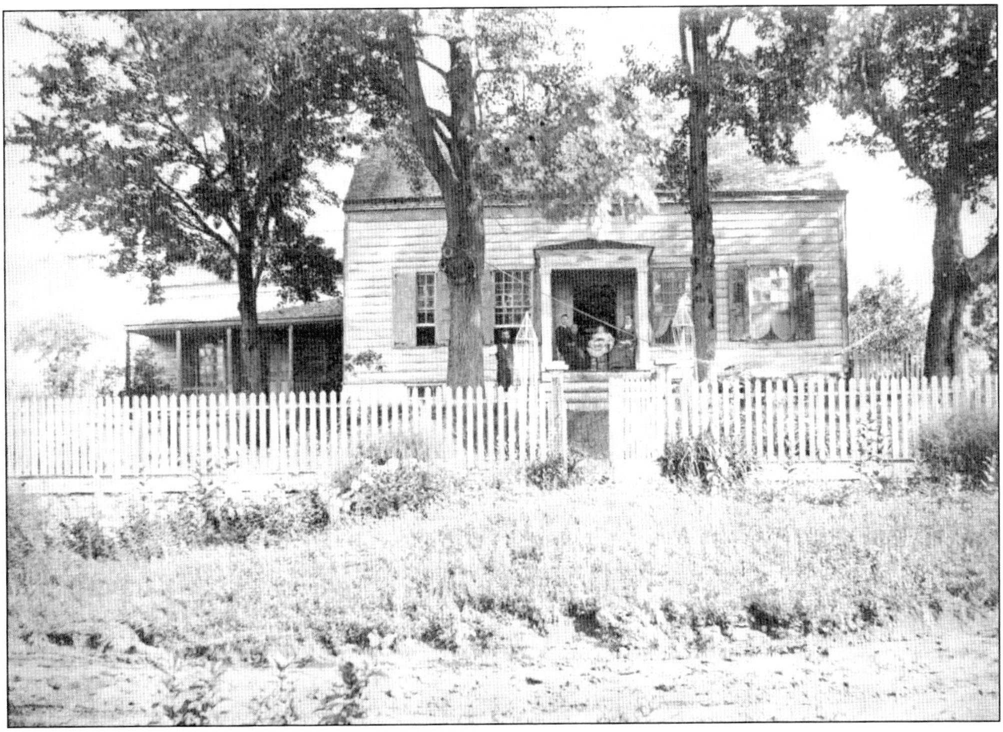

The Butterville neighborhood was not settled until around 1812. It was often called the Quaker Neighborhood on account of the number of members of the Society of Friends who settled in that region. The William F. Minard family were Quakers who built and lived in this house at 145 Mountain Rest Road. (Courtesy of Rosalie Nelson.)

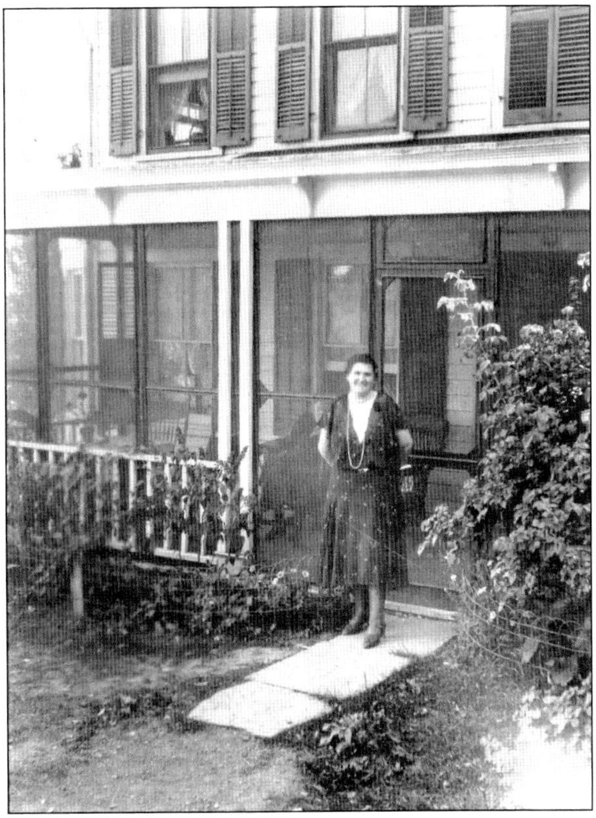

The Steen family grew apple, cherry, peach, pear, and plum trees for market. Part of the farm was bought in 1902 by the New Paltz Waterworks Company to build a reservoir for the village. More land was taken for the building of the aqueduct. Katherine Siegel (pictured) and her husband, Rudolf, bought the much smaller farm in 1929 and ran a boardinghouse there for several years. (Courtesy of Randy Siegel.)

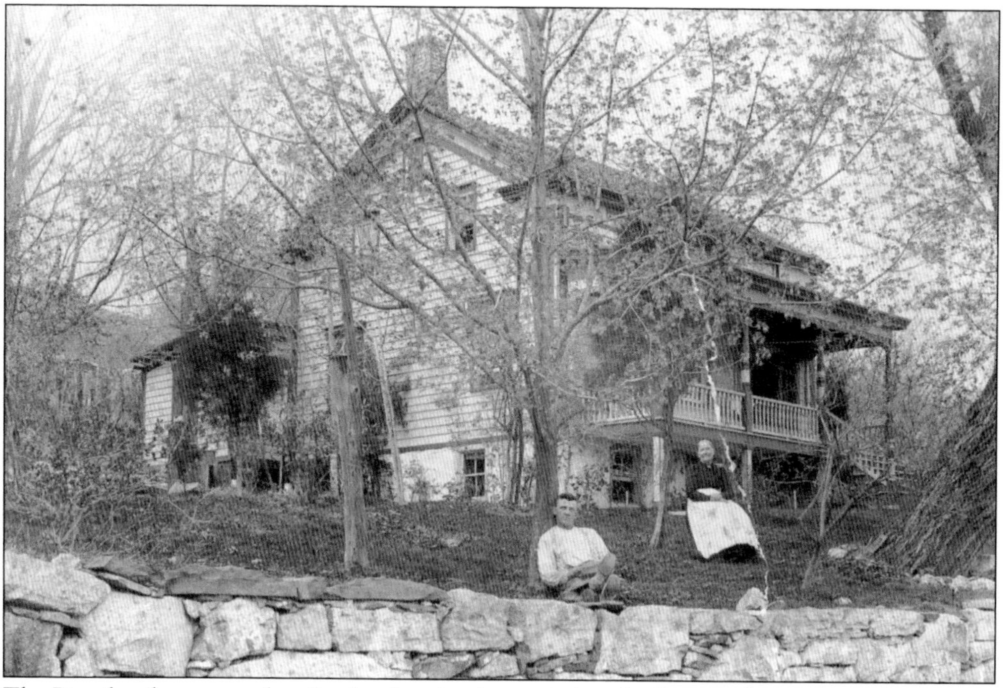

The Pine family was another Quaker family who settled in the Butterville area. Ennis DuBois, a tenant farmer, worked the farm in 1893. His wife, Catherine, and son Daniel are shown above. In 1909, this house was moved across the road and was used as the paymaster's house for the building of the Catskill Aqueduct. Its foundation can still be seen when hiking on Lenape Lane. (Courtesy of Rosalie Nelson.)

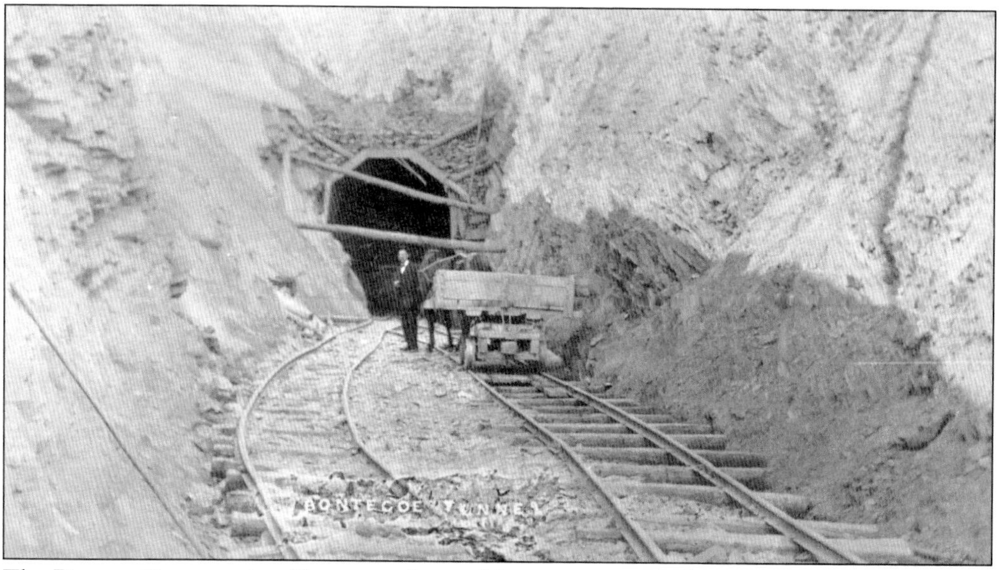

The Degnon Construction Company obtained by competitive bid a contract to build the local portion of the Catskill Aqueduct. This included tunnels through the mountain at Bonticou and under the Wallkill River at Libertyville. The Degnon Company built a narrow-gauge railroad along the pipeline's right-of-way to transport the steel, cement, lumber, and other necessary supplies for construction.

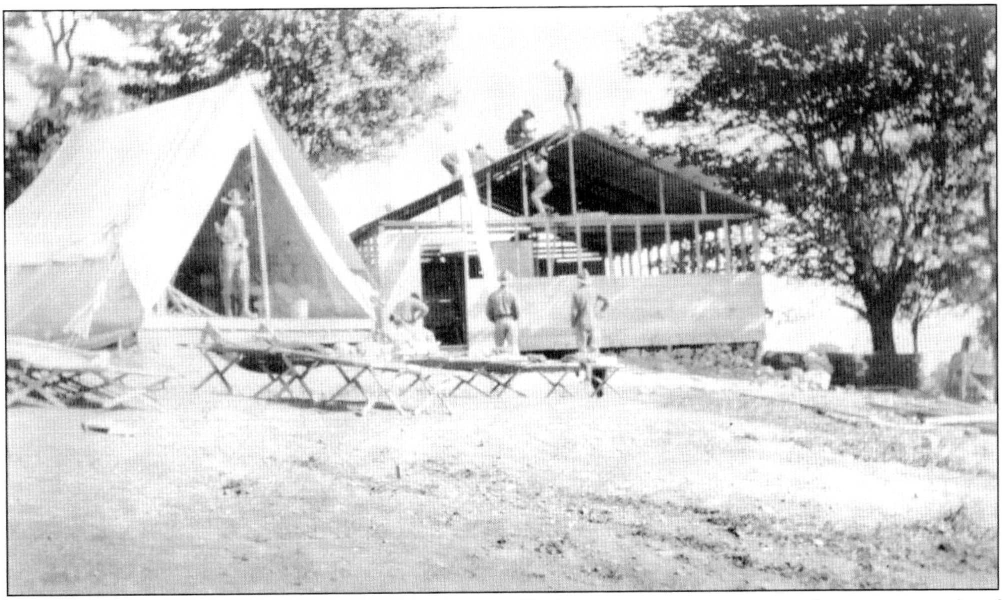

During World War I, the New York Guard was called into service to protect the water supply of the City of New York from feared German terrorist attacks. Camp Fort Orange, constructed by the men west of Butterville Road, consisted of barracks, a mess hall, and officers' quarters. Pvt. Hugh Taylor was accidentally shot and killed in February 1917 while on duty patrolling the aqueduct.

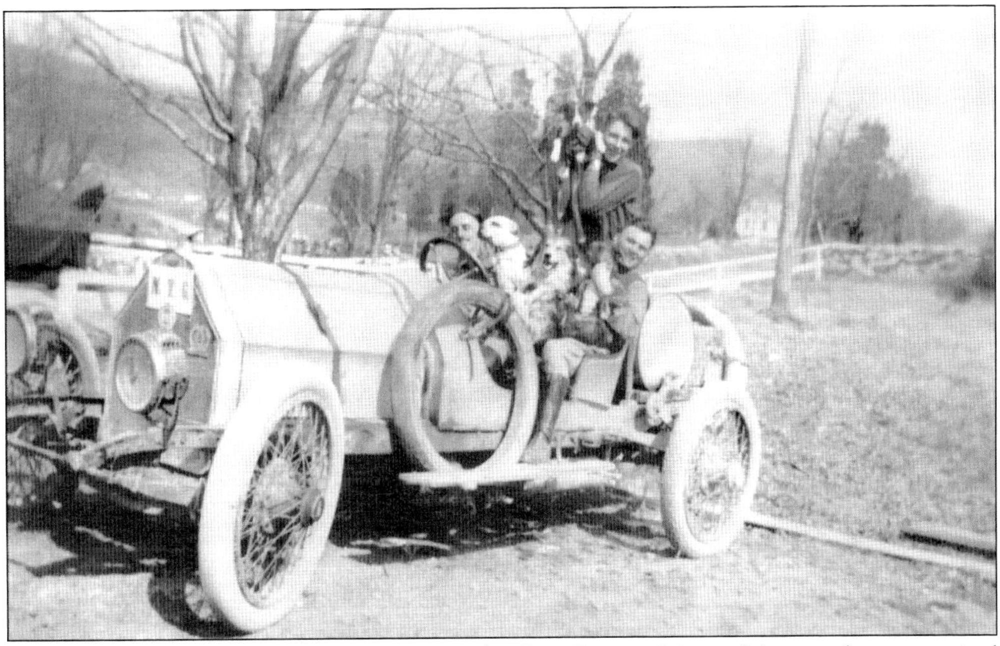

It was not all work and no play while stationed at Fort Orange. Many of the guardsmen acquired stray dogs while in New Paltz. The soldiers traveled into town quite often in this car, owned by Pvt. Lewis VanAlstyne. Pictured here are three of the soldiers parked beside Butterville Road with their newfound pets.

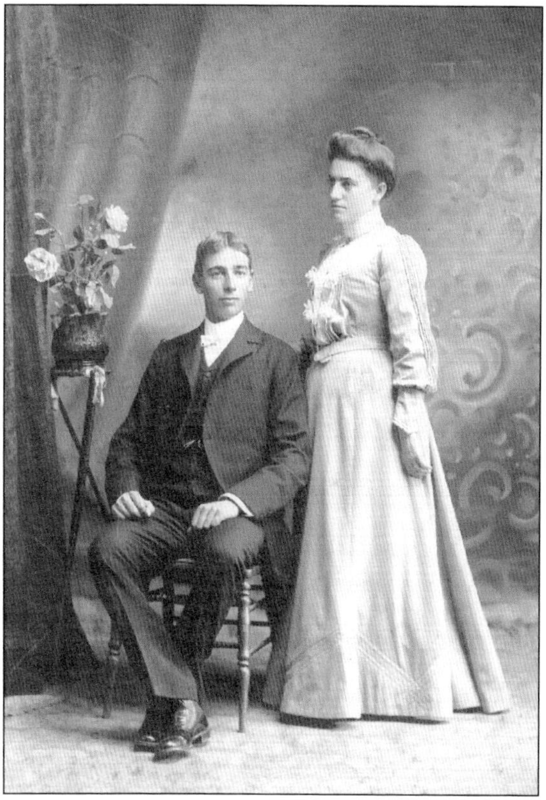

Although the Paltz Patent included approximately 40,000 acres of land, the patentees and their sons obtained grants of land to the south of the original patent. In June 1688, patentee Louis DuBois acquired land on both sides of the Wallkill from Gov. Thomas Dongan. Fred DuBois and his bride, Anna Buchanan (pictured at left), sit for their wedding portrait in October 1901. Their Maple Knoll Farm on DuBois Road was a part of this tract and was owned by several generations of the family. DuBois became one of Ulster County's most prominent agricultural figures and supervisor of the town of New Paltz from 1930 to 1933. Below, Robert DuBois, grandson of Fred and Anna, delivers milk from the DuBois Dairy. (Left, photograph by H. L. Schultz; below, courtesy of Vivian Wadlin.)

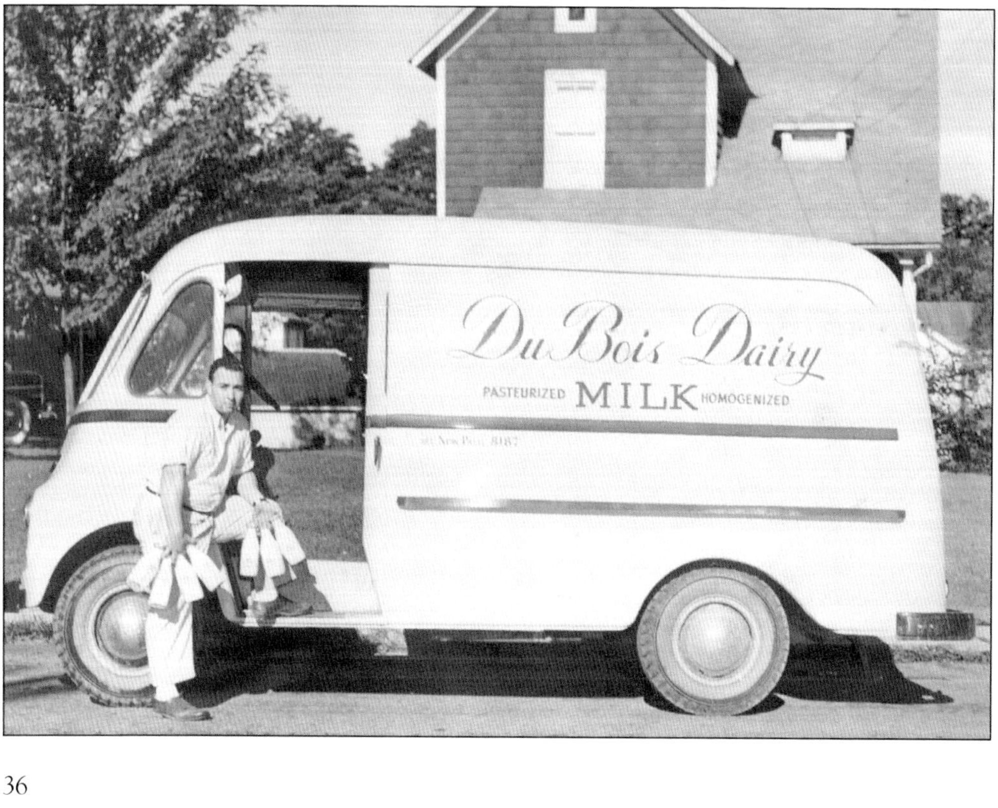

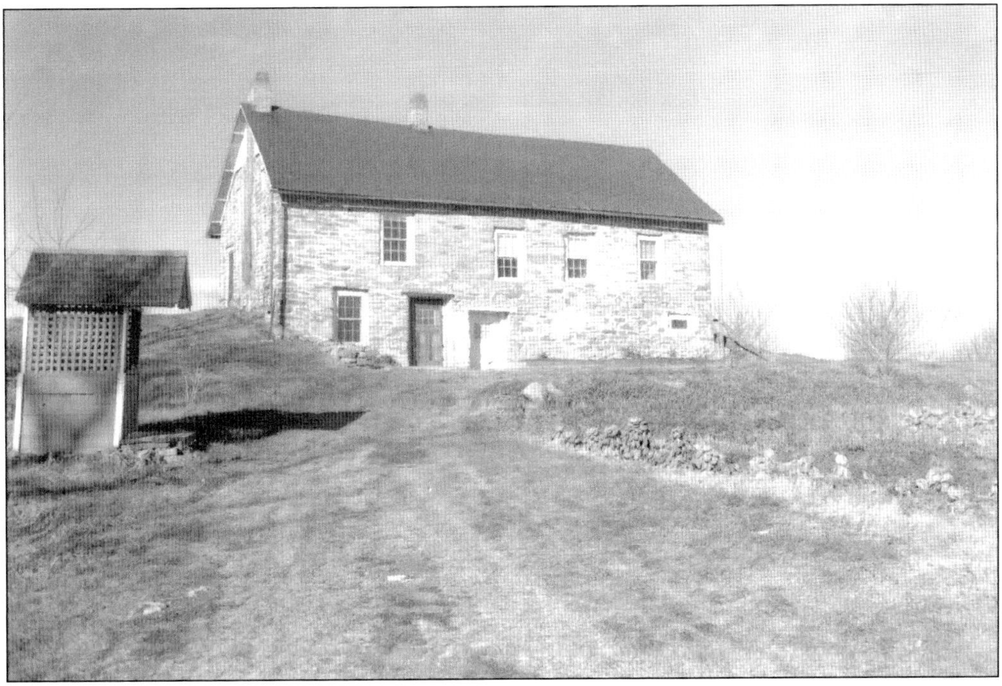

The Freer Patent consisted of 1,200 acres and adjoined the Paltz Patent on the south. It was granted on June 30, 1715, to Hugo Freer Sr., the son of New Paltz patentee Hugo Freer, and to his sons Hugo Jr., Thomas, and Isaac. Joseph Freer, the son of Isaac, built this home on Brookside Road in 1776. It stayed in the Freer family until 1945. (Photograph by Erma DeWitt.)

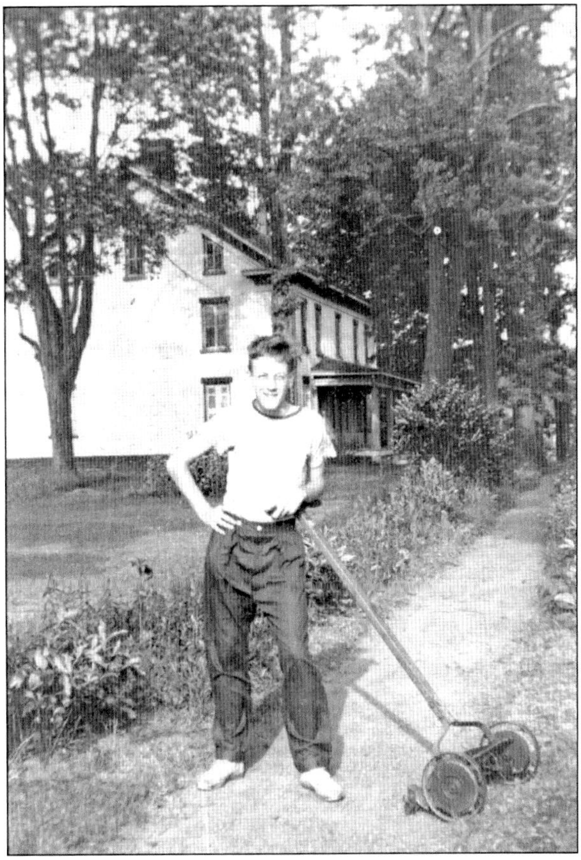

Noah Eltinge and Nathaniel LeFevre received a patent for 3,000 acres in 1748. This grant brought a great deal of trouble. It was claimed that the original New Paltz Patent covered part of the tract. The matter was settled in 1754, and they retained title to the land and to 22 acres on which Eltinge's home on Plains Road stood. Eltinge's descendant, Robert Lasher, is shown at right on the once-controversial land. (Courtesy of Kate Pepper.)

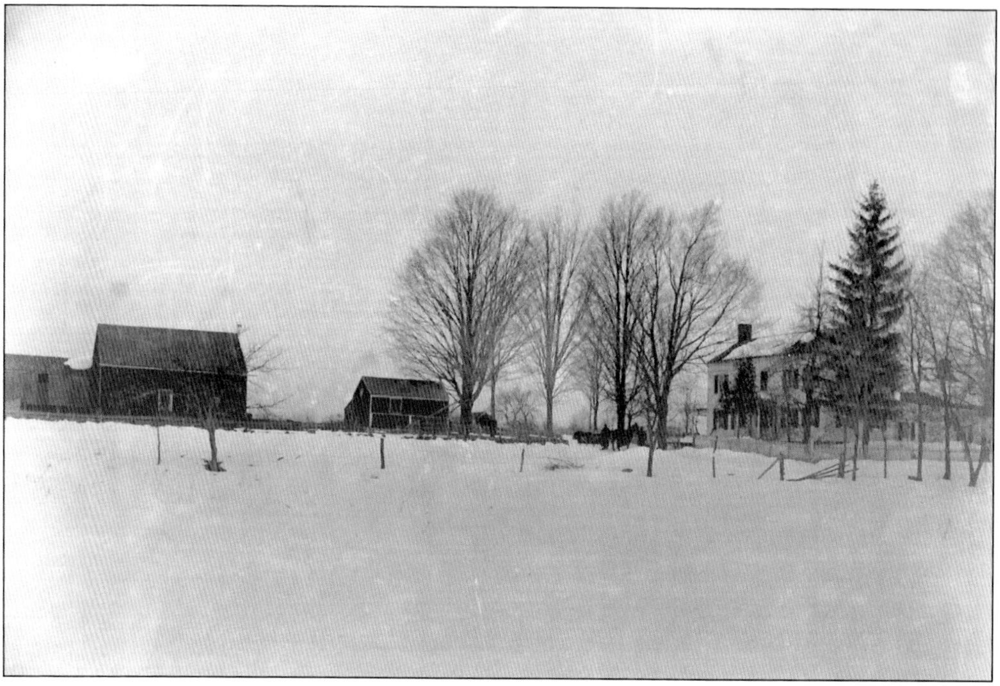

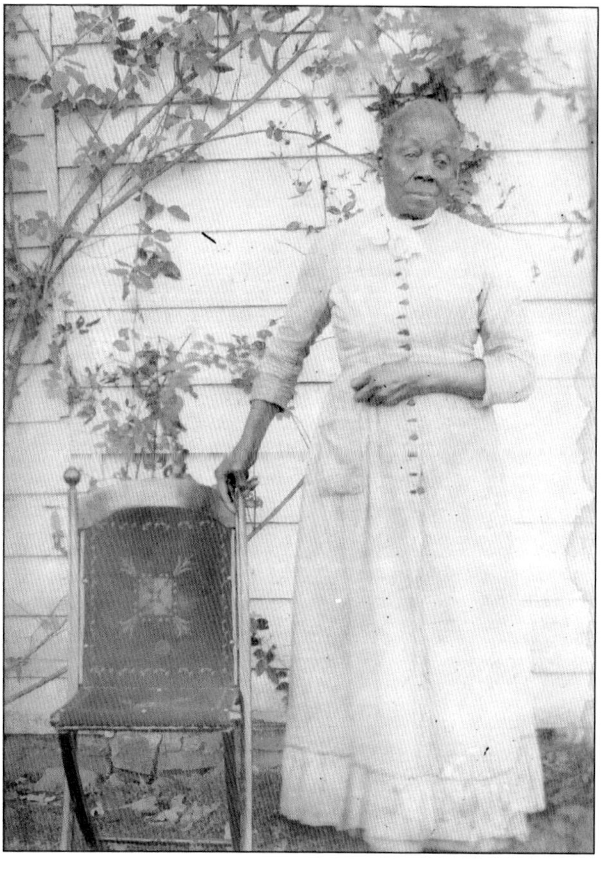

In the 1830s, an Irishman named William Crozier dug a ditch in the Black Creek east of Plutarch Road. This was a great engineering feat and made 2,000 acres of land the most fertile and productive in this vicinity. Roelif Eltinge's farm of 285 acres was on Plutarch Road. Only the stone house with the large frame addition remains of the farm today.

The back of this photograph identifies its subject as "Dinah Freer, daughter of Freer slaves." The earliest record found on Dinah is the 1855 New York census, where she is listed as a domestic servant for the Roelif Eltinge family. The last slaves in New York were emancipated in 1848. Many former slaves adopted the surname of their former owners. (Courtesy of Amy LeFevre.)

Capt. John E. Messmer Jr. poses with his father, John Sr., while home on furlough from World War II. The Roelif Eltinge farm was sold in 1925 to John Messmer Sr. Called "The Humus King," John Sr. owned one of the largest humus beds in all of New York. He frequently found relics in the swamp, including an old flintlock musket bearing the date 1812, a Revolutionary-era sword, copper coins, bronze statutes, and an old-fashioned hunting watch.

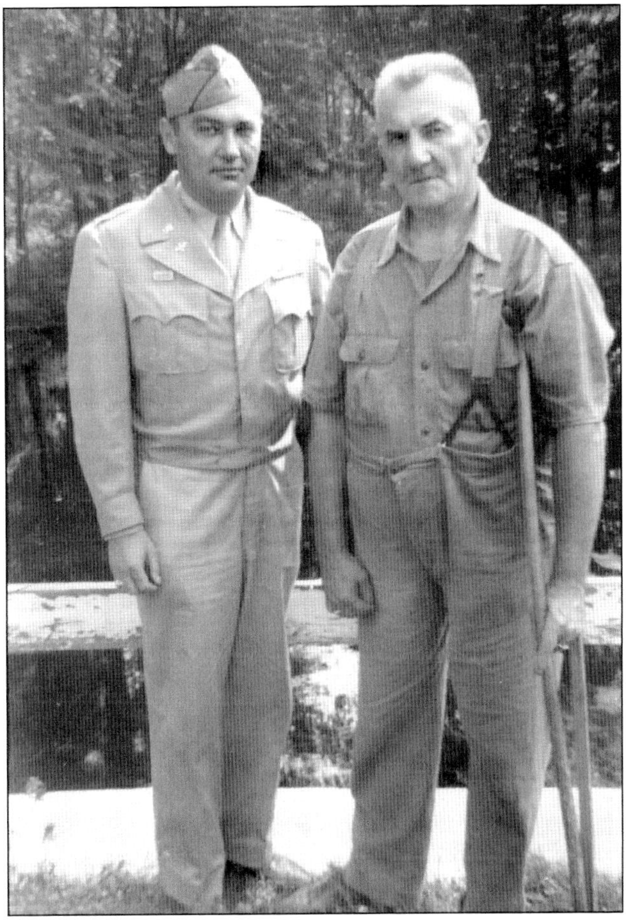

Below, Chester DeGraff sits at the wheel of a car parked next to the Oscar DeGraff home at 425 Plutarch Road. The hamlet of Plutarch was once a thriving farming community, with a store, a blacksmith, a school, a church, a fire department, and a post office. Only the Plutarch Methodist Church remains today. Most of the fields have been subdivided, and it is now a growing bedroom community. (Courtesy of Ethel Savago.)

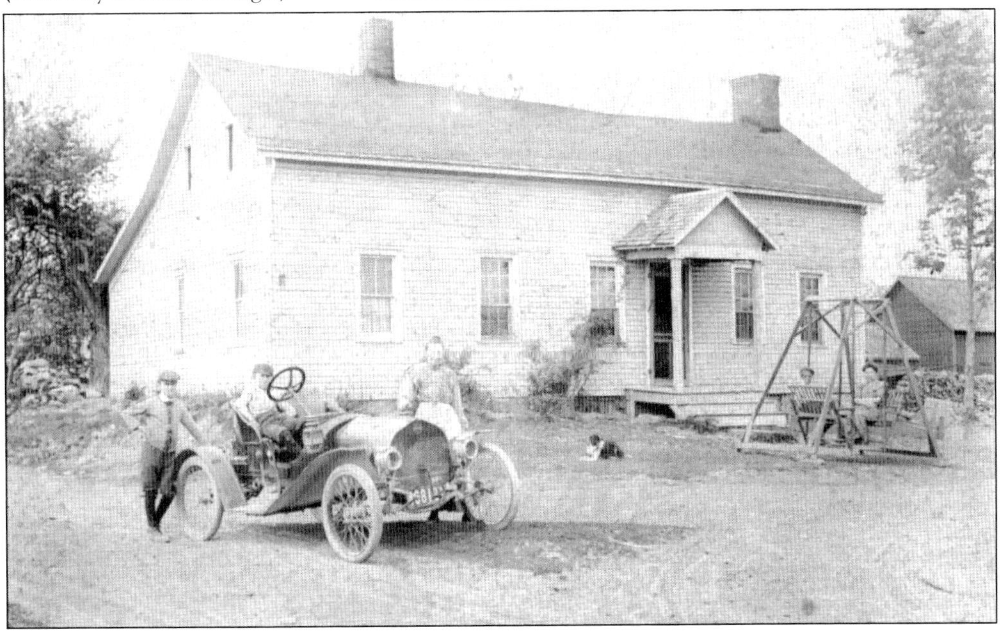

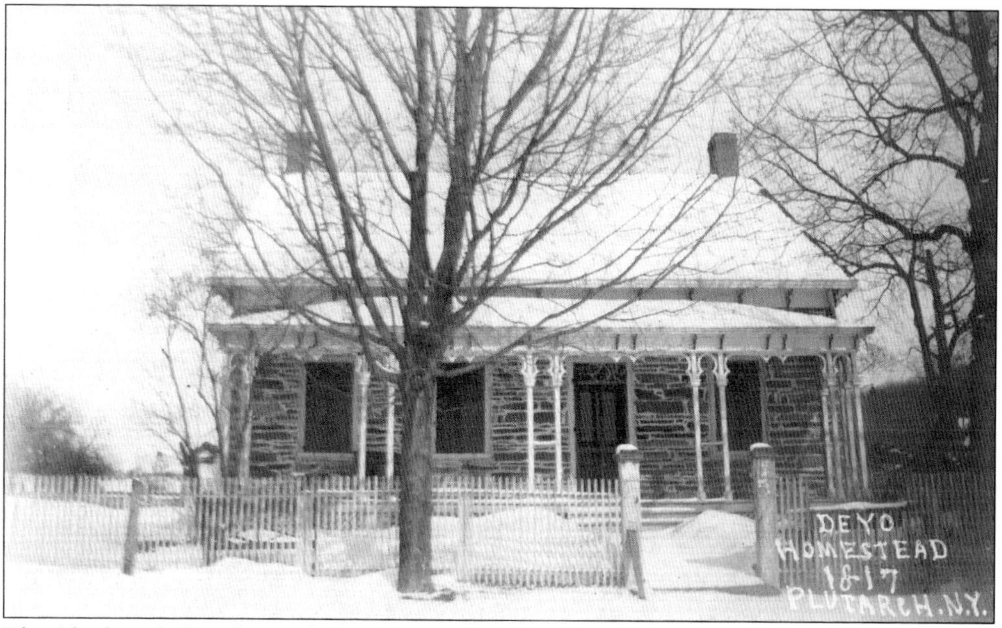

The Abraham J. Deyo house, built in 1812, was "quite certainly the last stone house built in New Paltz," according to the writings of Ralph LeFevre in 1903. On April 15, 1845, the town of Lloyd was formed from the town of New Paltz. Crozier's ditch became the official boundary between the two townships. Everything east of the ditch, including this home, is now considered part of the town of Lloyd. (Courtesy of Vivian Wadlin.)

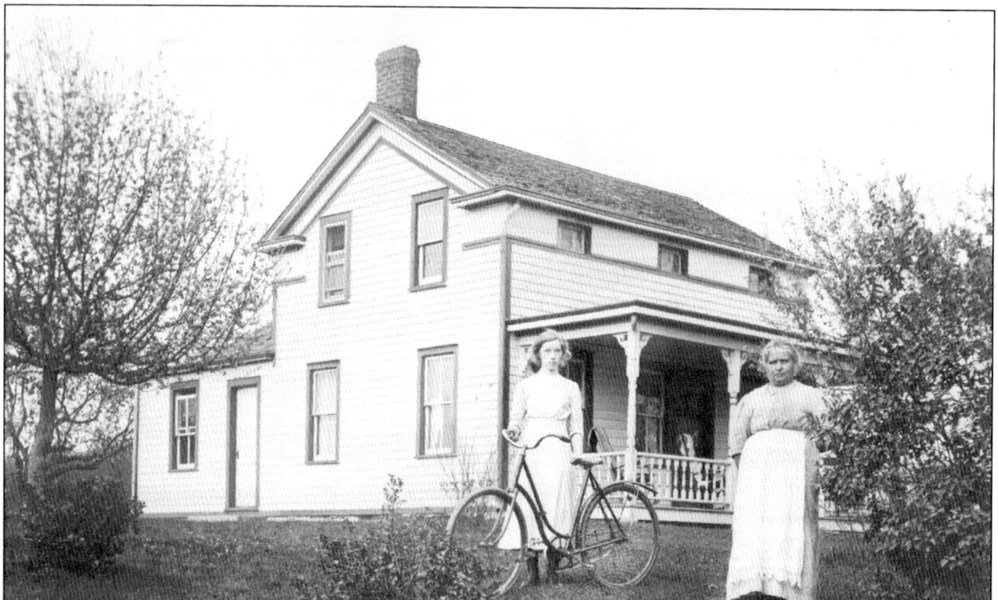

Farms like Abraham J. Deyo's in Plutarch were so big that they needed a tenant farmer to run the day-to-day operations. Because Deyo's tenant house (pictured here) was on the west side of the ditch, it remained in New Paltz. The tenant house stayed in the Deyo family until 1898, when it was bought by the Axel Lillberg family. Edith Lillberg is pictured with her bicycle; her sister-in-law Ida is on the right.

Janet Bracken, the teacher of first through sixth grades at the Plutarch School, took this picture of (from left to right) Bonnie, David, and Linda Elliott raising the flag outside the school in the fall of 1955. A year later the voters of the Plutarch School District voted 22 to 18 to close the school. Bracken went on to be the librarian at Elting Memorial Library from 1957 to 1974.

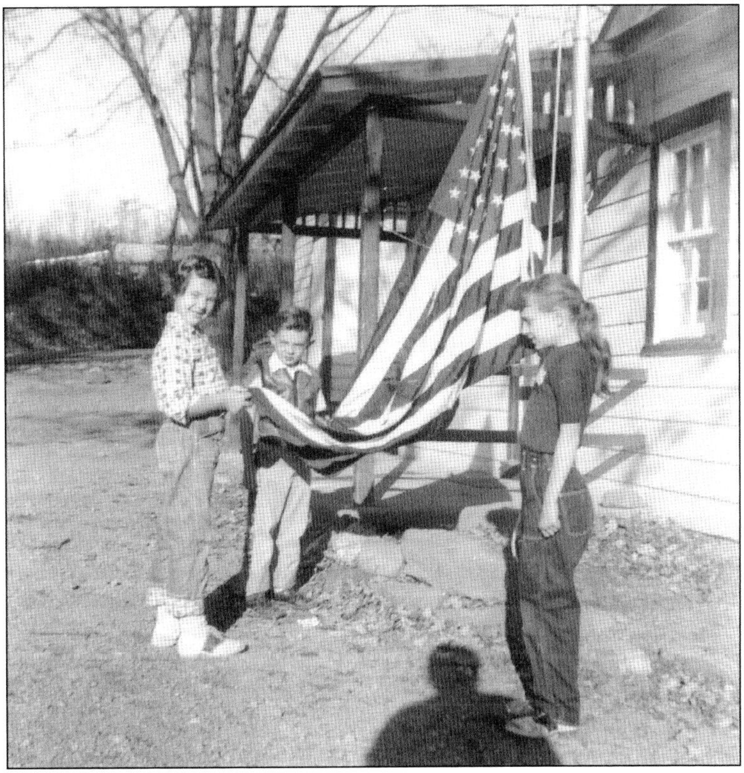

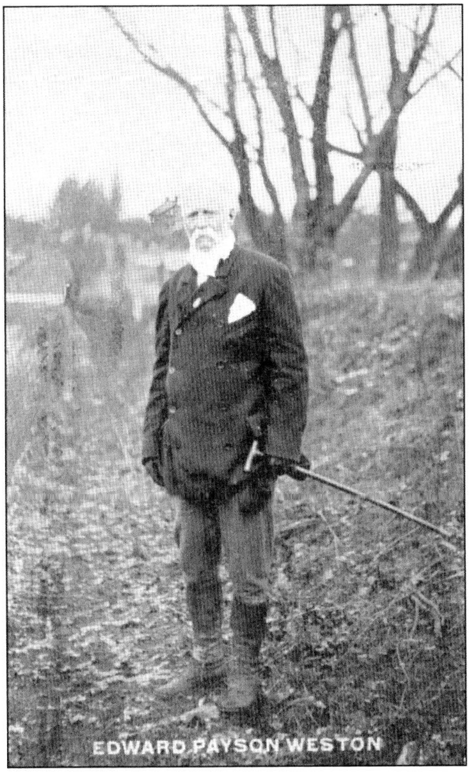

A famous resident of Plutarch was Edward Payson Weston (1839–1929), "the great pedestrian." Weston began his career as a walker while serving in the Civil War as a spy. He entered many walking competitions, which were popular after the war, including contests in which he would walk 200 miles backwards. He walked across the United States several times, including when he walked from New York to San Francisco at age 70 in 104 days and seven hours. On several occasions he was able to cover more than 100 miles per day. At age 74, he walked 1,500 miles from New York to Minneapolis in 60 days. Three hundred thousand people showed up in Minnesota to cheer him. His fame even spread to England and Scotland where he also walked thousands of miles. In 1924, the 86-year-old was shot when a band of armed men attacked his farmhouse on the Rifton Road (now Weston Road). Weston, unarmed, fled to an upstairs bedroom and locked the door. The men broke in and he was severely beaten. (Courtesy of Vivian Wadlin)

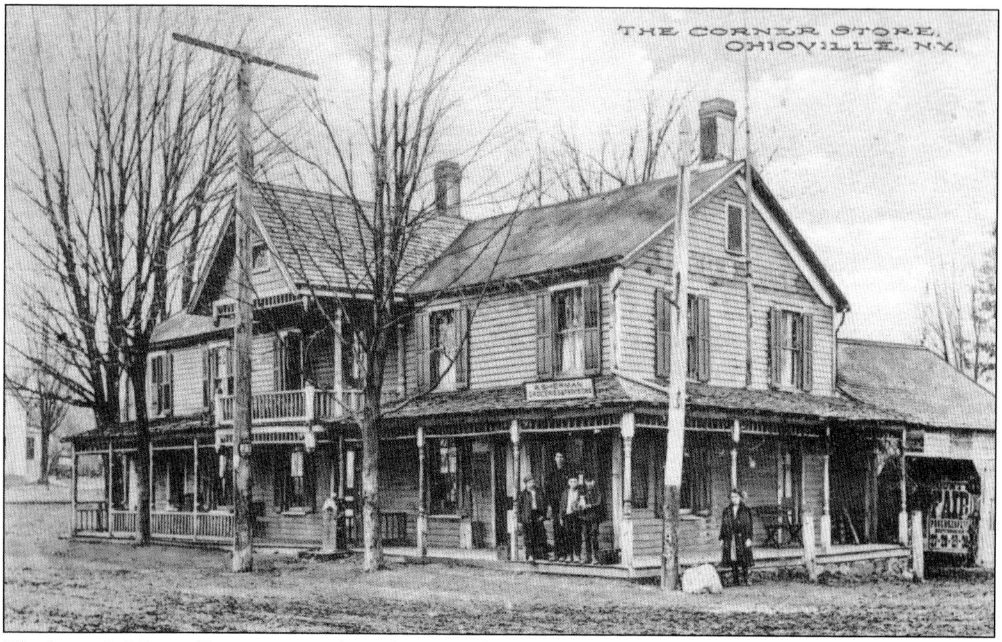

Blacksmith Moses Freer returned to this area from Ohio and settled in what was locally known as "Helltown," but he quickly changed the name to "Ohioville." He set up a blacksmith shop and also made carriages and sleighs. I. C. Dayton bought the property in 1891 and called his hotel the Dayton Rum House. Webb Sherman bought the hotel in 1909 and ran a grocery store in the building.

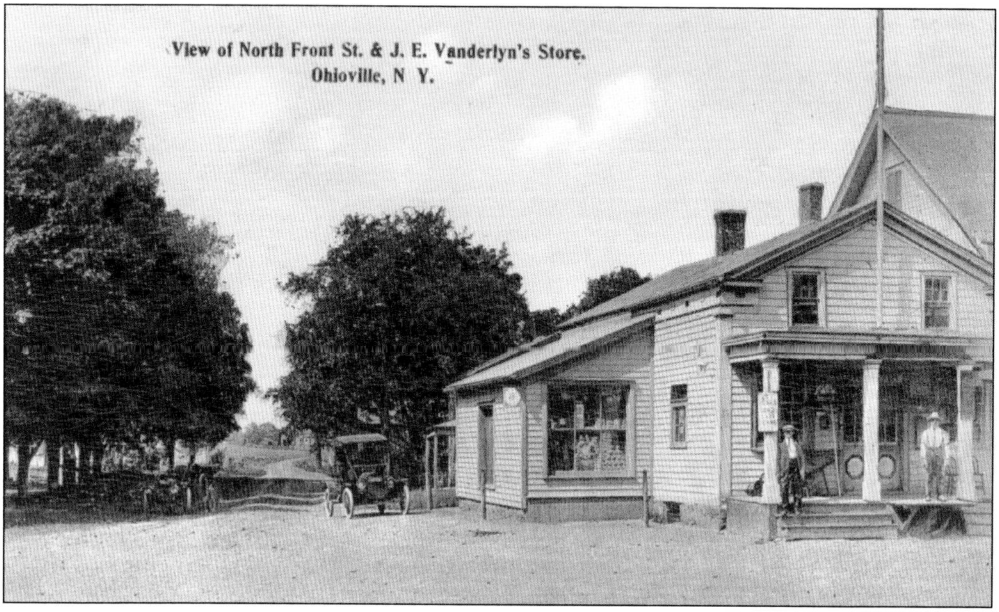

Across the street from Webb Sherman's store was another grocery store, owned by John E. Vanderlyn, a staunch Republican. Sherman was a lifelong Democrat. Depending on the political climate, the post office would shift from one store to the other. Official post office signs were permanently hung outside both establishments. This was confusing for outsiders, but locals knew where to get their mail. (Courtesy of Vivian Wadlin.)

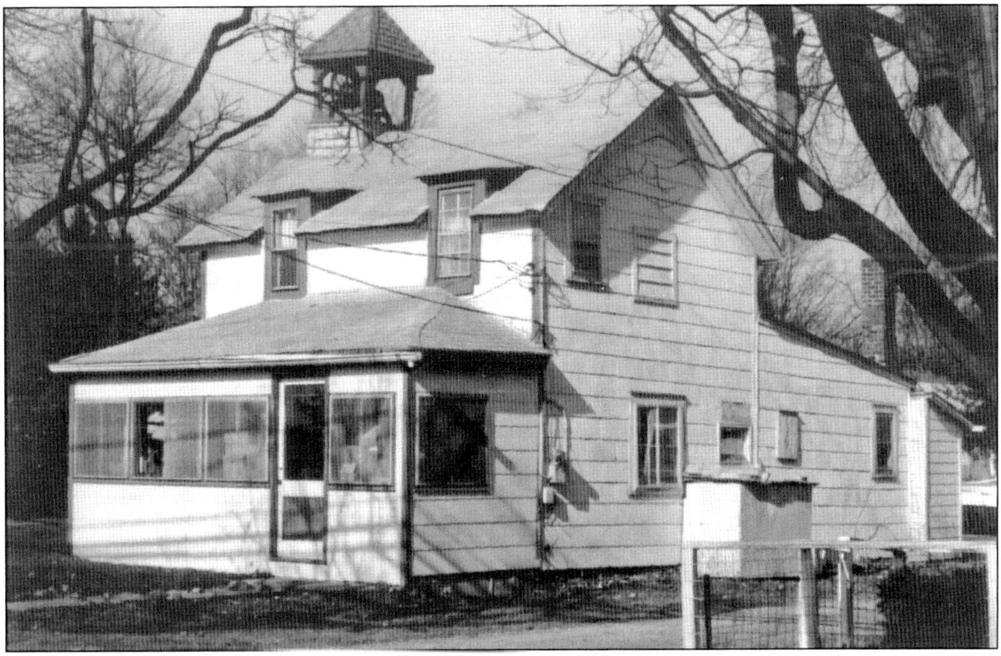

Few people pass by this small country cottage without noticing the bell perched on the roof. John Vanderlyn installed the bell on his harness repair shop so that residents could be summoned in case of a fire. During World War II, the bell was sounded as an air raid alert. A warden would ring the bell, usually at night, telling area residents to turn off all their lights and to take cover indoors. (Photograph by Marion Ryan.)

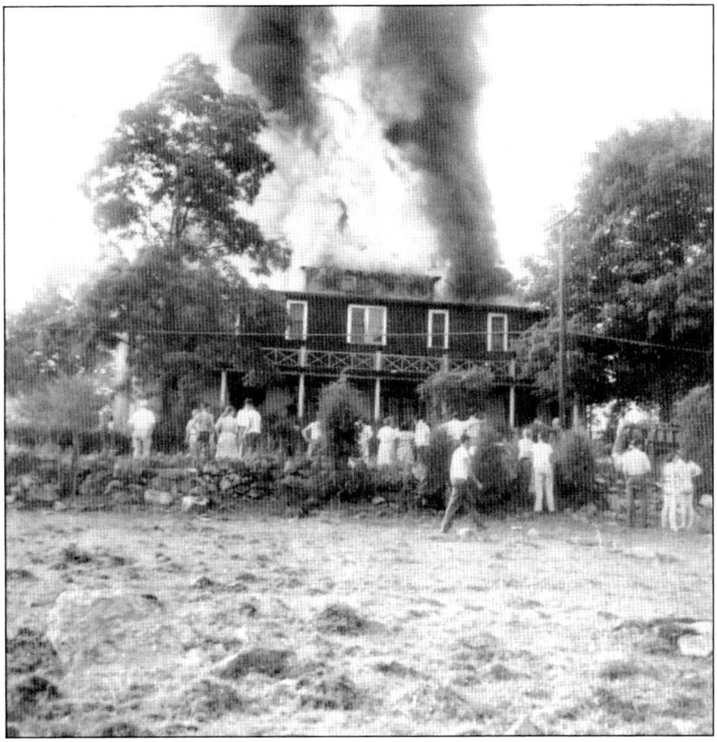

The Tusa Hotel went up in smoke on July 4, 1949. The 29-room boardinghouse was filled to capacity for the holiday weekend. The blaze, which started on the second floor of the two-and-a-half story building, destroyed the entire structure, along with a barn and a garage within an hour. The volunteer firemen's efforts were hampered by a lack of water. (Courtesy of Dede Smith.)

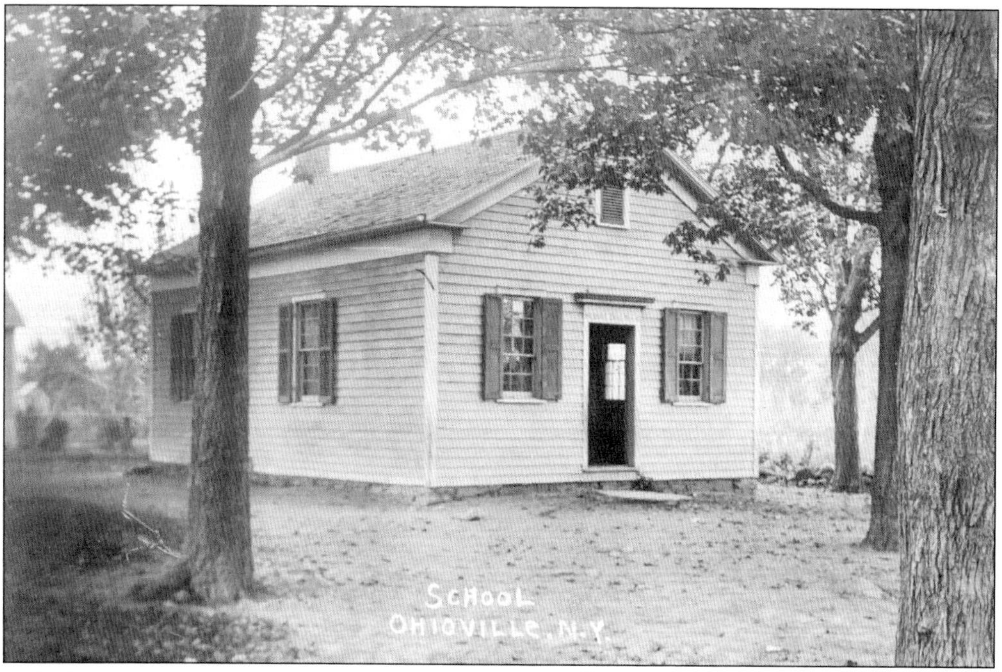

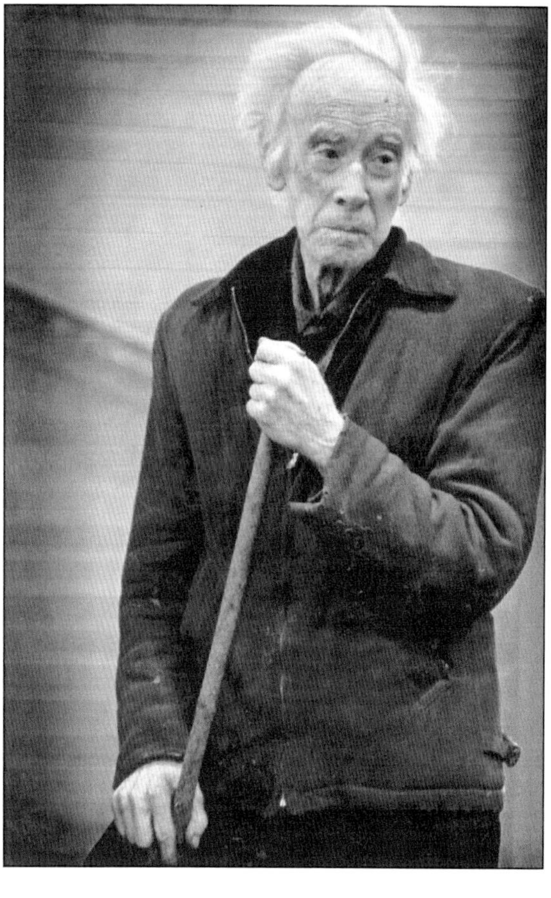

One-room schoolhouses, like this one in Ohioville, began dotting the countryside in the early 1800s. These schools had a basic curriculum, just reading and writing. The curriculum was expanded in 1827 to include geography, grammar, and arithmetic. Cooperative teachers would later travel from school to school and teach art, music, and physical education. The Ohioville School closed in 1946.

Byron J. Terwilliger (1867–1962) graduated from the New Paltz Normal School in 1894. He taught at country schools in Kettleborough, New Hurley, Lamontville, Ruby, Brunswick, and Ohioville. Terwilliger was also a collector of all items that he believed were of historical value. He wrote the book *Old Gravestones of Ulster County* with Dr. J. Wilson Poucher in 1931. (Photograph by Morris Rosenfield.)

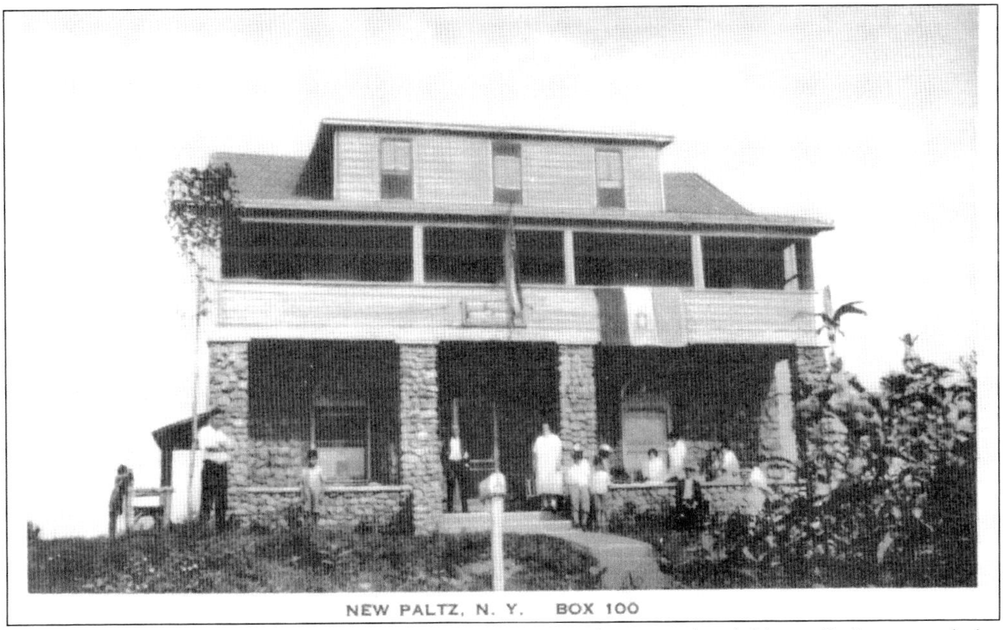

"There are at least six or eight houses in the Italian colony south of Ohioville," reported the *New Paltz Independent* on August 12, 1920. "Most of the houses are of cobblestone. These houses are large and substantial looking. The peculiar style of architecture is, no doubt, Italian. These Italians are noted for their industry and large families. It is said that about half of the children in the Ohioville school district are Italians."

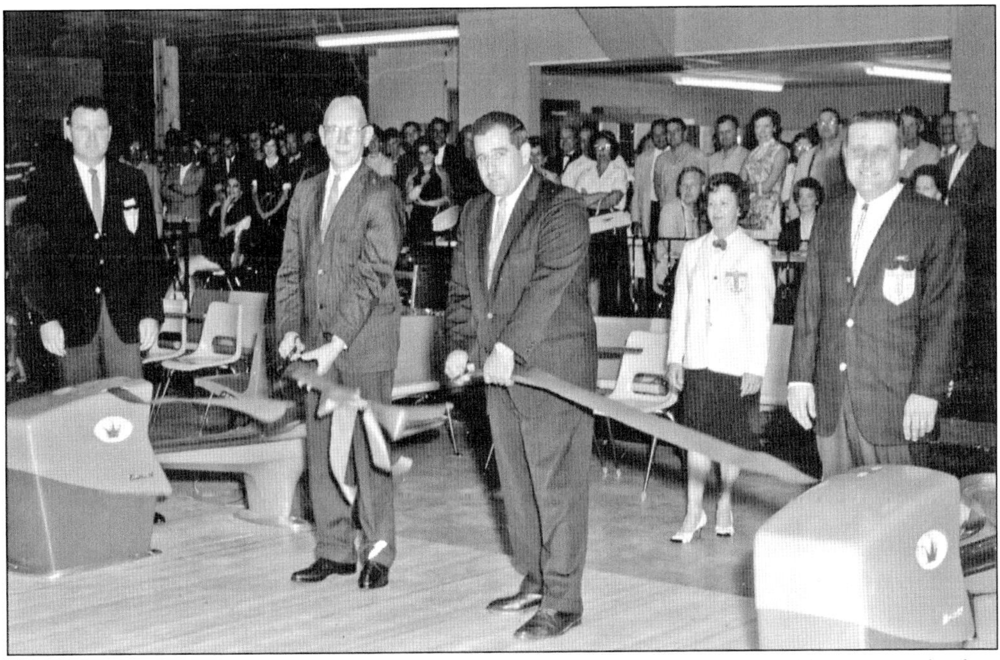

Mayor Henry W. DuBois (left) and Town Supervisor Peter J. Savago cut the ribbon across the first two lanes at the grand opening of the College Lanes Bowling Alley in 1963. They also bowled the first gutter ball and first strike. After the ceremony, guests were invited for refreshments and dancing in the Hasbrouck Room to the music of the Lew Schaffert Orchestra.

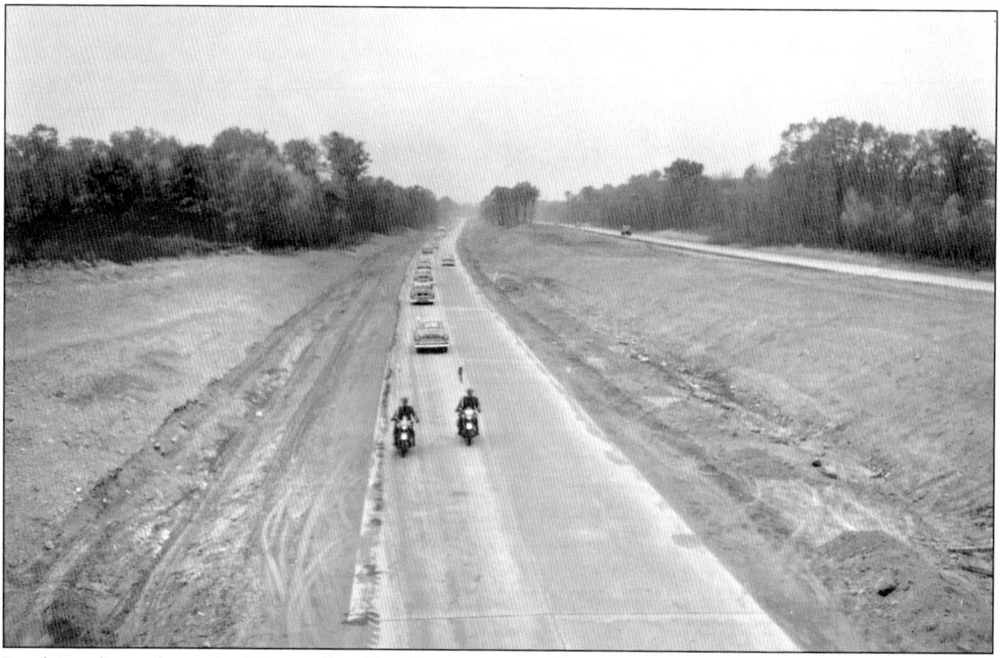

Looking down from the Horsenden Road overpass on the morning of October 26, 1954, one would have seen a 500-car cavalcade led by Gov. Thomas E. Dewey, marking the grand opening of the Newburgh-to-Utica section of the New York State Thruway. When it opened, the toll was 1.25¢ per mile. (Courtesy of the Lent family.)

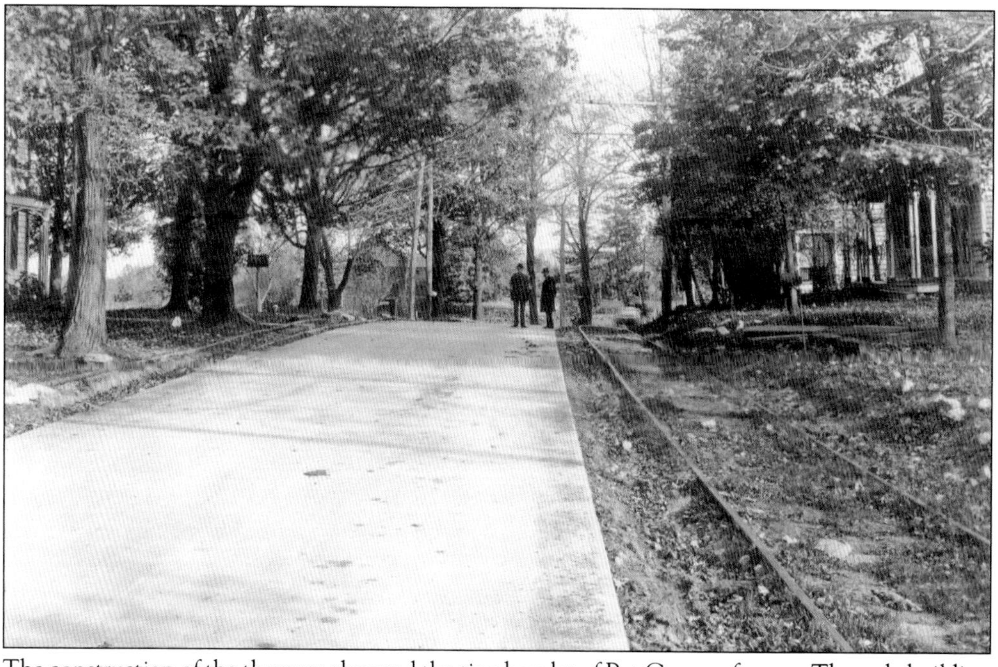

The construction of the thruway changed the tiny hamlet of Put Corners forever. The only building still standing from this 1924 photograph is now the home of Empire State Bank at 275 Main Street (far left). The homes on the right were replaced by the Shop-Rite Plaza. The trolley tracks have been removed, and Main Street was substantially widened. (Courtesy of the Lent family.)

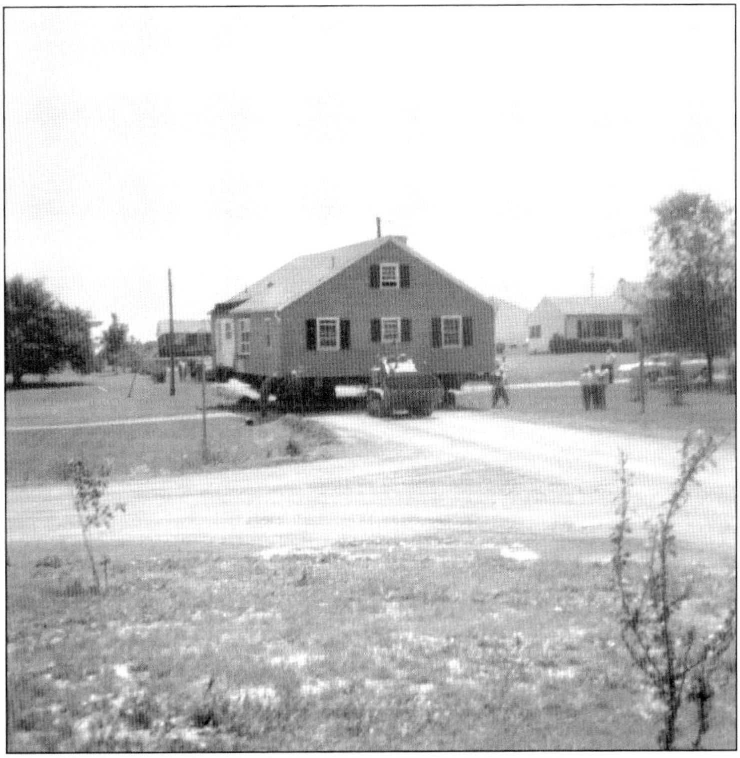

The house located at 3 Cicero Avenue was moved in 1971 to make way for a Friendly's Ice Cream Shop. Frank LoCicero owned orchards on "Cherry Hill" and slowly parceled off his property. He had hoped that the streets in the development would bear the names of his children, but instead they are inexplicably named Bruce, Rita, Howard, and Gardner Streets. Early maps show Cicero Avenue as LoCicero Avenue. (Courtesy of Audrey Roach.)

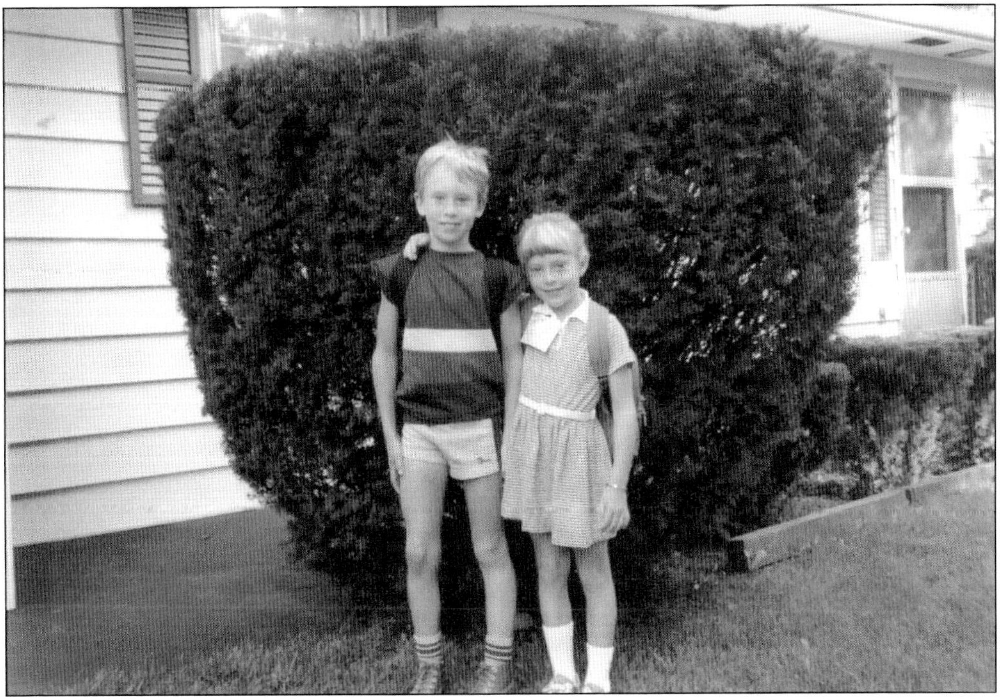

David and Kim Ziegler wait in front of their home on Duzine Road for the school bus to Duzine Elementary School. Both the school and the road are named for the Duzine, the twelve men who founded and governed the early community. (Photograph by Donna Ziegler.)

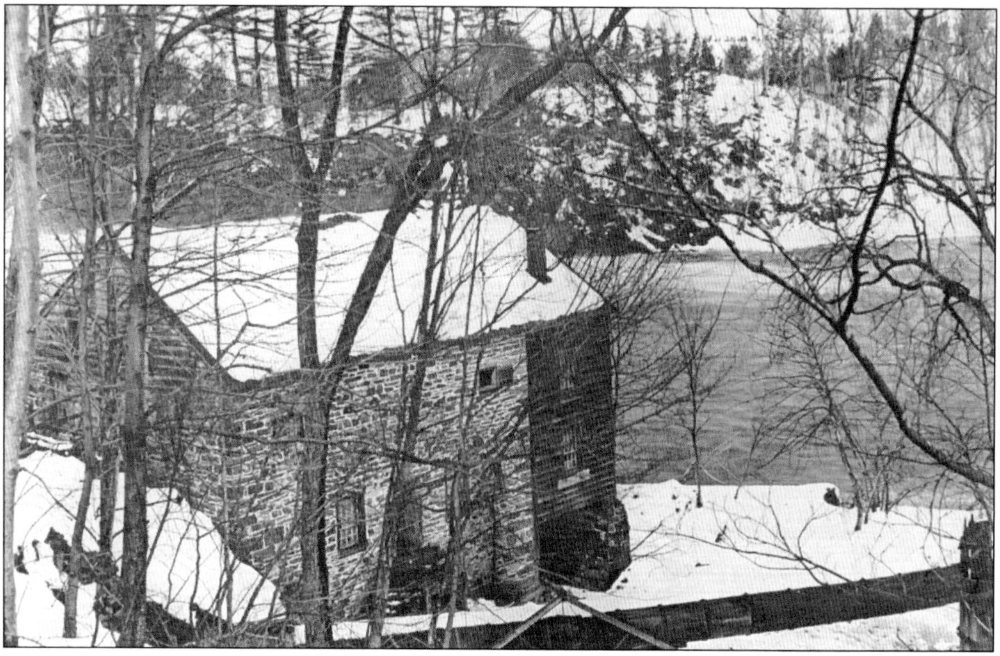

Pieces of the towns of Gardiner, Esopus, and Rosendale also came from the town of New Paltz. The town of Gardiner was formed in 1853, and the little hamlet of Libertyville was split between New Paltz and Gardiner. The Libertyville mill was built before 1790 by Nathaniel DuBois. Its ruins can still be seen along the west bank of the river. (Photograph by H. L. Schultz.)

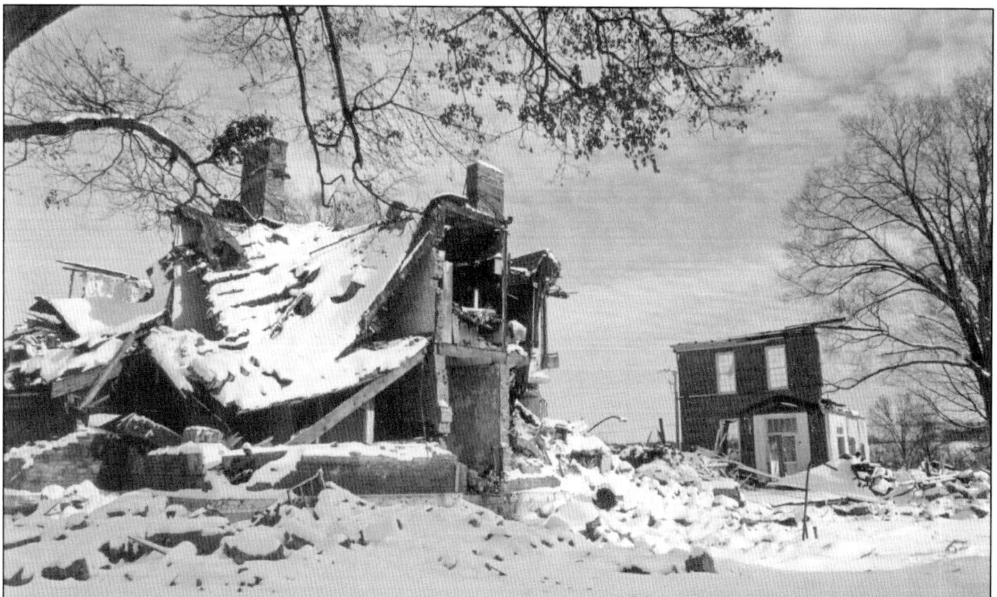

The former Ulster County Home was torn down in February 1985, after being declared unsafe due to a fire that happened three years earlier. The buildings served as an adult residence for home relief recipients until 1978, and one wing was used as a migrant childcare center until 1981. The building complex had been constructed in 1888 to replace the old county poorhouse and insane asylum. (Photograph by Jon Margolis.)

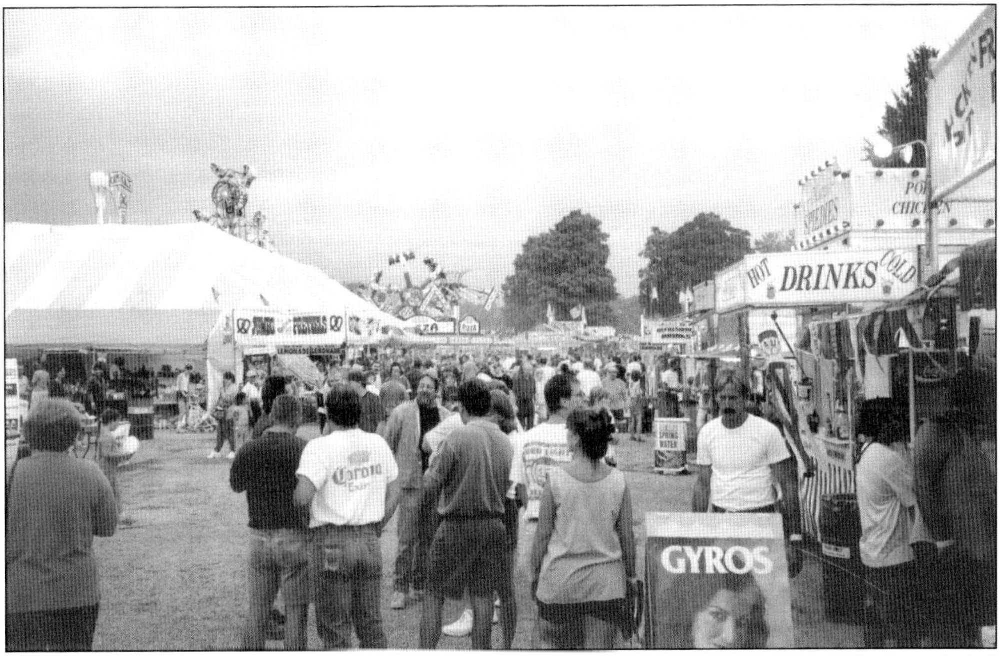

The Ellenville Driving Park played host to several small fairs beginning in 1869, which included horse racing and agricultural exhibits. The newly founded Ulster County Agricultural Society began the first official Ulster County Fair in 1886. The fair was held first in Ellenville and then in Kingston before coming to New Paltz in 1967. (Photograph by Dennis O'Keefe.)

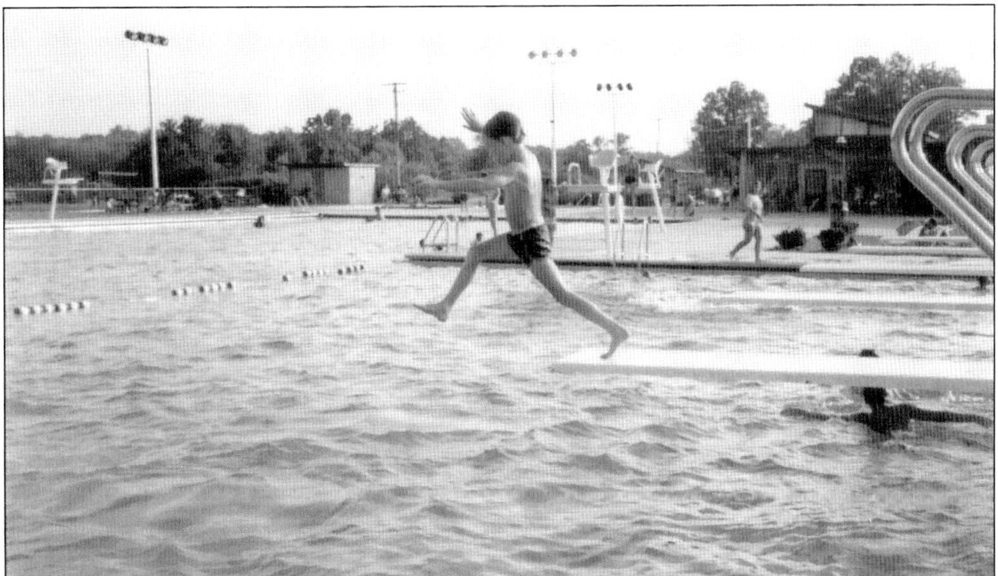

Young David Ziegler jumps into the Ulster County Pool. The pool was the first stage of a park master plan that included the pool complex, a pond for fishing and ice-skating, picnic areas, an amphitheater for summer concerts, a canoe launch, a golf course, and camping areas. The poorhouse cemetery, with more than 2,000 grave sites, was destroyed when the pool was built in 1976. (Photograph by Donna Ziegler.)

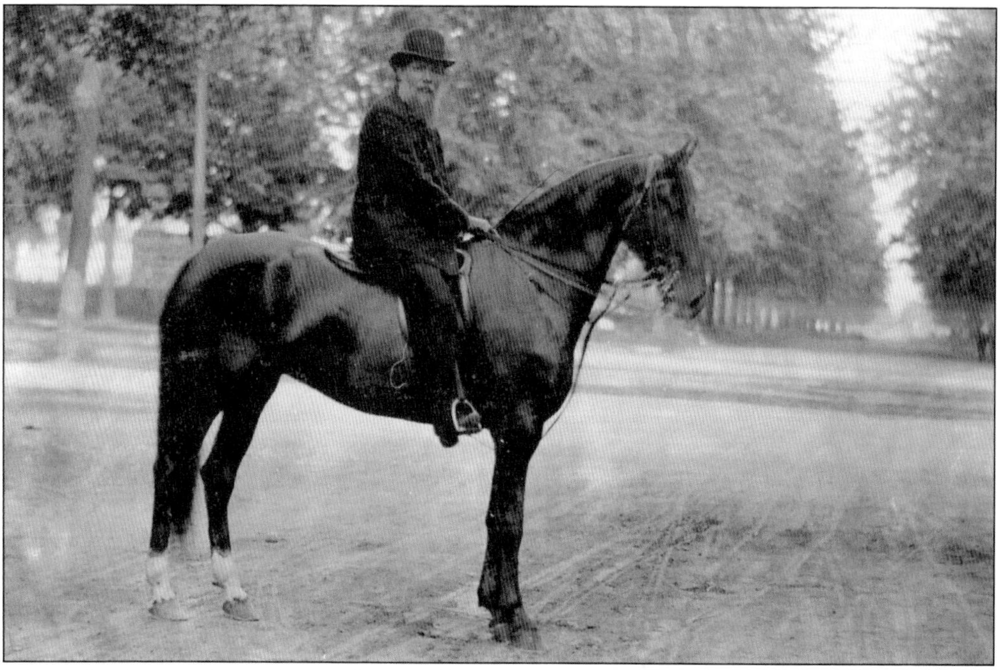

John Arbuckle was the leading coffee and Cuban sugar importer to the United States in the early 20th century. In his later years, he was a celebrated philanthropist. He purchased several farms west of the Wallkill and established a program that brought 40 underprivileged children at a time for a free two-week vacation in the country. When he died in 1912, his estate was estimated to be $20 million. (Courtesy of Geri Buck.)

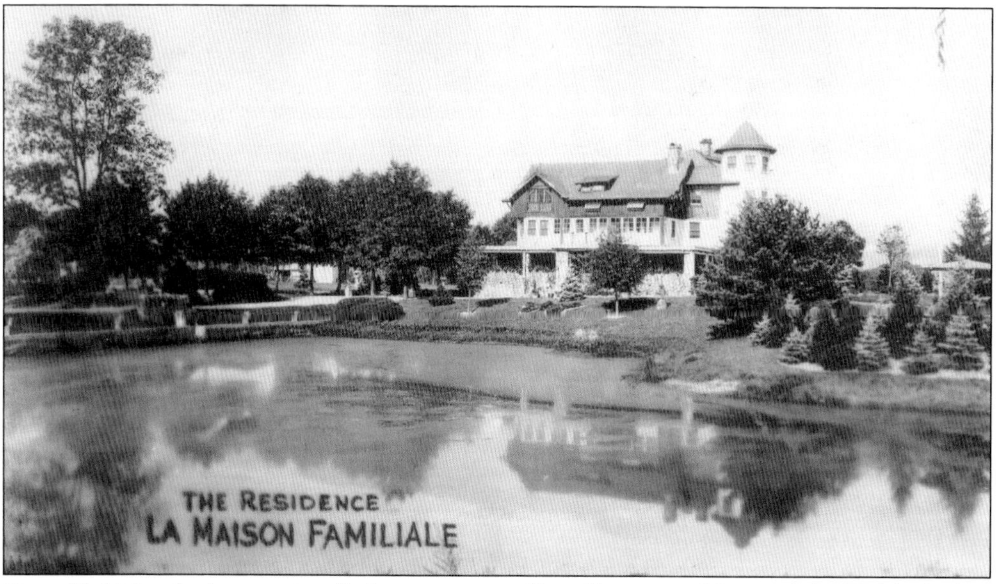

Oscar Tschirky, the internationally famous maitre d'hotel known as "Oscar of the Waldorf," died here at his home in 1950. Despite popular illusions, Oscar never was a chef, although he is credited with concoctions such as Veal Oscar, Waldorf Salad, and Thousand Island salad dressing. He deeded his beautiful home to the Societe Culinaire Philanthropique, and it serves as a retirement home. (Courtesy of Vivian Wadlin.)

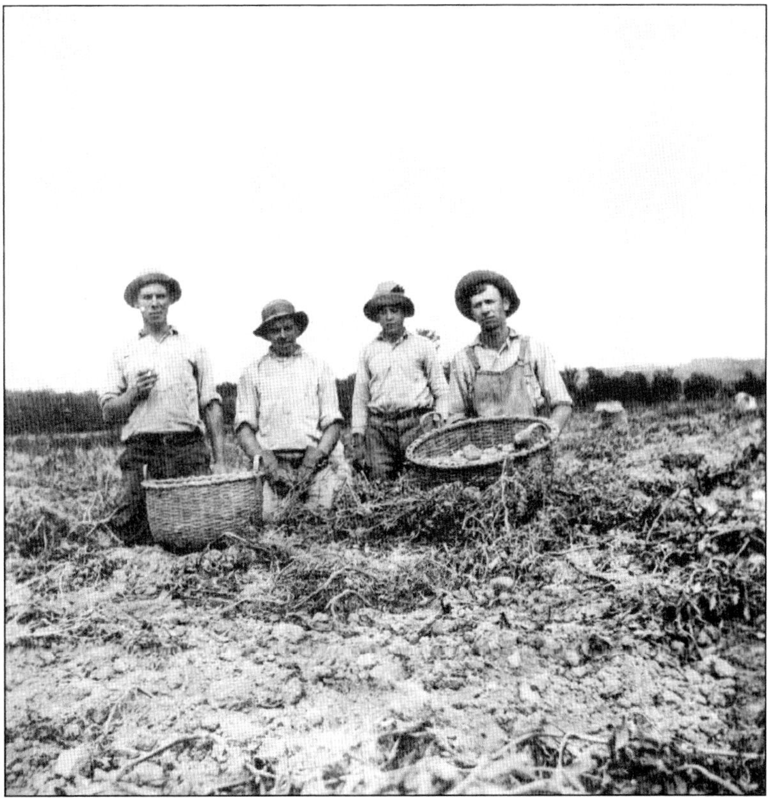

Potatoes and onions were the principal crops of the Springtown farmer. In 1914, Oscar Deyo harvested a crop of approximately 4,000 potatoes. The price of a bushel of potatoes at that time was approximately 80¢. At the Tim Sullivan farm, pictured at right, workers are filling their baskets with ripe potatoes ready for market. (Courtesy of Janet McDermott.)

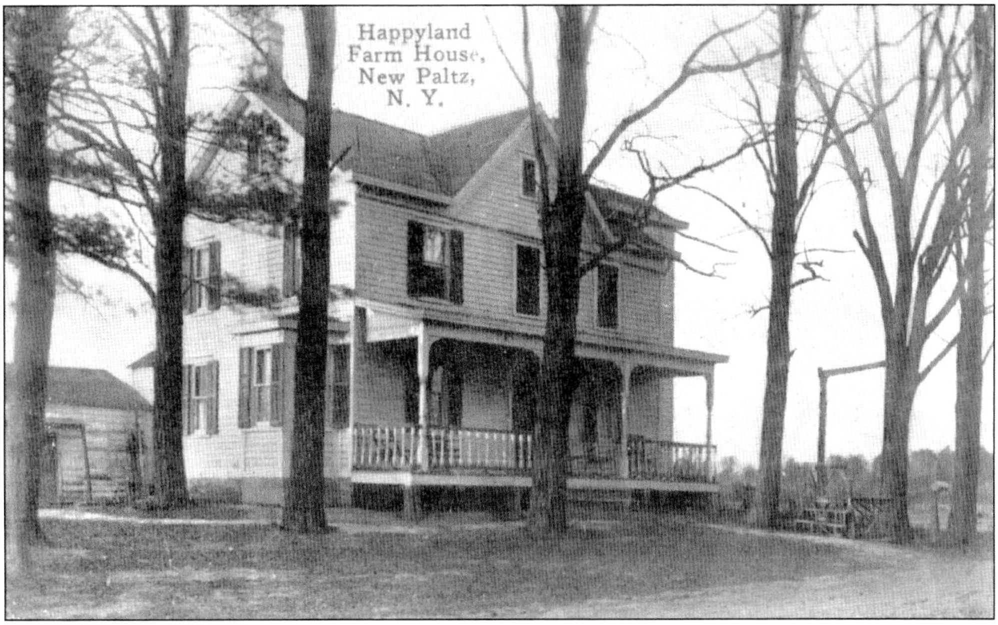

For a 60-year period starting around 1875, Springtown was known for its hotels and boardinghouses. Tourists would flock to establishments like Happyland on Dug Road for the summer. Owned first by Tjerck Deyo and then by the Oscar Shuttrick family, the *New Paltz Independent* reported that 40 summer boarders were vacationing there in 1914.

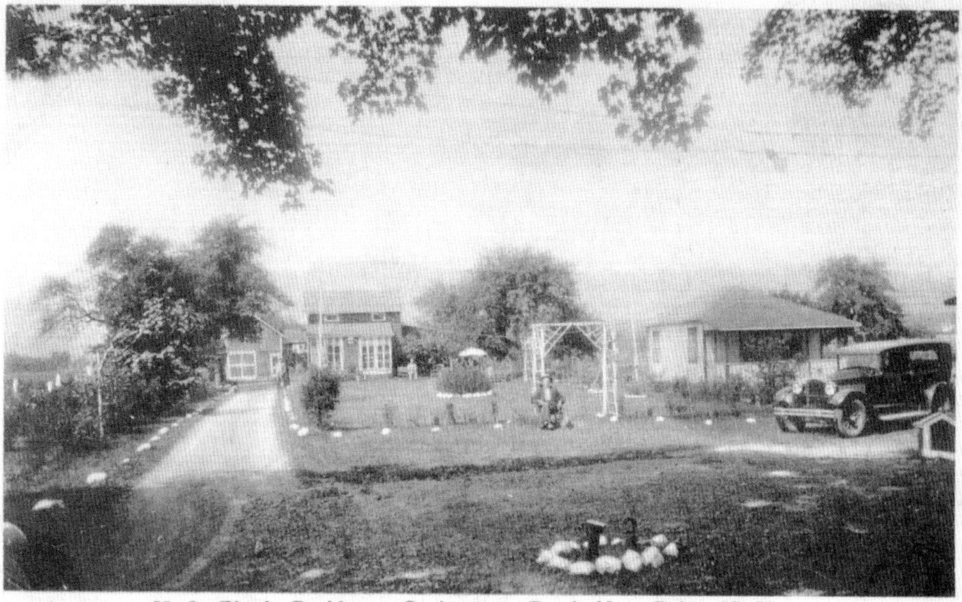

H. L. Eberle Residence, Springtown Road, New Paltz, N. Y.

Harry Eberle sits in front of his Maple Lodge Farm, at 317 Springtown Road, in 1929. Chief Provost, an Native American chief who spent his weekends at the Maple Cottage, presented Eberle with a talking, whistling parrot in July 1928 that was much admired by the other boarders there. Chief Provost was with Buffalo Bill's Wild West Show for 25 years as an interpreter.

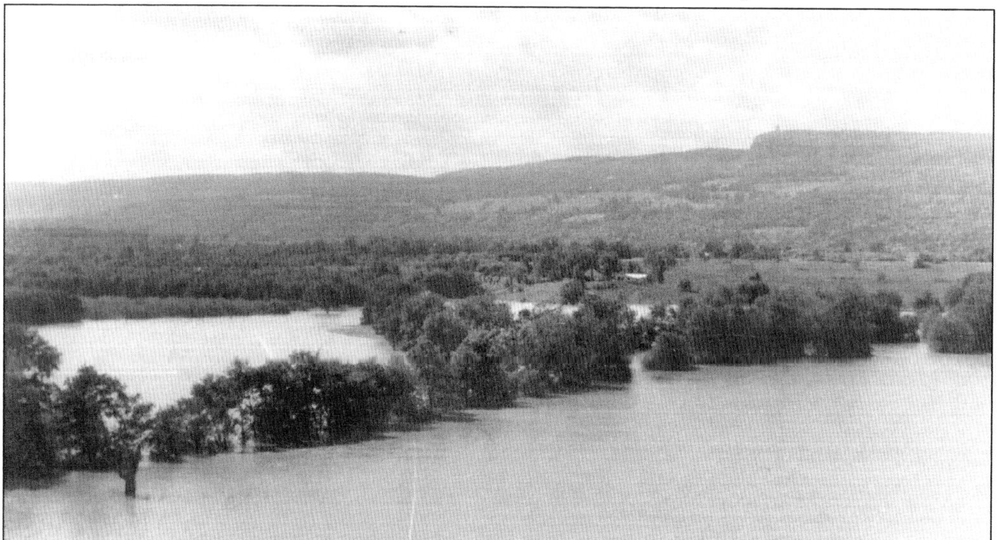

Springtown was especially hard hit by the Wallkill River floods. Two storms hit the Wallkill Valley in 1955, each causing record flooding, death, and destruction. Firemen and volunteers in boats evacuated people from the low-lying areas. A boat ride on the river found several houses with water nearly up to their first-floor windows. One farmer lost a flock of 1,400 chickens in the August flood.

Three

The Village of New Paltz

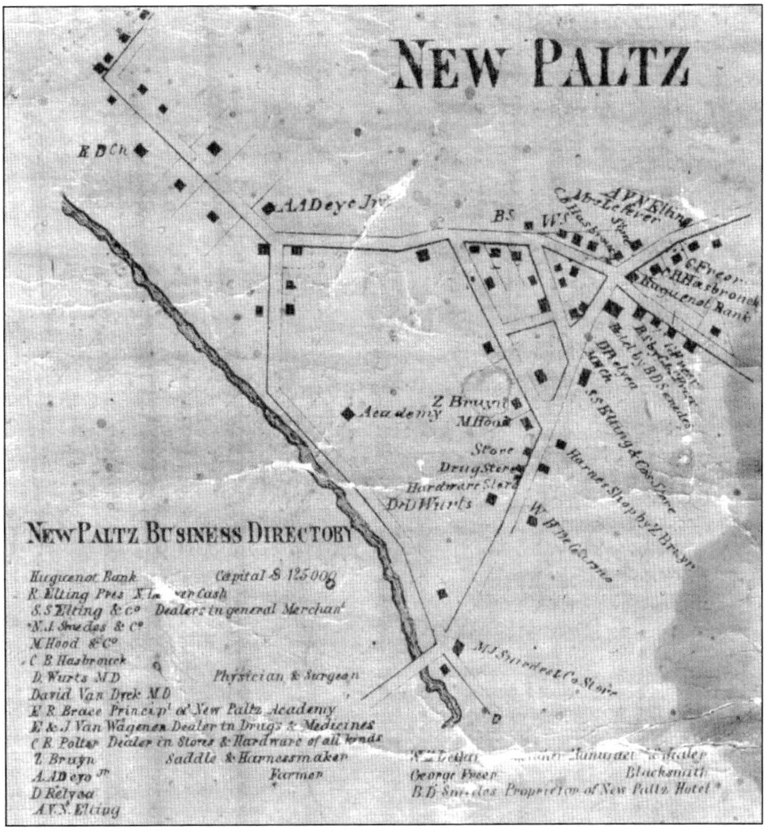

Two events led to the spread of the village away from Huguenot Street and the formation of the present downtown area. The first was the building of the New Paltz Turnpike from New Paltz to Highland in 1831. The second was the building of the old covered bridge in 1845 over the Wallkill River, away from the site of the old scow crossing. This map shows the village of New Paltz in 1858.

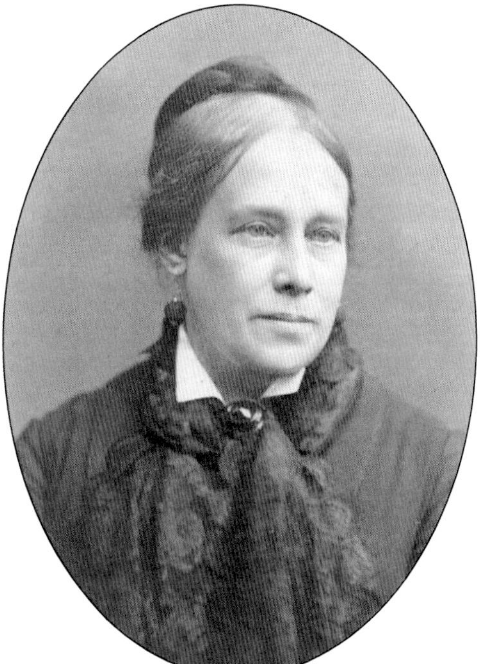 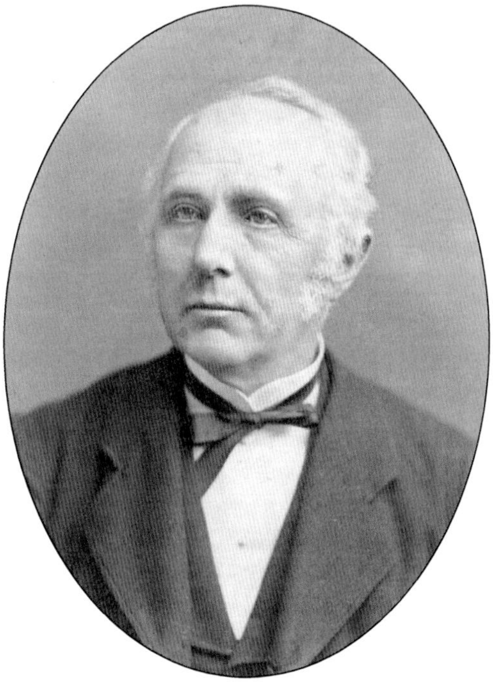

Edmund Eltinge (1817–1897) and his wife, Magdalene Deyo (1819–1878), were the parents of 12 children. Perhaps no other man in New Paltz has been identified with so many aspects of the growth and success of the town. Edmund was the first in New Paltz to embark largely in the grape-growing business. When the railroad came, he bought a large tract on the southern end of the village and laid out building lots. He was active in the work of promoting the building of the Wallkill Valley Railroad. Eltinge was a trustee of the New Paltz Academy and the first president of the Huguenot Bank. He helped organize the Huguenot Memorial and the Ulster County Historical Societies. Below, Edmund sits on the front porch of his home, known as the Locusts, surrounded by his family in 1887. (Below, courtesy of Kate Pepper.)

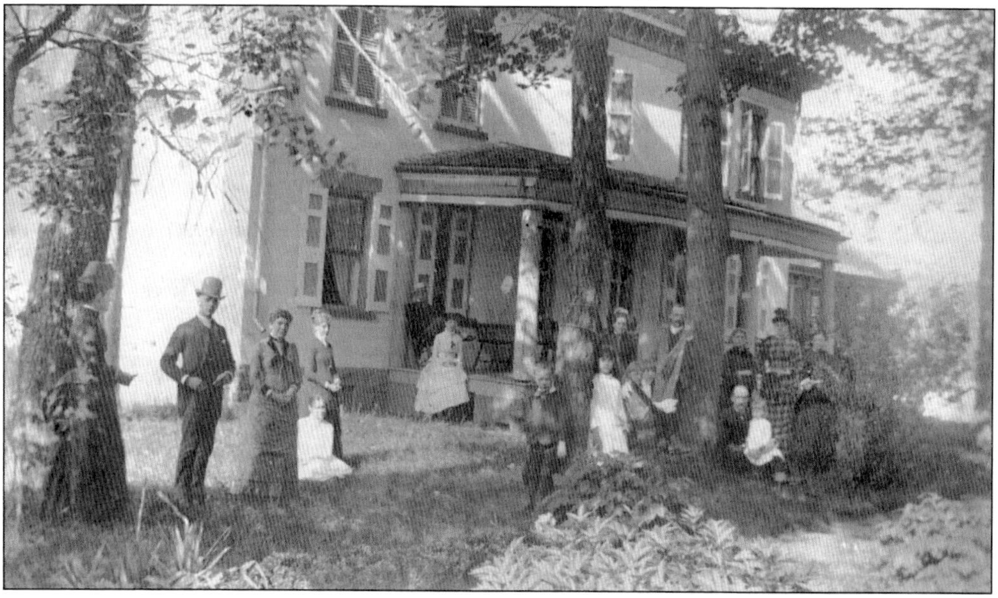

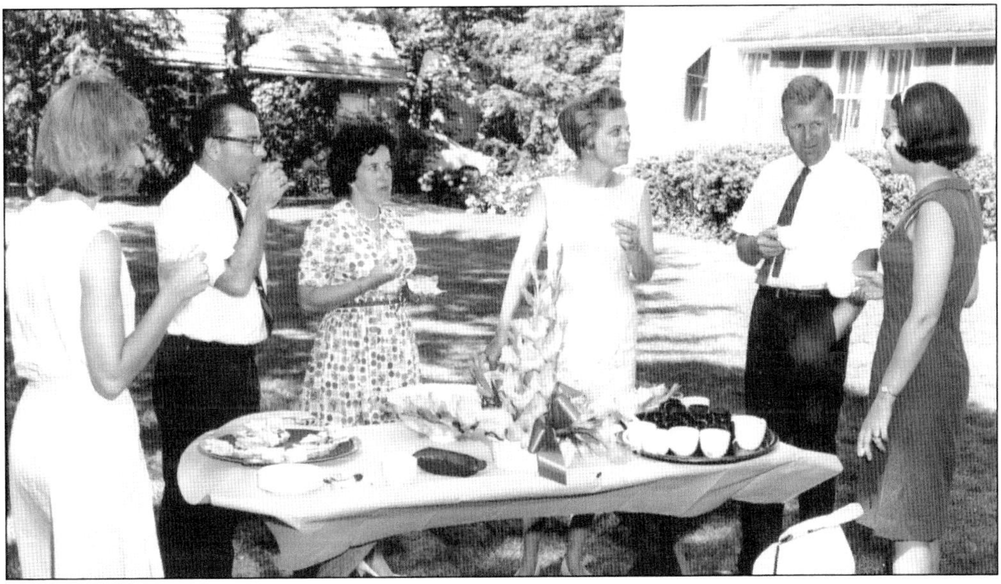

The first house built on Edmund Eltinge's Vineland tract on the south side of the village was the home of Civil War veteran John L. Rosencrans, at 51 Elting Avenue. Later owners Vera and William Irwin (fourth and fifth from left, respectively) would entertain college faculty members and students in their beautiful backyard.

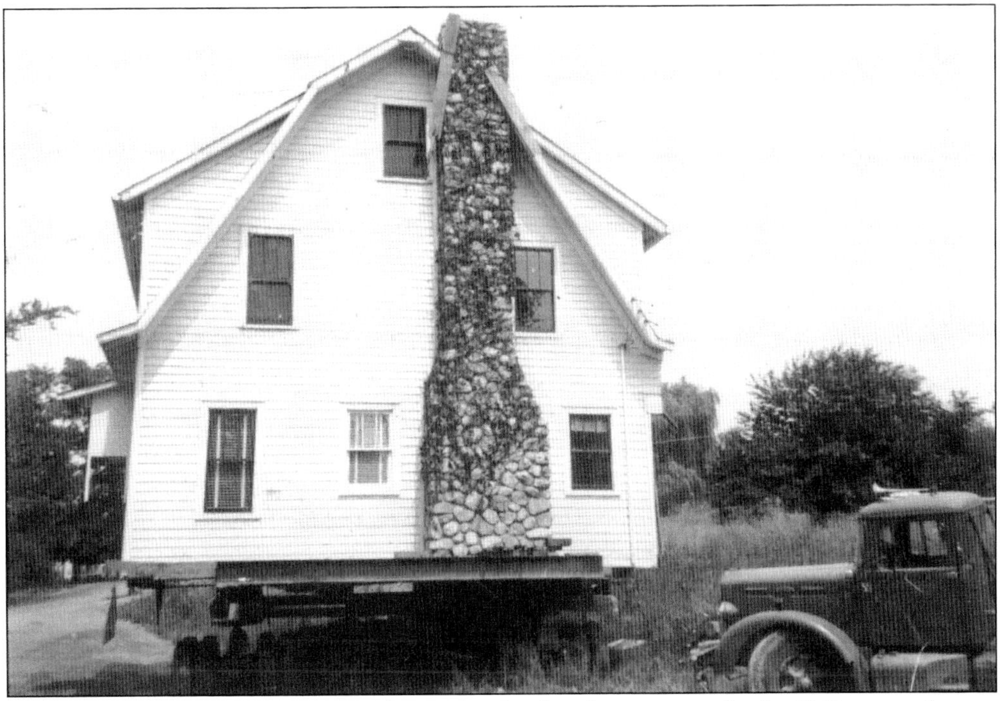

Many of the streets laid out in the Eltinge Vineland no longer exist. In the 1960s, many houses were either moved or torn down for the expansion of the State Teachers College. On the flatbed of a truck is the Lloyd Smith house. This house, along with the house of Howard Mosier and the apartment building of Marinus Peterson, was moved from Excelsior Avenue to South Chestnut Street in 1963. All the other houses on Excelsior were demolished.

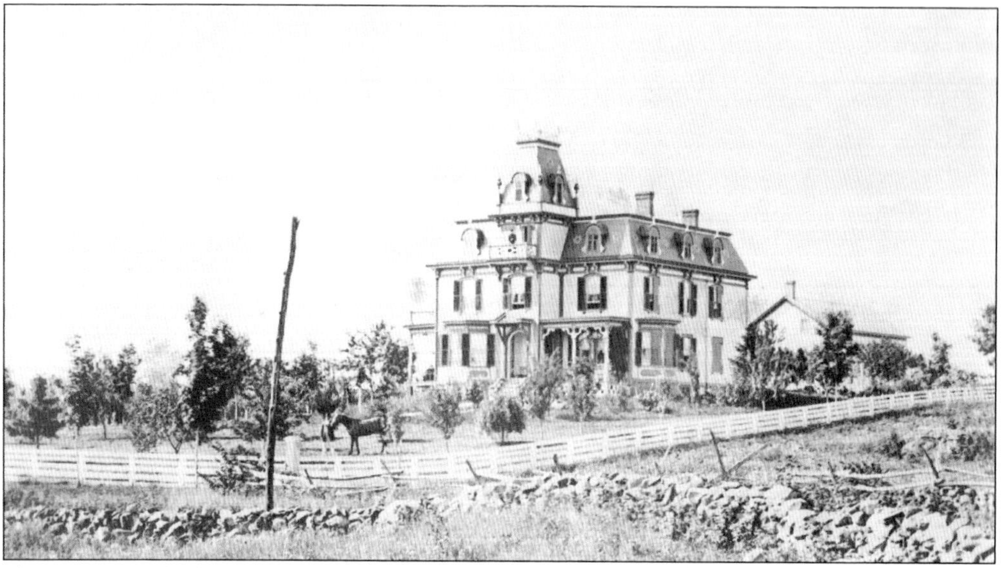

Elting T. Deyo built his own home in the Eltinge Vineland in 1870–1871 at a cost of $11,000. He later ran an undertaking business in the home from 1880 to 1894. In 1947, the house was purchased by the state and became a part of the State Teachers College campus. First used as a dormitory for men, then as offices, it was razed in 1966. (Courtesy of Susanna Lent.)

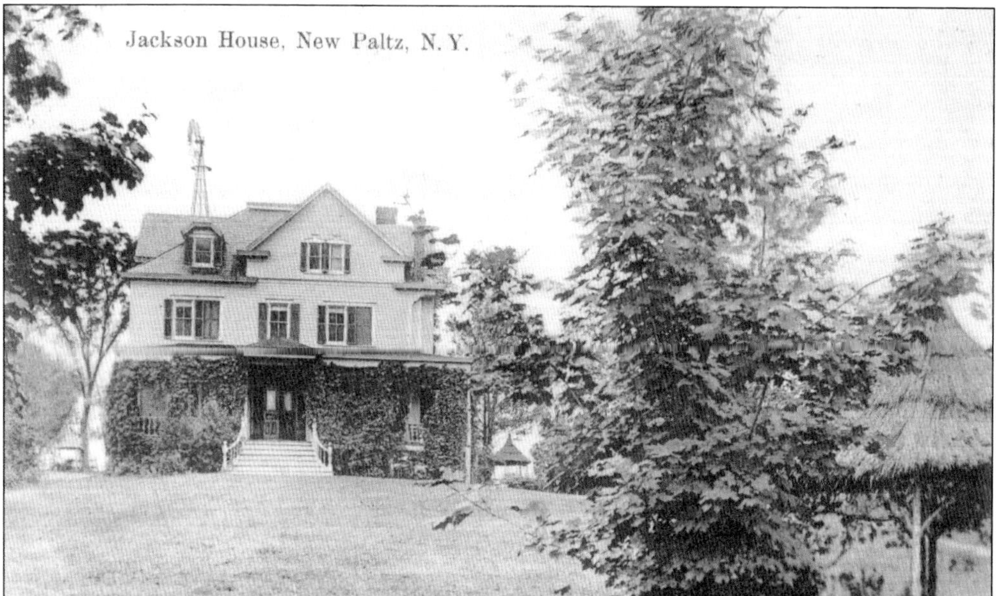

High on the hill overlooking Elting Avenue stood the Jackson boardinghouse. It was the scene of a hostage situation in the early 1960s. A man with a gun held up the house and kept the college girls living there hostage overnight. The large house was later razed, and a parking lot was built on the spot.

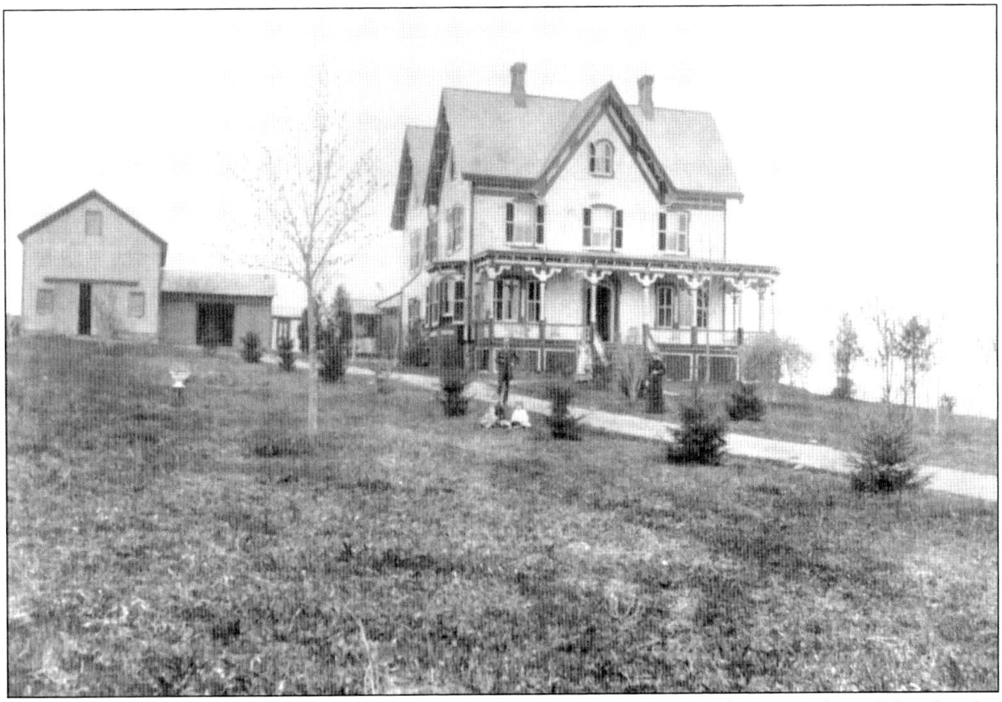

Peter LeFevre built this house in the Eltinge Vineland in 1870. It was later purchased first by the McKinstry family and then by the Lewis H. Woolsey family. In 1920, Peter LeFevre's daughter, Jane, and her husband, Daniel R. Gerow, bought the house. In this image, the Lewis H. Woolsey family is in front of the house, at 14 Southside Avenue.

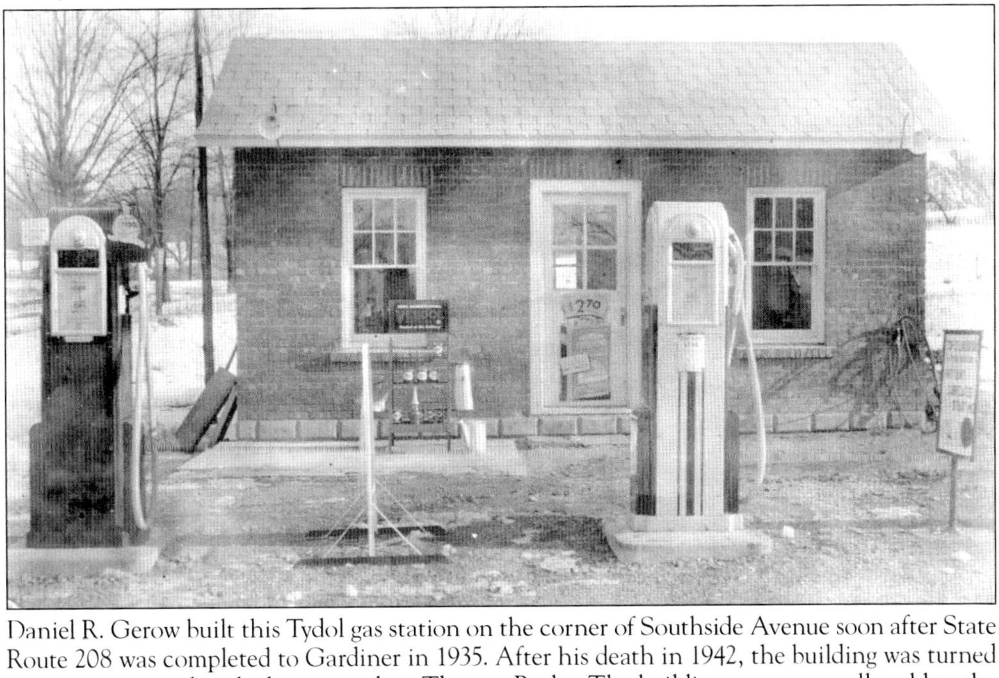

Daniel R. Gerow built this Tydol gas station on the corner of Southside Avenue soon after State Route 208 was completed to Gardiner in 1935. After his death in 1942, the building was turned into an antiques shop by his son-in-law, Thomas Burke. The building was eventually sold to the college and was torn down in June 2002.

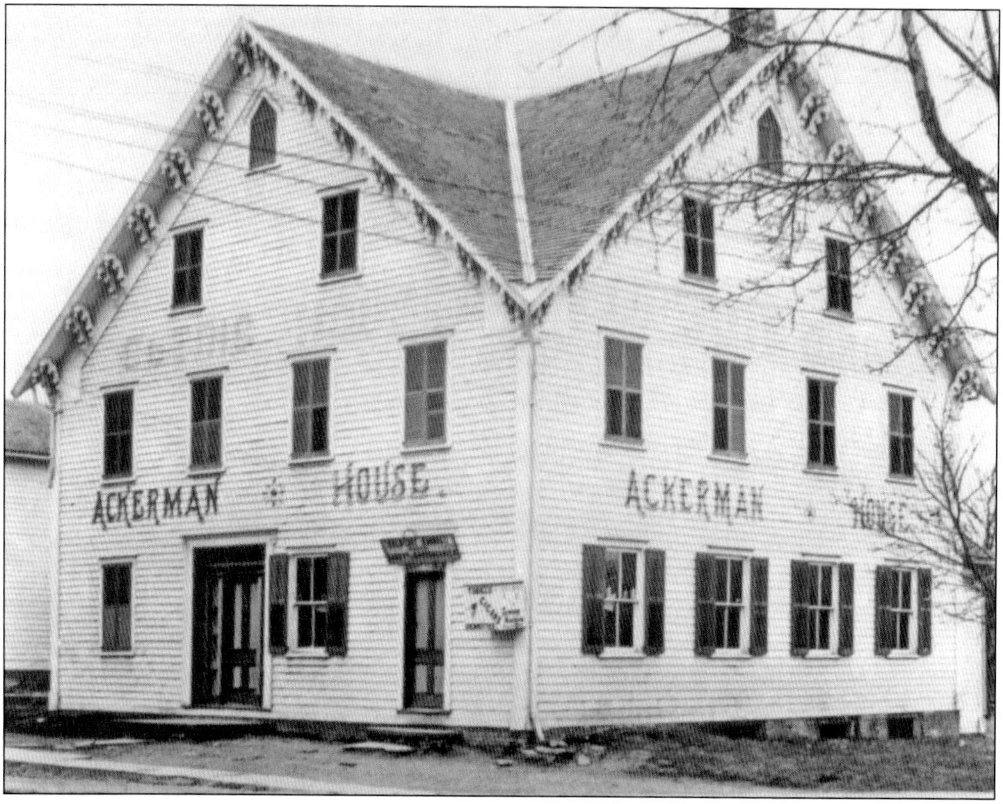

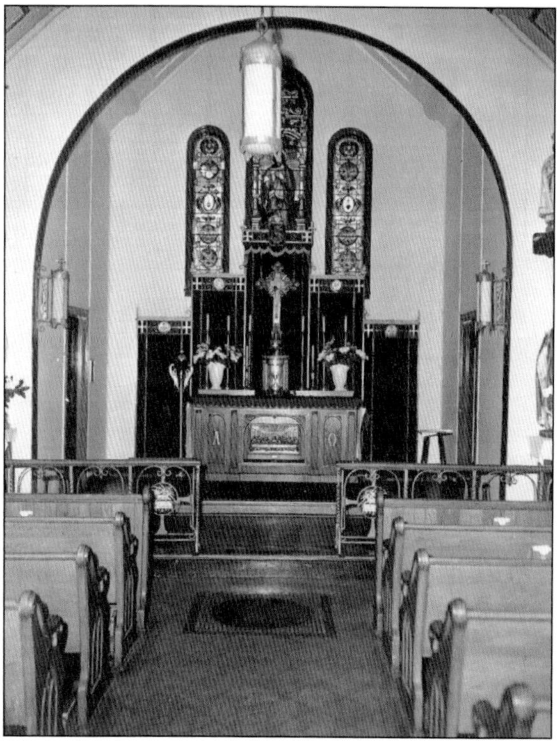

"The Catholic people of this vicinity held services in the hall of the Ackerman House, on Sunday morning last, Rev. Father Browne officiating," according to the January 24, 1883, *New Paltz Independent*. "This hall will hold about 150 people, and was well filled on the above occasion." The Ackerman House was located on the corner of North Chestnut and Front Streets.

Archbishop Michael Corrigan conducted the opening services for the original Catholic church in 1894. By 1965, the congregation had outgrown the original church, and it was torn down to make room for the present, much larger, church. Pictured at left is an interior view of the old St. Joseph's Catholic Church in New Paltz. (Courtesy of St. Joseph's Catholic Church.)

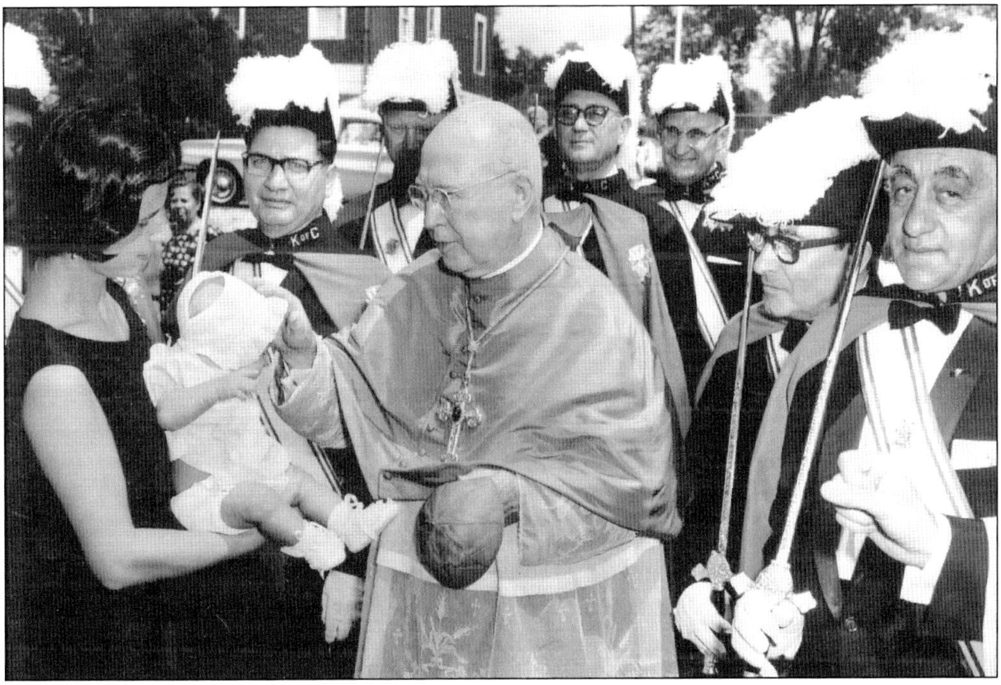

When Cardinal Francis Spellman arrived to dedicate the new St. Joseph's Catholic Church on Sunday, June 5, 1966, he was greeted by some 1,500 parishioners and friends. While on his way inside, he stopped to bless little Leonora Spies. (Courtesy of St. Joseph's Catholic Church.)

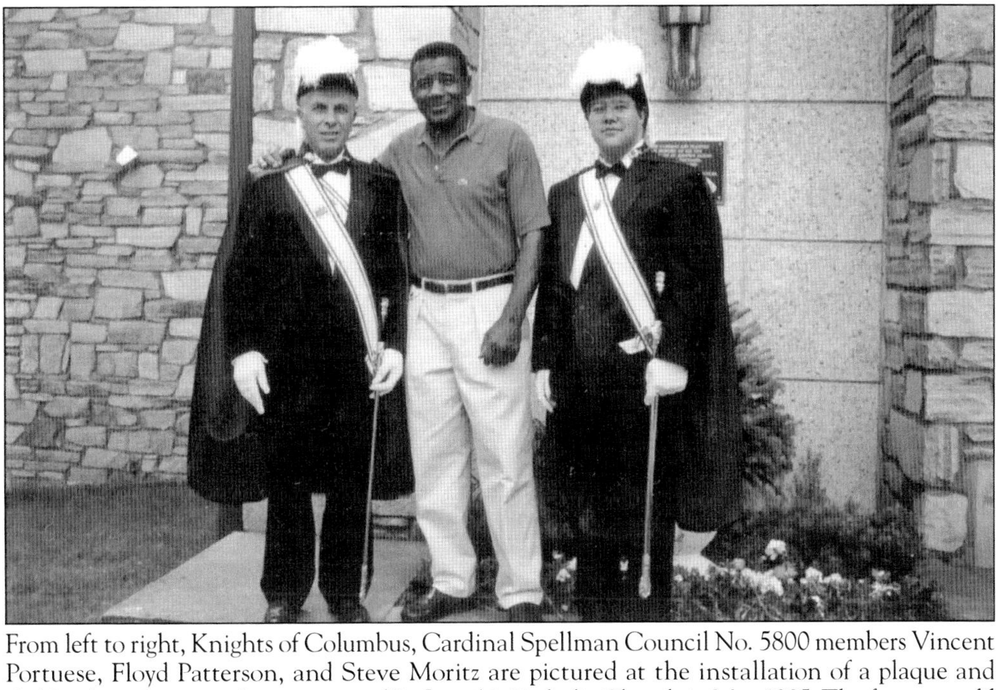

From left to right, Knights of Columbus, Cardinal Spellman Council No. 5800 members Vincent Portuese, Floyd Patterson, and Steve Moritz are pictured at the installation of a plaque and children's garden near the entrance of St. Joseph's Catholic Church in May 1995. The former world champion heavyweight boxer, Floyd Patterson became a member of the Knights of Columbus in 1988. (Courtesy of Vincent Portuese.)

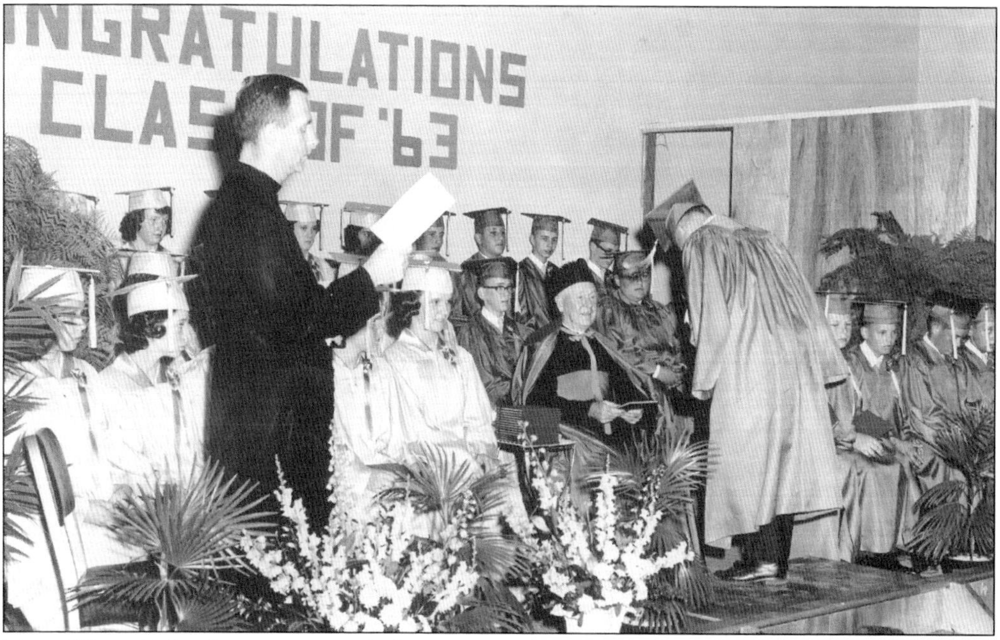

Msgr. Edward Monckton presents diplomas to graduates of St. Joseph's Parochial School while Fr. Joseph Hickey assists in June 1963. The ceremony took place at St. Joseph's Center on North Chestnut Street, which was owned by the church from 1929 to 1966. St. Joseph's Center was the social hall for the parish, and many dances, bazaars, and graduations were held there. The building now houses Barnaby's Restaurant. (Photograph by Leo Spies.)

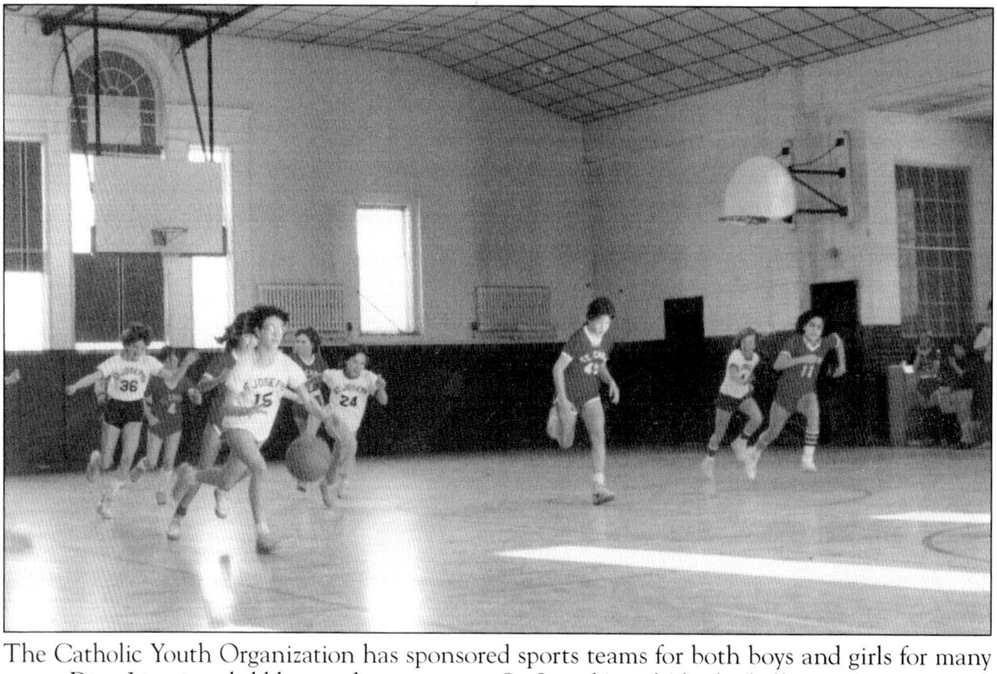

The Catholic Youth Organization has sponsored sports teams for both boys and girls for many years. Dina Ligotino dribbles up the court in a St. Joseph's girls' basketball team game against St. Christopher's of Red Hook in the van den Berg Annex Gymnasium. (Photograph by Linda Ackert.)

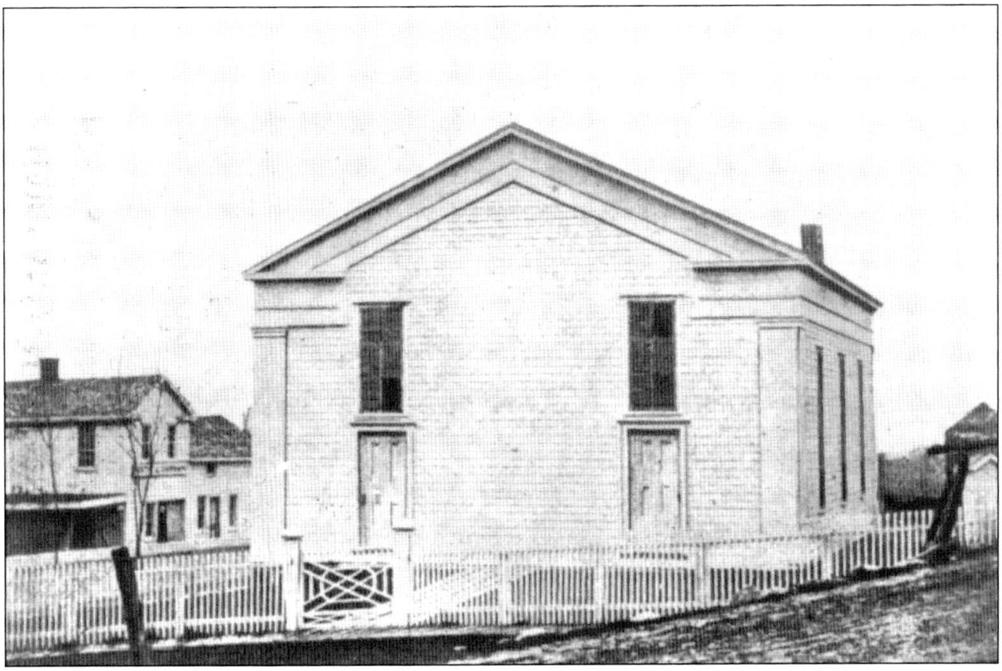

The first Methodist church was located near 69 Main Street. It was erected in 1839, when Martin VanBuren was president, William H. Seward was governor, and Abram P. LeFevre was town supervisor. The church was remodeled in 1870 and was moved in order to front what is now called Church Street. A 70-foot steeple was added to the building, and a parsonage was built next door to the church at the same time.

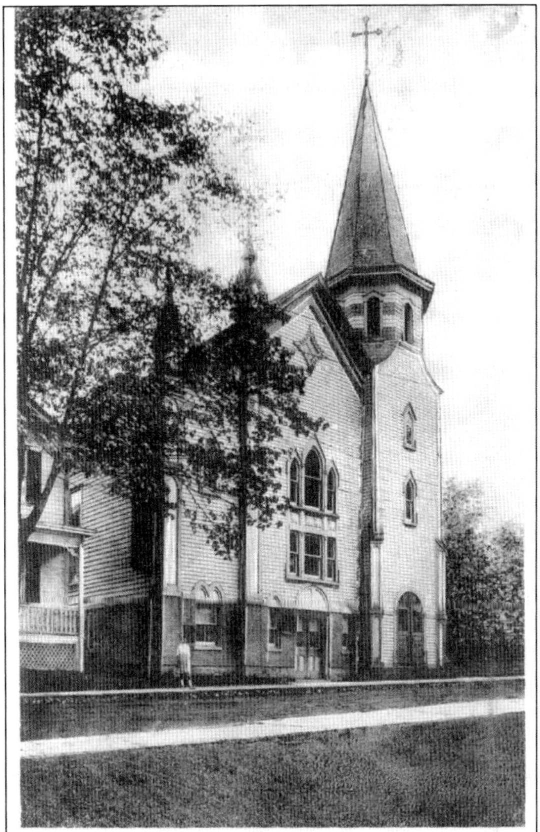

No. 8. METHODIST CHURCH. 1840-1924. NEW PALTZ, N. Y.

The Methodists sold the building in 1928 to the local American Legion post. The building was modernized in 1947 and the steeple removed. In 1960, the American Legion hall was purchased by the Redeemer Lutheran Church, and it served as a place of worship once again. In 1964, the Jewish Congregation of New Paltz began worshipping there, along with the Lutherans. Congregation Ahavath Achim acquired the building in 1965.

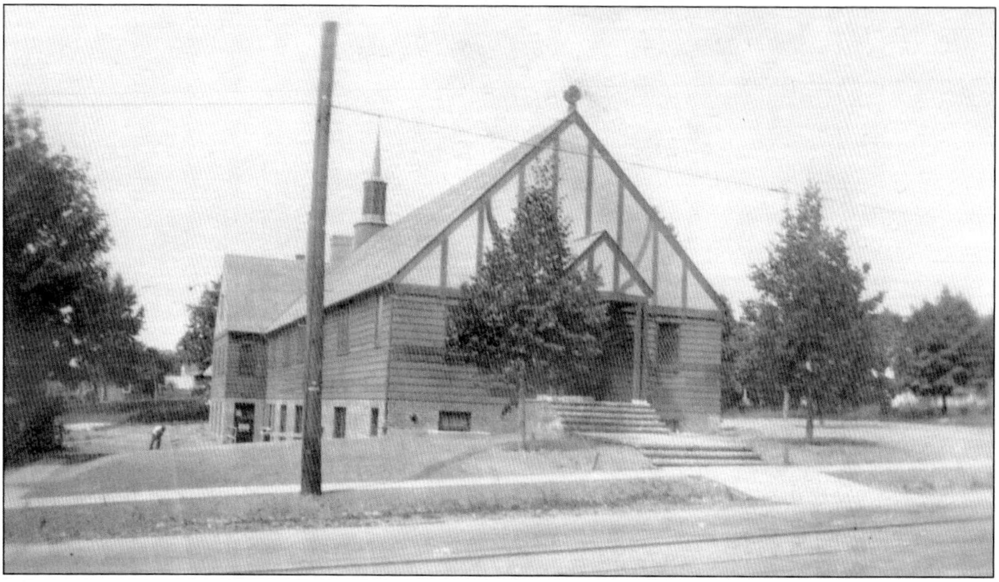

The cornerstone of the new Methodist church, on the corner of Main and Grove Streets, is unique. It has two dates—1839, the date of the original church's construction, and 1929, the year the new church was built. In the cornerstone are keepsakes from two of the first church's cornerstones, including a three-cent piece and articles relating to the 1929 ceremony. An education wing was added to the church in 1961. Rev. Willett R. Porter (below) gives the baccalaureate sermon to graduates at the church in June 1962. Reverend Porter was the minister at the church from 1951 to 1964.

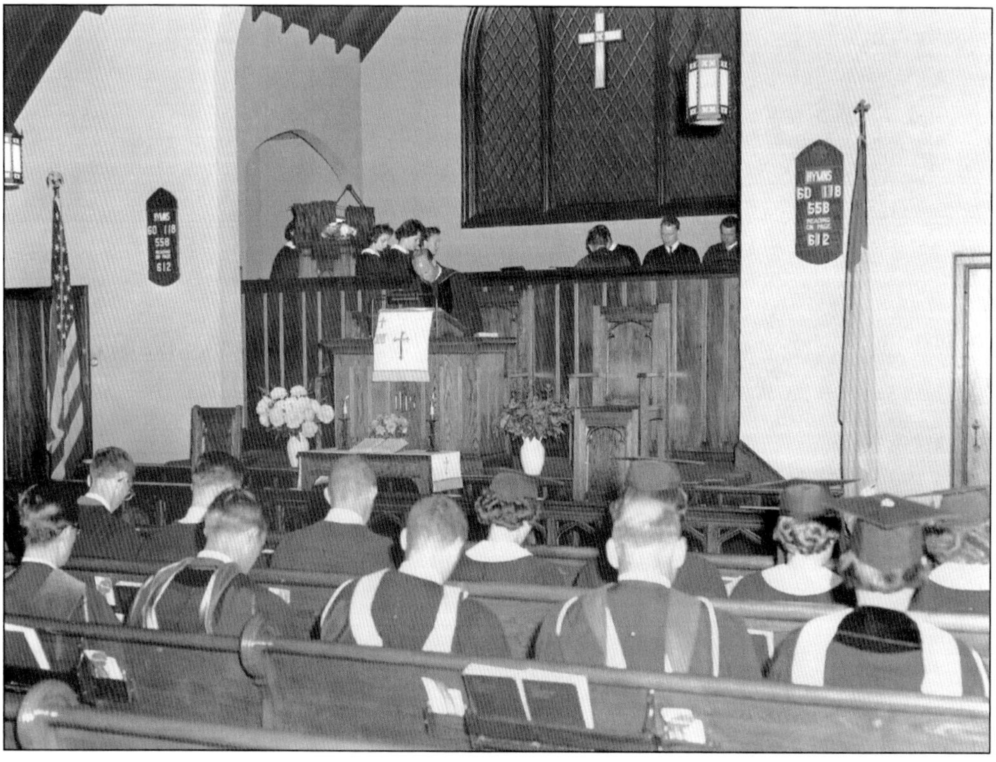

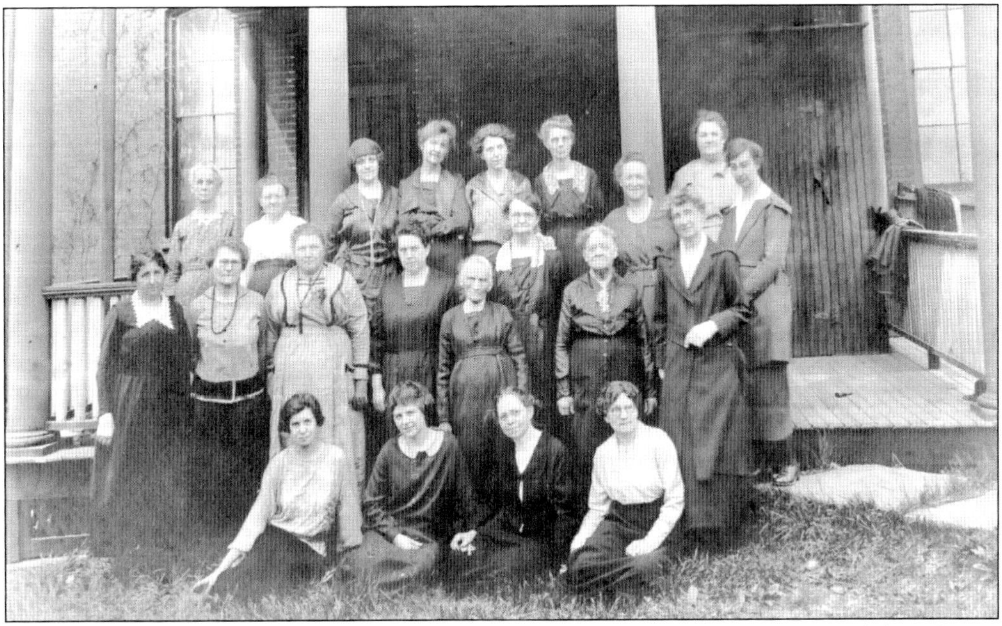

The Seekers class of the Methodist church Sunday school stands on the steps of the Church Street Elementary School on May 8, 1923. The school opened in February 1875, with 89 children assembling for the last time at the old school on North Front Street. They then marched in a column two abreast, headed by their teachers Jennie Schoonmaker and Maggie DuBois, into the new schoolhouse on Church Street. (Courtesy of Elaine Kniffen.)

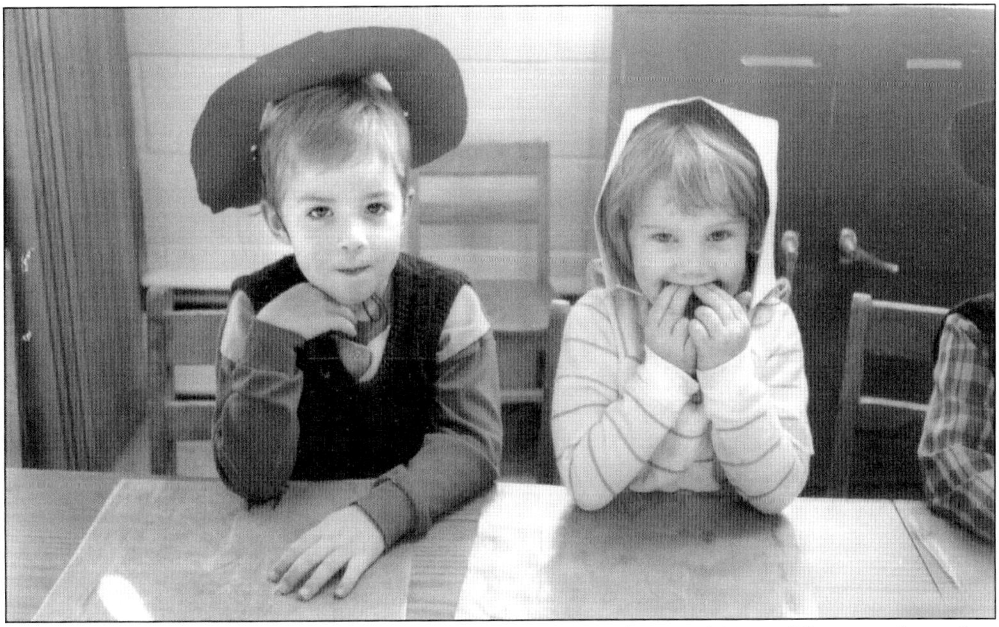

At the Methodist Playschool in November 1988, Sean Corbett and Karen Blase are dressed in pilgrim hats waiting for their Thanksgiving snack to be served on their self-made place mats. The place mats have turkeys embellished on them, made from silhouettes of their hands. Sean and Karen were in the nursery school class taught by Linda Ackert and Virginia Harrison. (Photograph by Linda Ackert.)

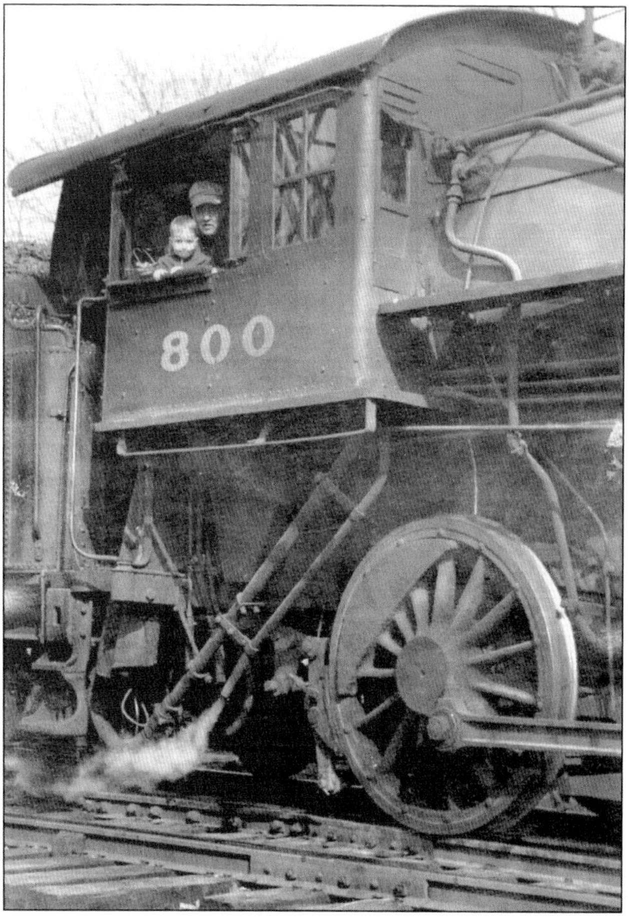

Edmund Eltinge advocated for the Wallkill Valley Railroad to go through the village of New Paltz. When it was built in 1870, it marked a new era in New Paltz's growth and development. Several passenger and freight trains would travel to town daily, with the last train going through in 1978. Pictured at left is young Dirk DeWitt with "Casey" the train conductor in 1944. (Photograph by Erma DeWitt.)

Below, George Millham's truck is loaded with newly made apple barrels in front of the New Paltz Cooperage on Water Street. His son, Schuyler, would go almost every day with a truckload of barrels, 170 or more, to Highland, Milton, Marlborough, and elsewhere. He sold the barrels to the apple growers, who needed them to ship their apples to market. (Courtesy of Faire Hart.)

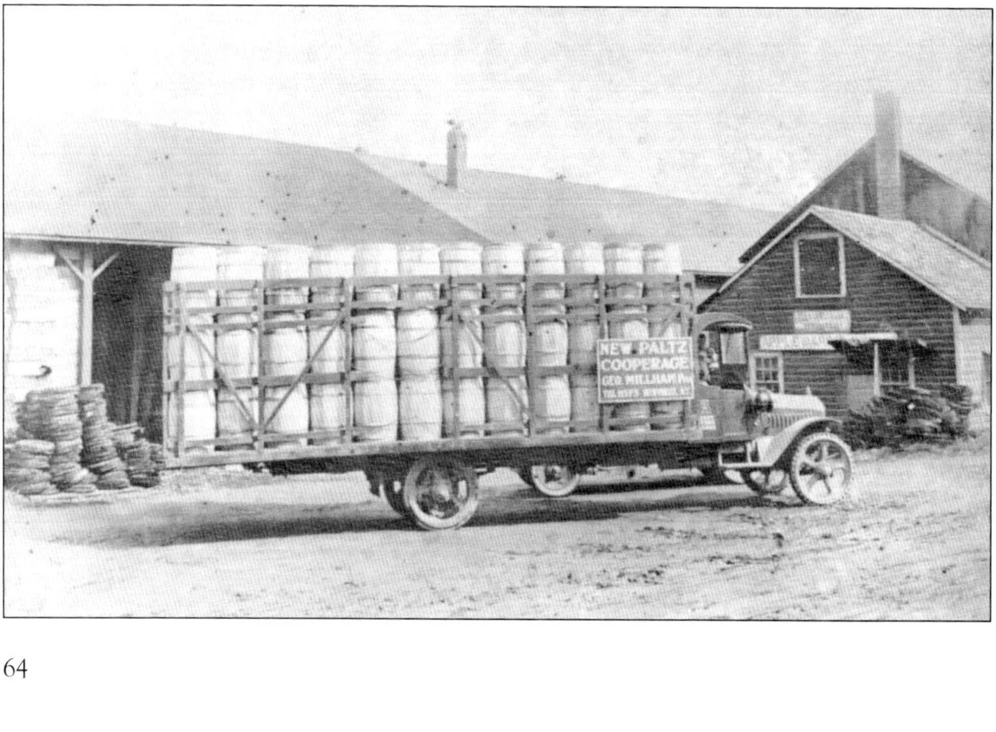

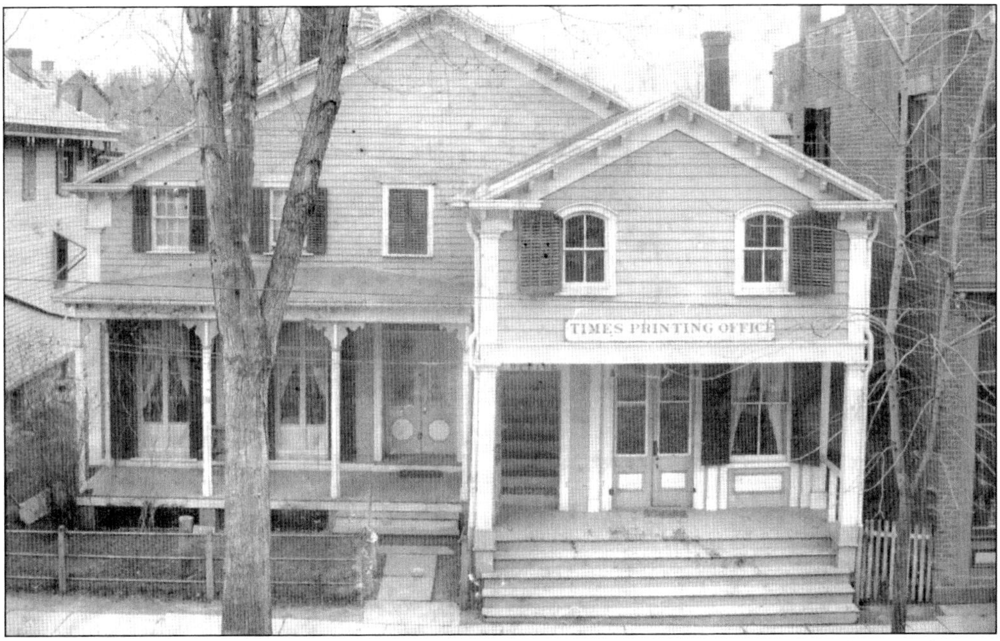

The *New Paltz Times* was the town's first newspaper, published by Democrat Charles J. Ackert in this building at 40 Main Street. For many years after the Civil War, political issues were bitterly contested in New Paltz. The newspapers were in the forefront of these disagreements, and the discourse between Ackert and the editor of the *New Paltz Independent*, Republican Ralph LeFevre, was legendary.

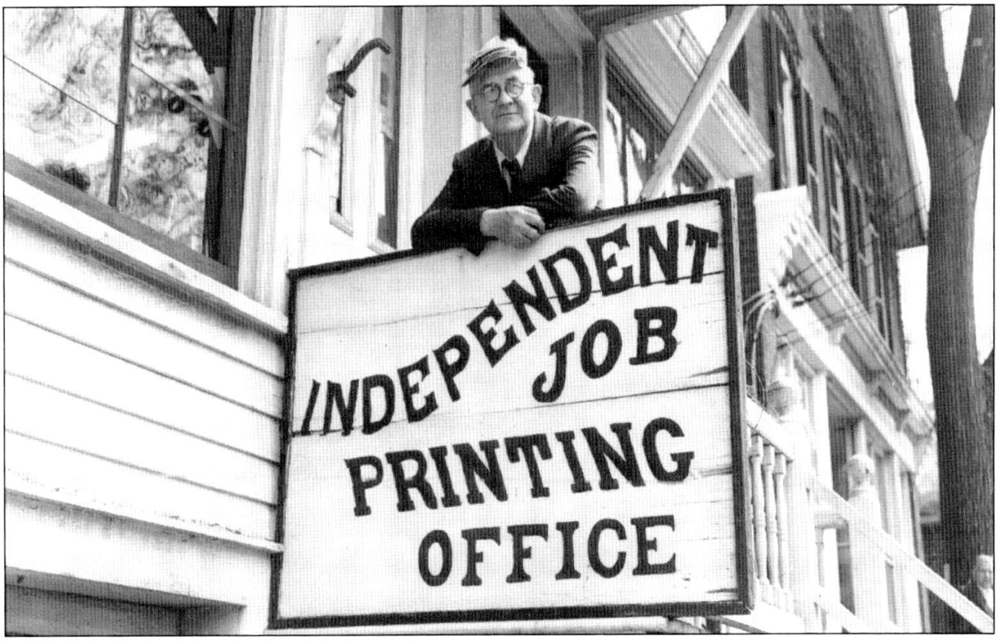

Ralph LeFevre purchased the *New Paltz Times* in 1919 and combined it with his own paper, the *New Paltz Independent*. James O. LeFevre (pictured) published the *New Paltz Independent and Times* after the death of his father in 1925. The offices of the *Independent* were located at 2 South Chestnut Street. James O. LeFevre died when struck by a car on Upper Main Street in 1956.

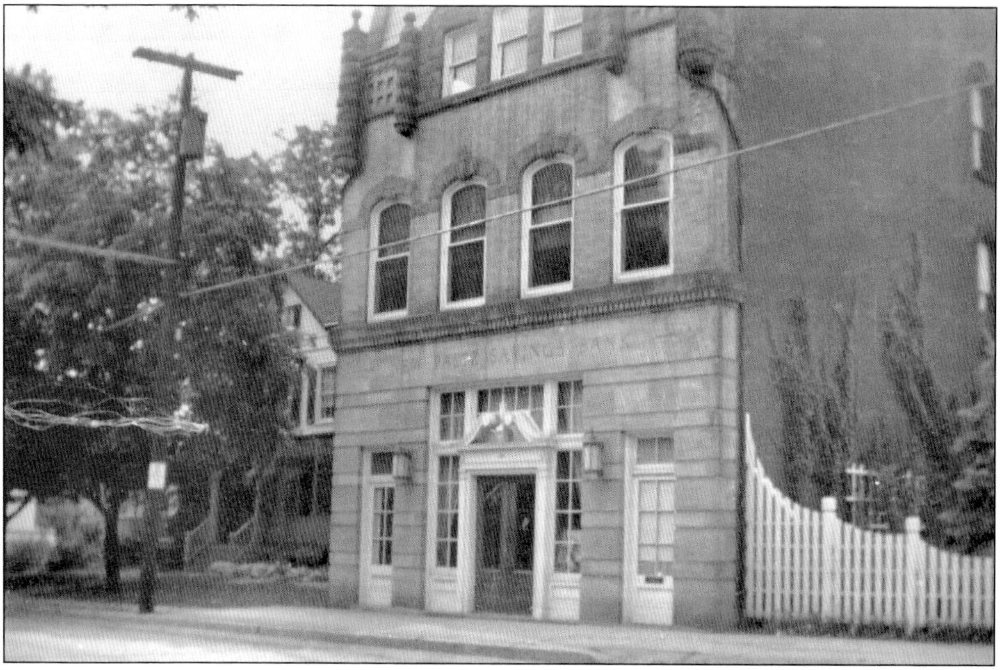

Etched in the stone over the front door of the bank at 29 Main Street is "New Paltz Savings Bank." The building was originally three stories high, comprised of 144,000 bricks made at the New Paltz brickyard. In 1950, the second and third floors were removed, and a large addition was erected to the east. An addition to the west was added in 1967. (Courtesy of Rosalie Nelson.)

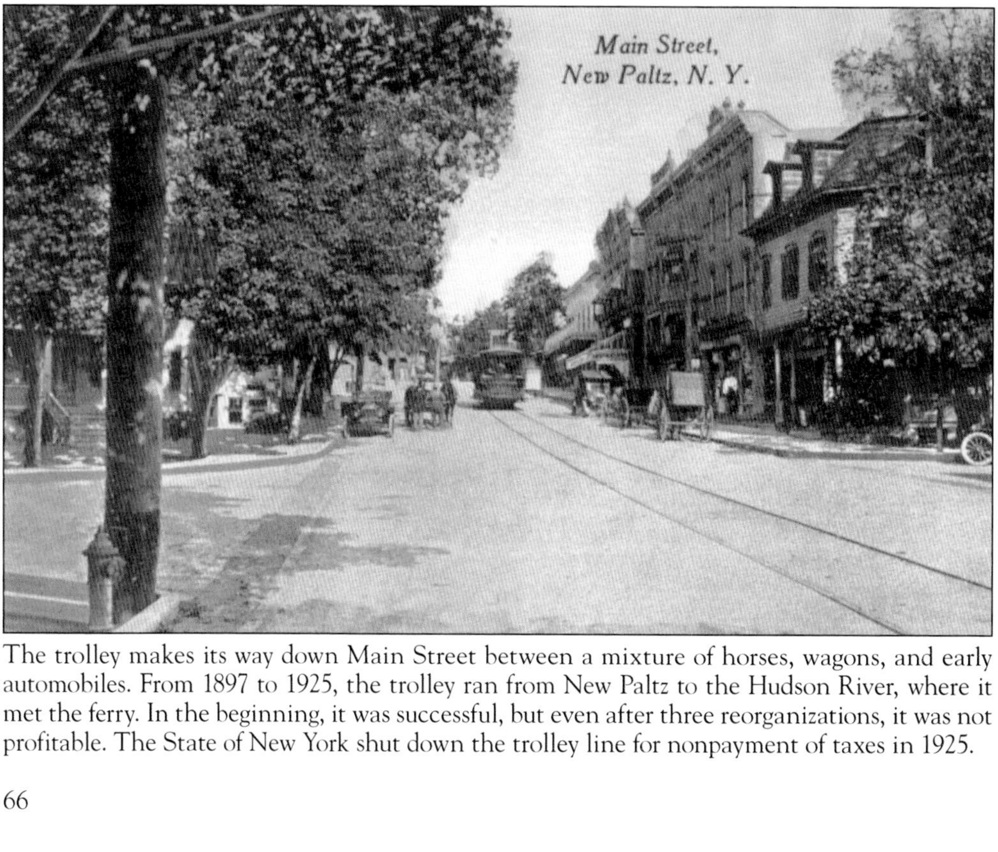

The trolley makes its way down Main Street between a mixture of horses, wagons, and early automobiles. From 1897 to 1925, the trolley ran from New Paltz to the Hudson River, where it met the ferry. In the beginning, it was successful, but even after three reorganizations, it was not profitable. The State of New York shut down the trolley line for nonpayment of taxes in 1925.

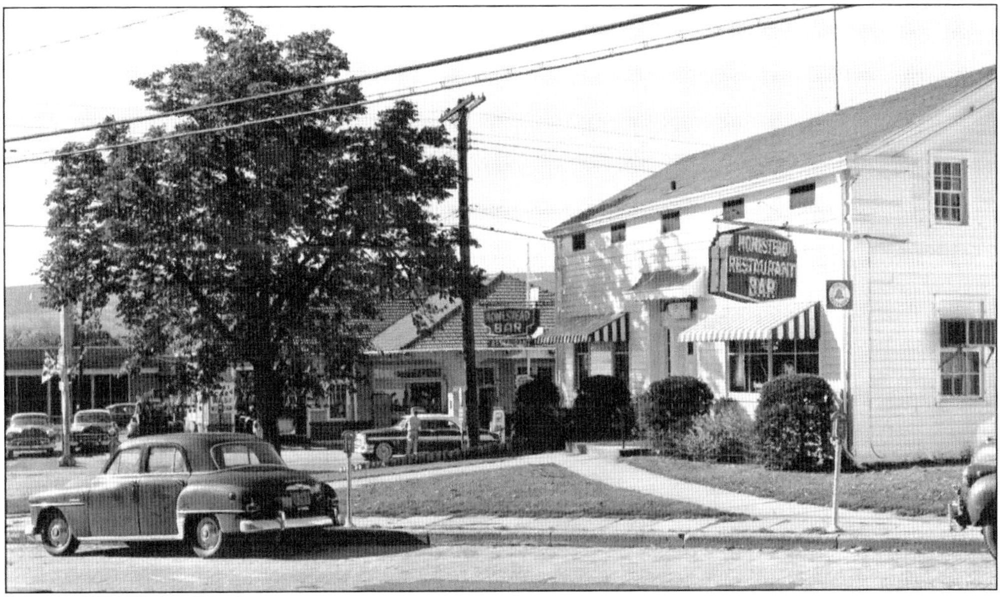

Bill Lorenzen opened the Homestead restaurant and bar at 49 Main Street in 1946. A village landmark, it was built in 1842 and was occupied by the Elias Coe family for nearly 60 years. Emily Coe was a dressmaker, and for 40 years she made the wedding dresses of most of the brides who lived in New Paltz. (Photograph by Morris Rosenfield.)

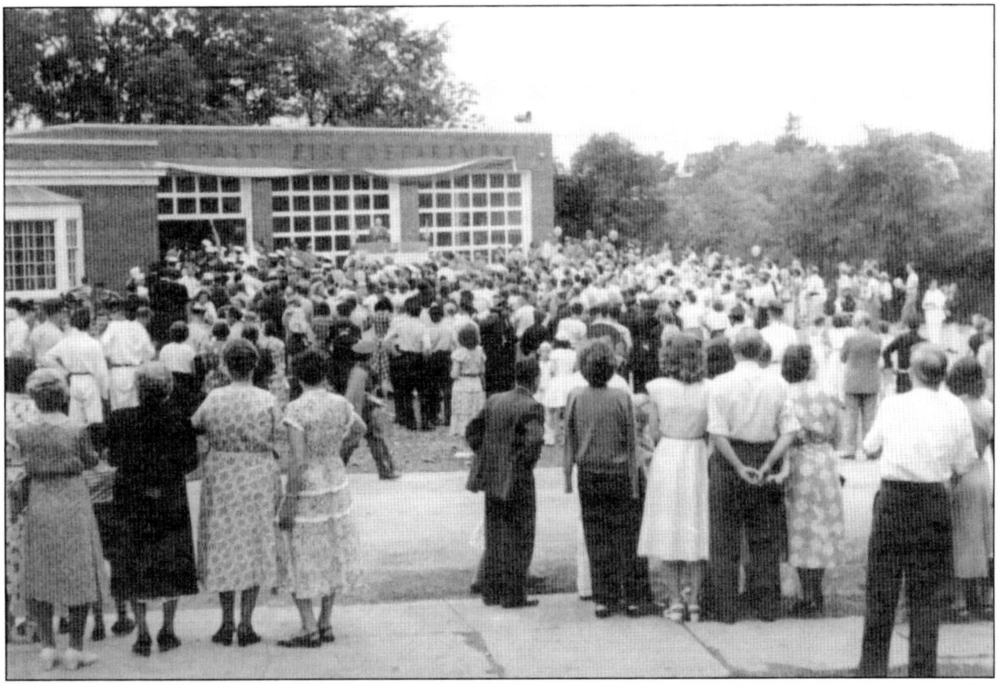

The new municipal building was constructed by Stanley Hasbrouck. After a parade in the morning sponsored by the fire department, the dedication services were held on the afternoon of July 4, 1950. Congressman Jay LeFevre was the principal speaker for the dedication. The day was capped off with a block party in the evening. The Town of New Paltz added a large addition to the building in 1962.

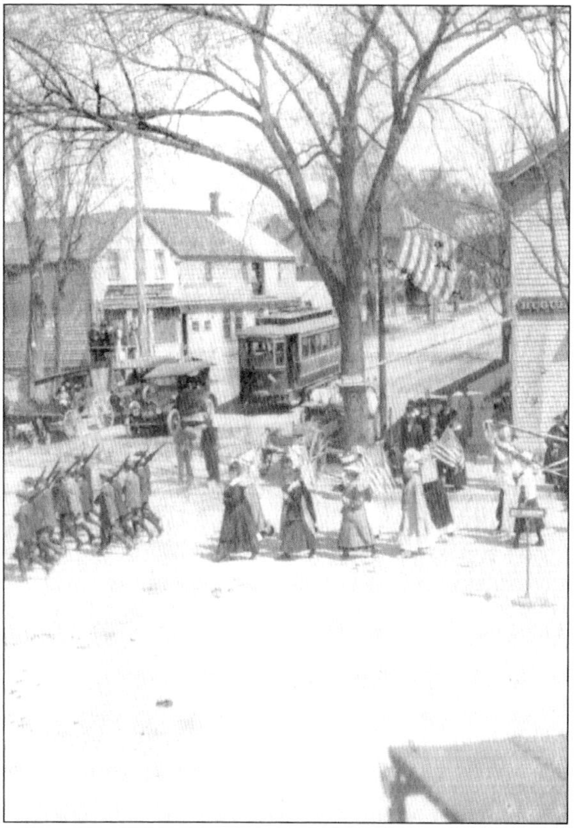

Huguenot Square, located at the junction of Main Street and Plattekill Avenue, has been the site of many special events, including block dances, carnivals, protests, and the Tour de Trump. Parades of all sorts have marched through this spot, including the one pictured at left around 1915. For several years, parades would begin on Huguenot Street, proceeding on Brodhead Avenue to North Chestnut Street. Marchers would then proceed on lower Main Street, Wurts Avenue, Mohonk Avenue, and South Chestnut Street. They would then go all the way up Main to North Manheim Boulevard, John Street, and North Oakwood Terrace, back to Main and down to Plattekill Avenue, past the reviewing stand, and end up at Hasbrouck Park. Below, on this reviewing stand are, from left to right, Mayor Robert Reid, Henry W. DuBois, Van Bogert, Roland Will, Jay LeFevre, I. C. Barnes, Dr. Edgar Beebe, and George Ackert. (Below, courtesy of Jeff Ackert.)

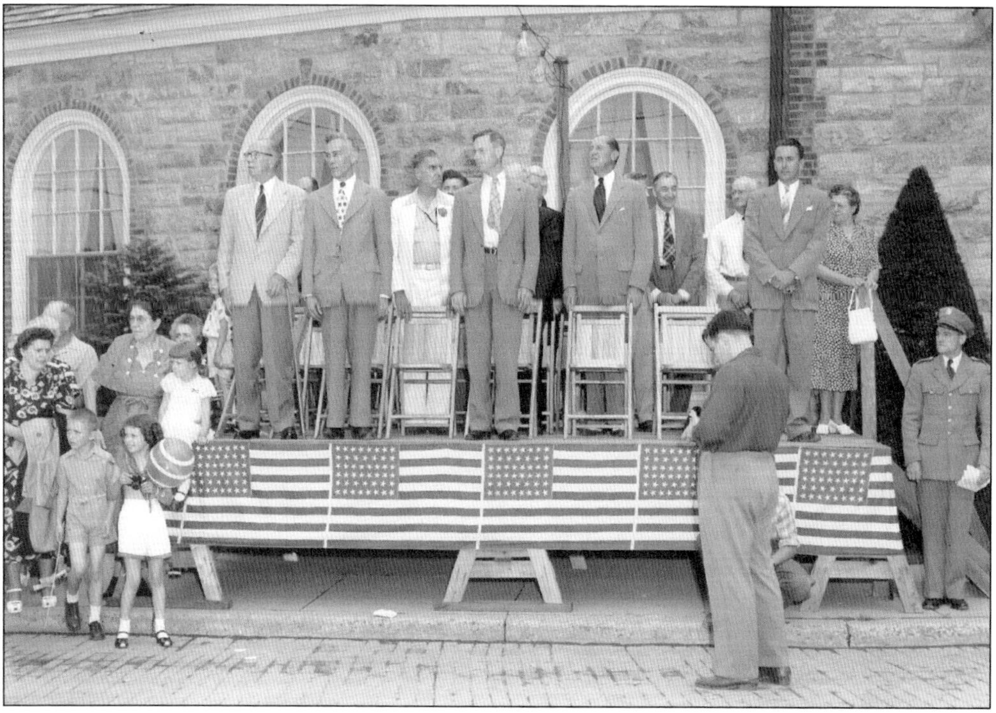

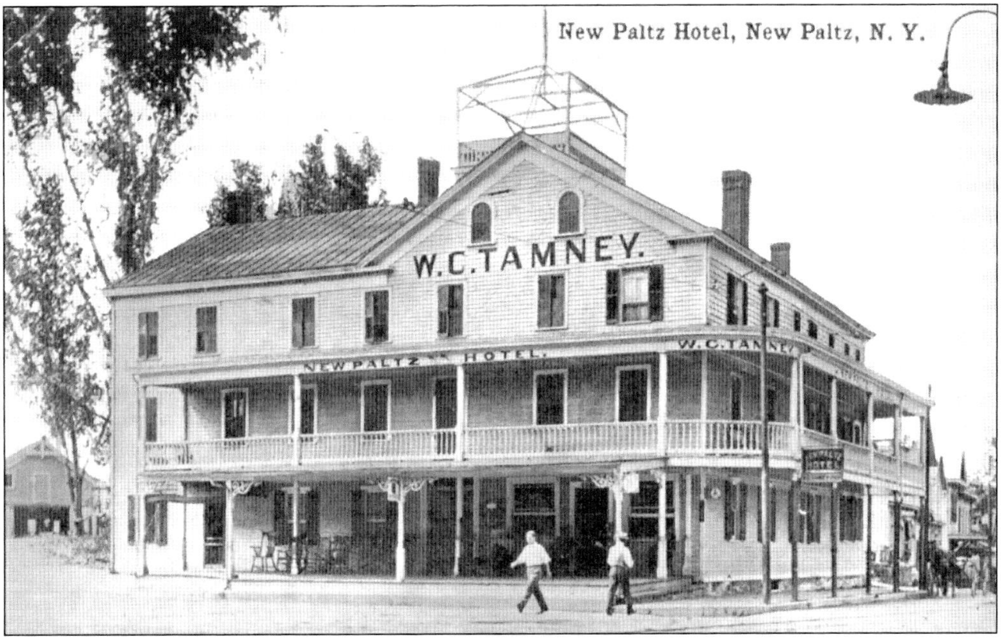

The New Paltz Hotel stood on the southwest corner of Huguenot Square for many years. This combination hotel, meeting place, and newspaper distribution center also served as the bus depot. This is where many local men lingered a few moments before boarding buses on their way to serve in World War II. When the war ended, the men returned and found a brand new gas station in its place.

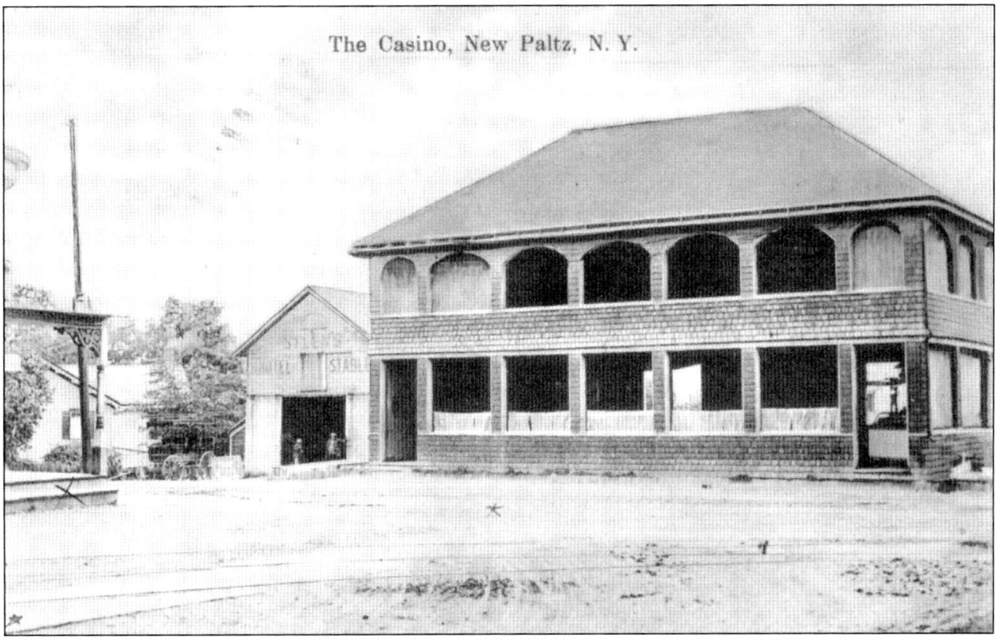

Home of P&G's Restaurant since 1947, the "Casino," or bandstand, was built by John H. Hasbrouck in 1900. There was a fountain on the first floor surrounded by palms, where ice cream, candies, soda water, and cake were served. A dance floor was located above, where concerts were given every afternoon. To the left of the Casino were the stables of the hotel situated across the street.

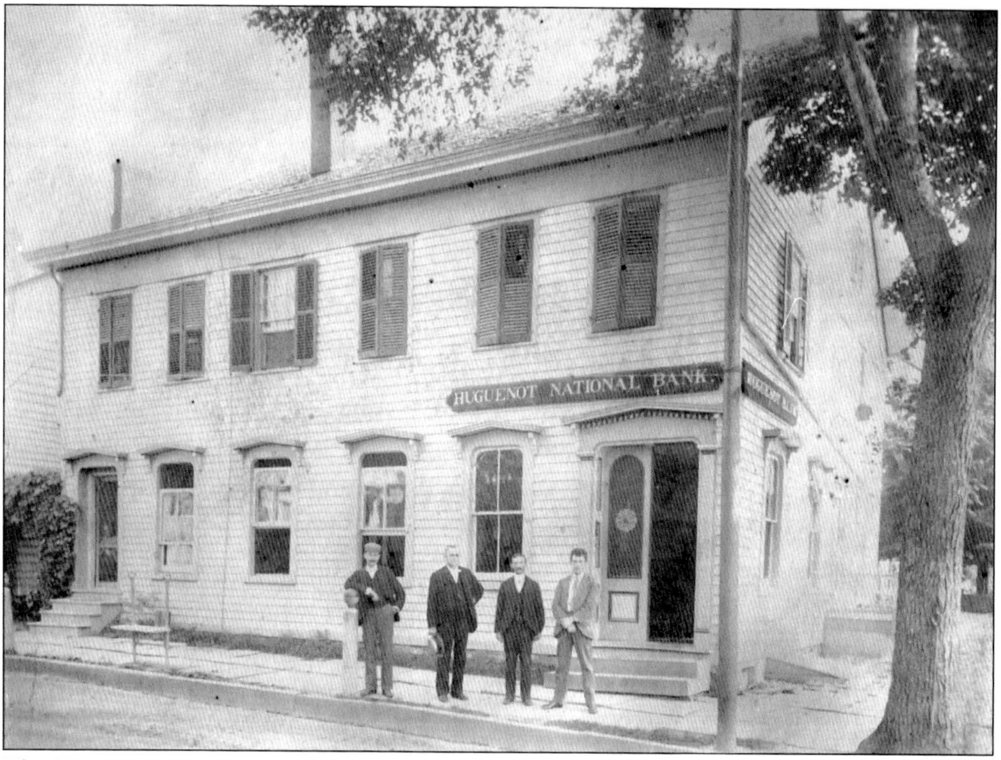

The Huguenot National Bank was organized in 1853, with Edmund Eltinge serving as its first president. Standing in front of the bank are Jacob Lefever (second from left) and his son, Frank J. Lefever (far right), who were the bank's presidents from 1874 to 1940. At the far right is the Village Elm Tree, which in 1997 was taken down because it suffered from elm disease.

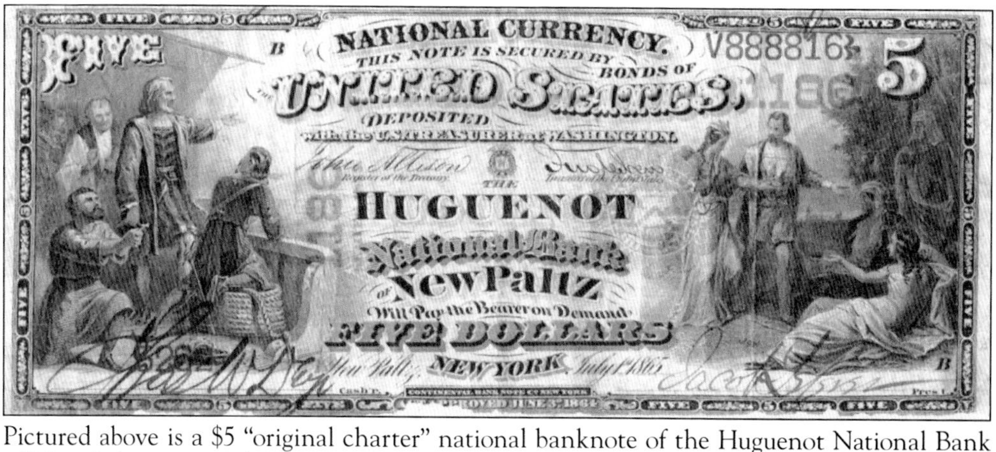

Pictured above is a $5 "original charter" national banknote of the Huguenot National Bank of New Paltz, as issued in 1865. The note is signed by cashier Charles W. Deyo and bank president Jacob Lefever.

The Village Elm Tree was spared when the new Huguenot bank building (below) replaced the old frame building in 1935. The new bank was built from native stone, quarried and laid by local masons. The cupola (shown at right) was crowned with a hand-wrought-iron weather vane bearing the silhouette of the *Gilded Otter*, the ship that carried Antoine Crispell to America. The bank merged with the State of New York Bank in 1961 and Bankers Trust in 1967. It is now a Chase Bank. Also visible below is the Elting Memorial Library, in the background at left. (Right, photograph by Dennis O'Keefe; below, photograph by Erma DeWitt.)

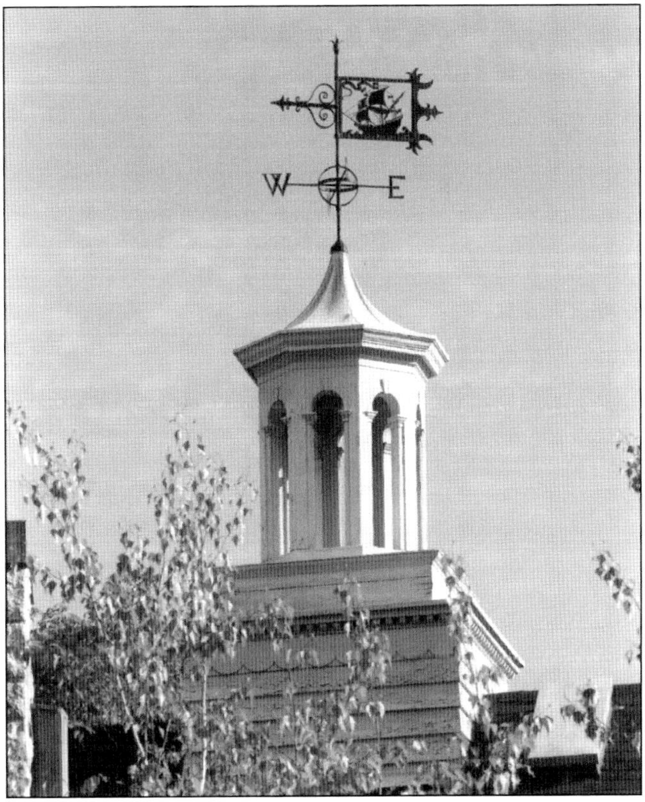

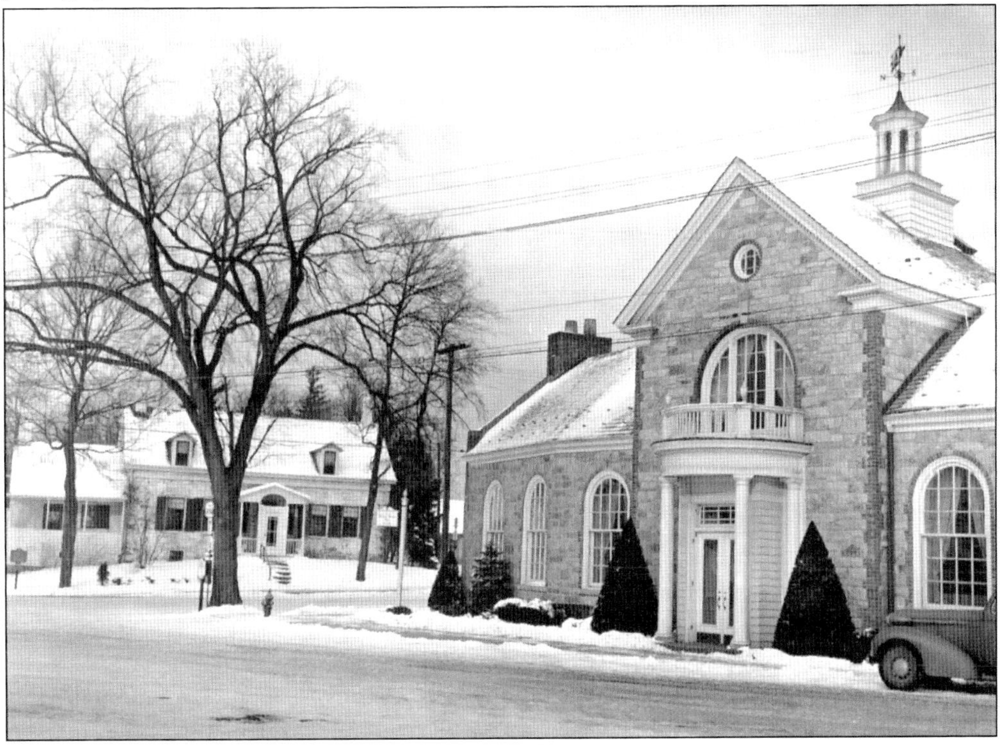

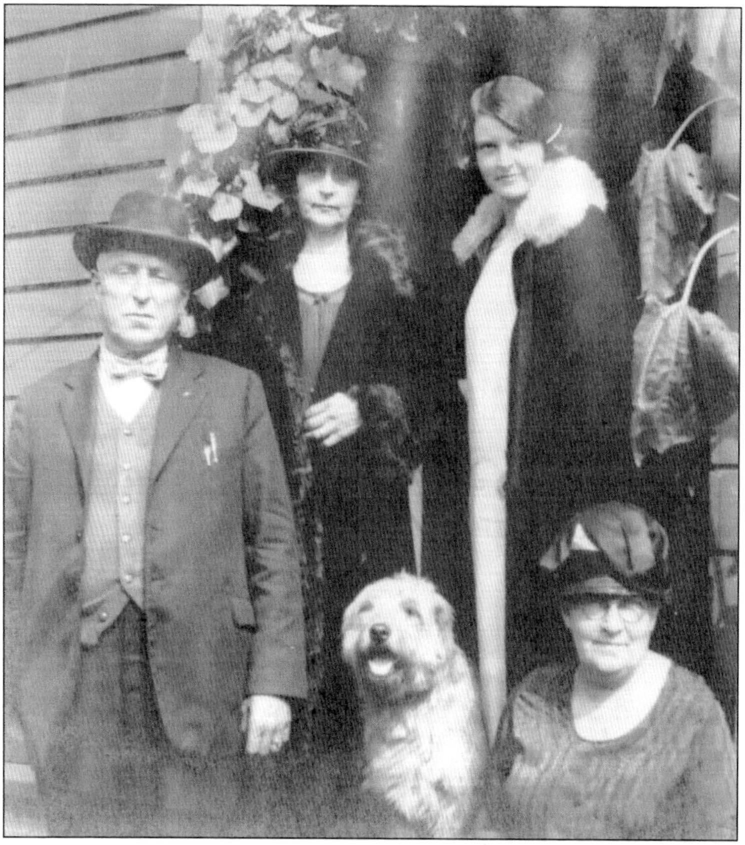

Lorin J. Conner and his wife, the former Elizabeth Deyo (seated at right), lived at 27 Church Street for 25 years. Her sister, Kittie Deyo Schoonmaker (standing second from left), and daughter, Mildred Schoonmaker, lived with them and inherited the house upon their deaths in 1932. Kittie Deyo Schoonmaker was Elting Memorial Library's second librarian, following in the footsteps of her husband's cousin, Ida Schoonmaker.

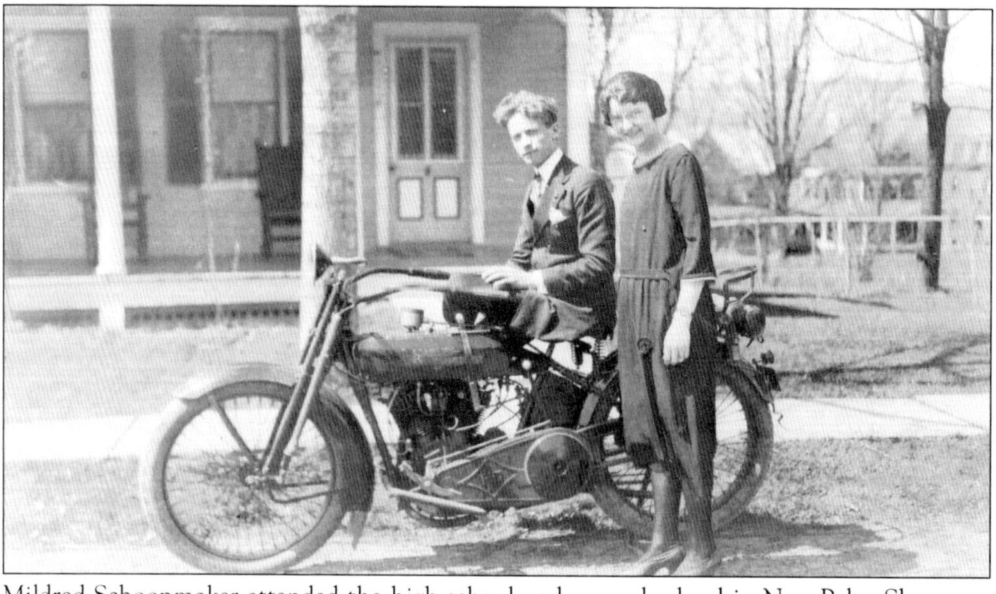

Mildred Schoonmaker attended the high school and normal school in New Paltz. She was a popular girl and had many suitors. Many photographs from her album show her on various dates, with her mother as a chaperone. Here she is standing in front of her house on Church Street next to one suitor on his Harley-Davidson.

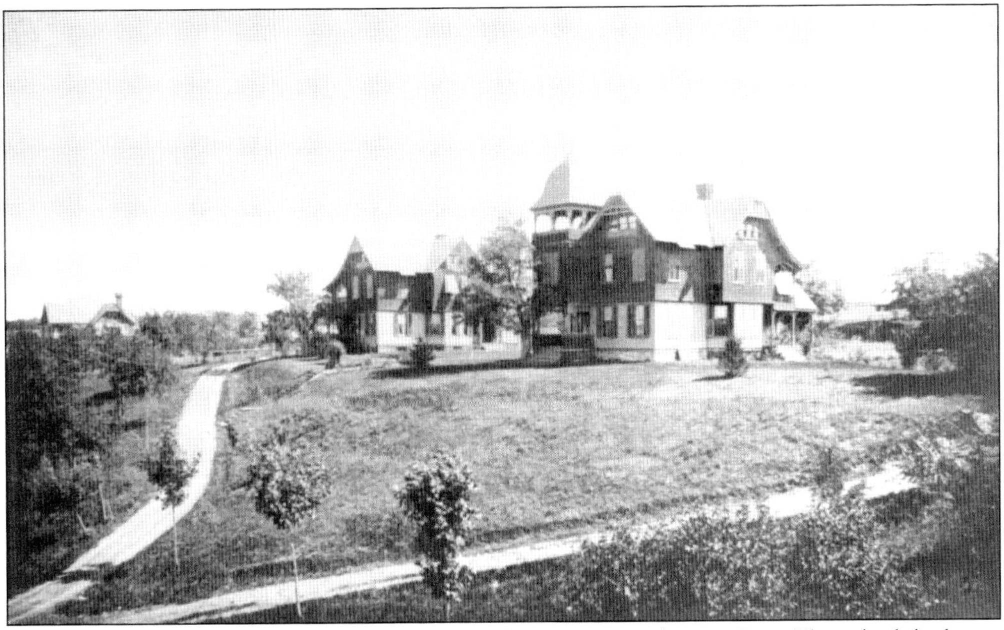

Across Church Street, on Orchard Heights, stand two Victorian houses. Jesse Elting had the home on the left built as a wedding present to his daughter, Gertrude, and new son-in-law, Jacob Deyo, in 1887. A year later, Jesse completed his own home right next door. The Eltings' house was the first house in New Paltz with indoor plumbing, meaning a sink upstairs and down.

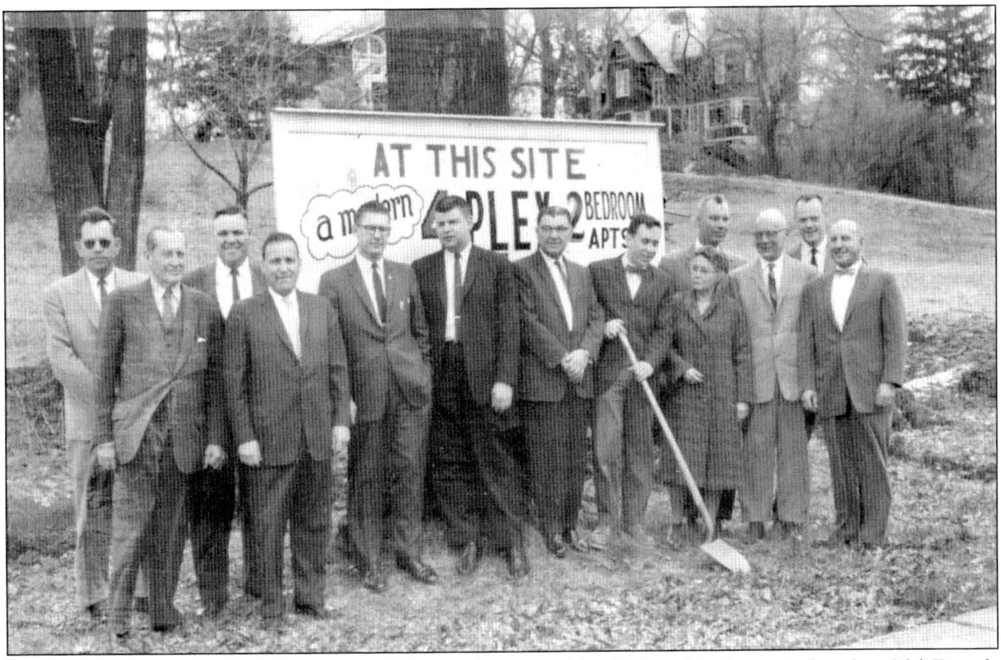

Ground was broken in 1962 on land formerly owned by Helen Hasbrouck for the Old Dutch Apartments. Other buildings were also planned for the site but never materialized. Participating in the ceremony are, from left to right (first row) Jay LeFevre, Clarence Jansen, Robert Glanz, Robert Harp, Herman Glanz, Van Pine, Helen Hasbrouck, Henry DuBois, and Lee Heinze; (second row) William Lukacik, Hugh McCowat, Carl Lillberg, and Robert Murray.

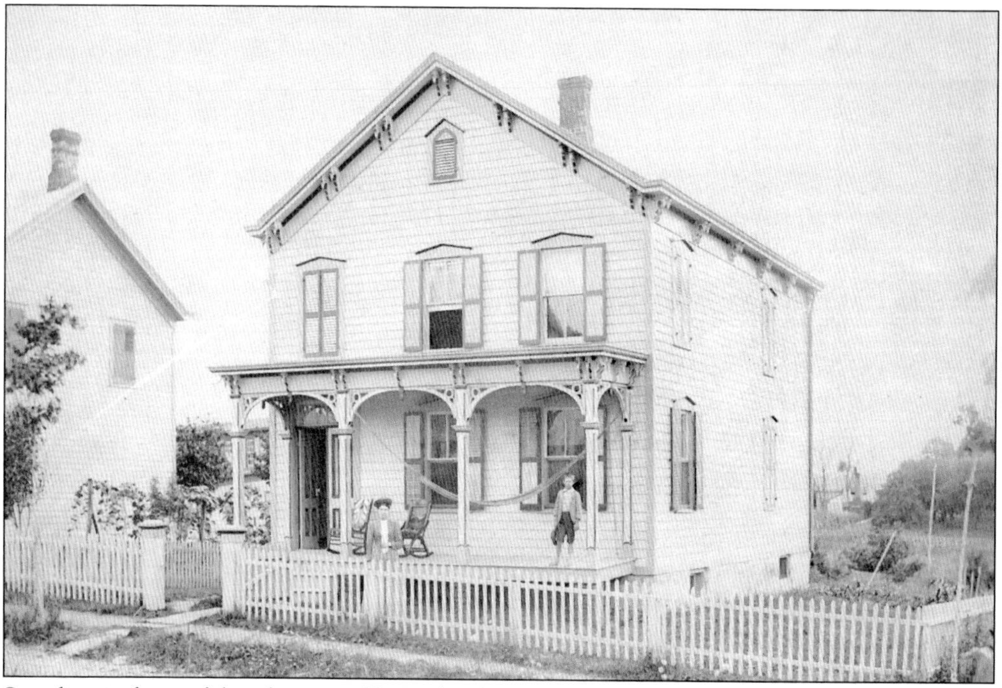

Standing in front of their house at 53 North Chestnut Street are May LeFevre and her son Jessie. When North Chestnut Street first opened beyond North Front Street, it was called Potato Street. The name was changed due to the number of horse chestnut trees located along it. The last horse chestnut tree along the street stood at the corner of Main and Chestnut Streets until it was cut down in 1988. (Courtesy of Rosalie Nelson.)

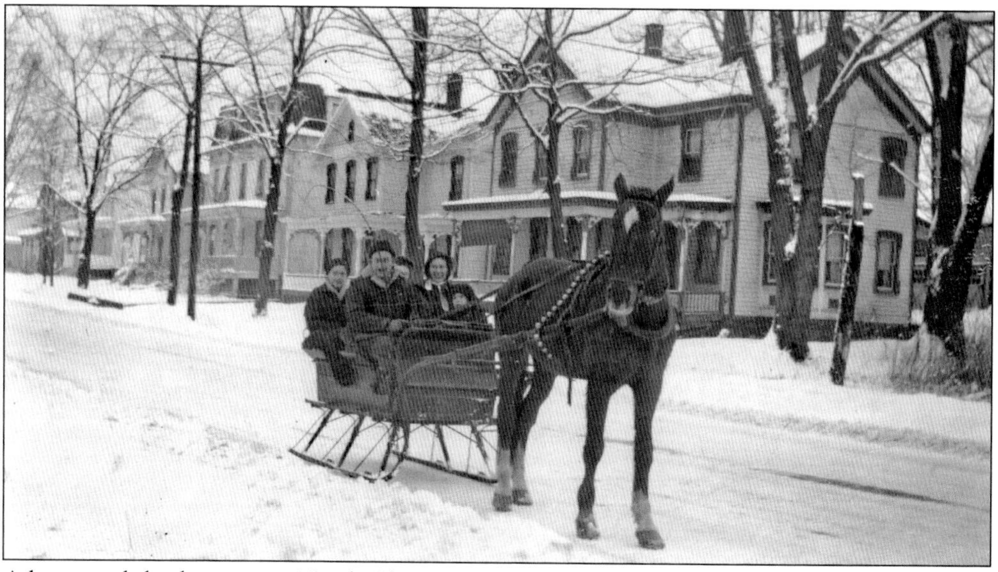

A horse and sleigh pause on North Chestnut Street just along enough to snap this photograph. Sleighing was a most-enjoyed mode of transportation in New Paltz. Many people put their cars away for the winter season and used sleds to get around town. Sleighs were used until the "muddy season," when the front comes out of the ground and transportation is at its most difficult. (Courtesy of Pat Walker.)

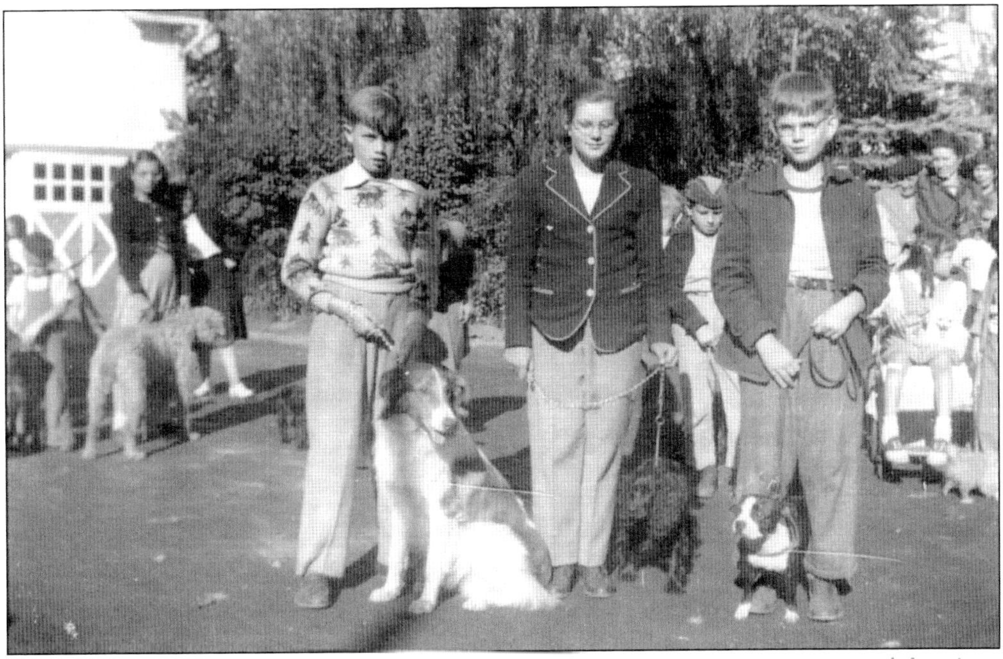

Sponsored by the Ralston Purina Company (maker of Purina Dog Chow), an annual dog show was held at the A. P. LeFevre and Son lumberyard. The LeFevres' lumber, coal, and feed company was founded in 1893. The feed business was prosperous locally but hit its peak in the 1920s. In 1957, Jay Lefevre Sr. decided to give up the feed business, and the dog show was discontinued. (Courtesy of Amy LeFevre.)

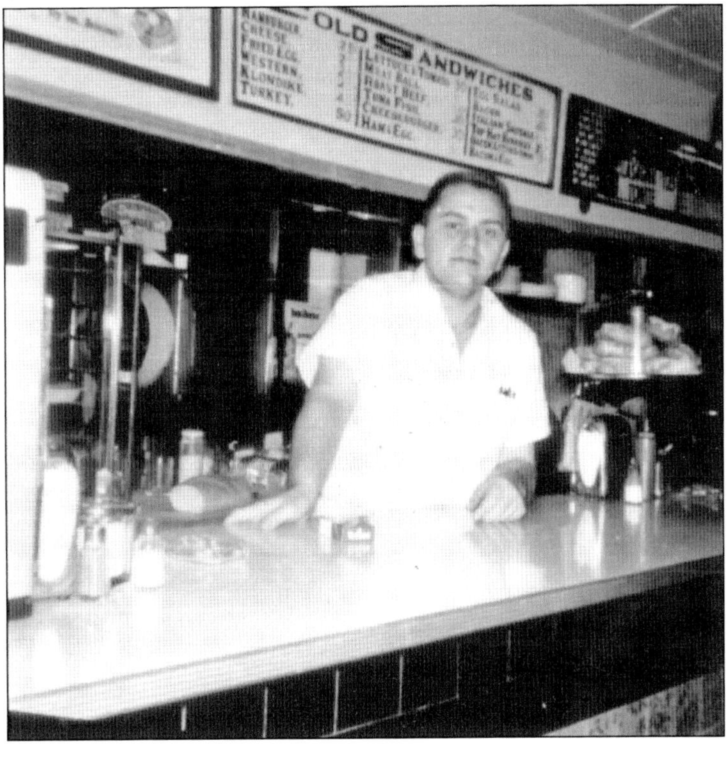

The Sfregola family opened the New Paltz Diner on North Chestnut Street in 1945. Dominick Sfregola, pictured in the diner in 1962, later built and opened a restaurant across the street in 1966. After 34 years of operation, Dominick's Restaurant closed in October 2000. (Courtesy of Joyce Sfregola and William Rhoads.)

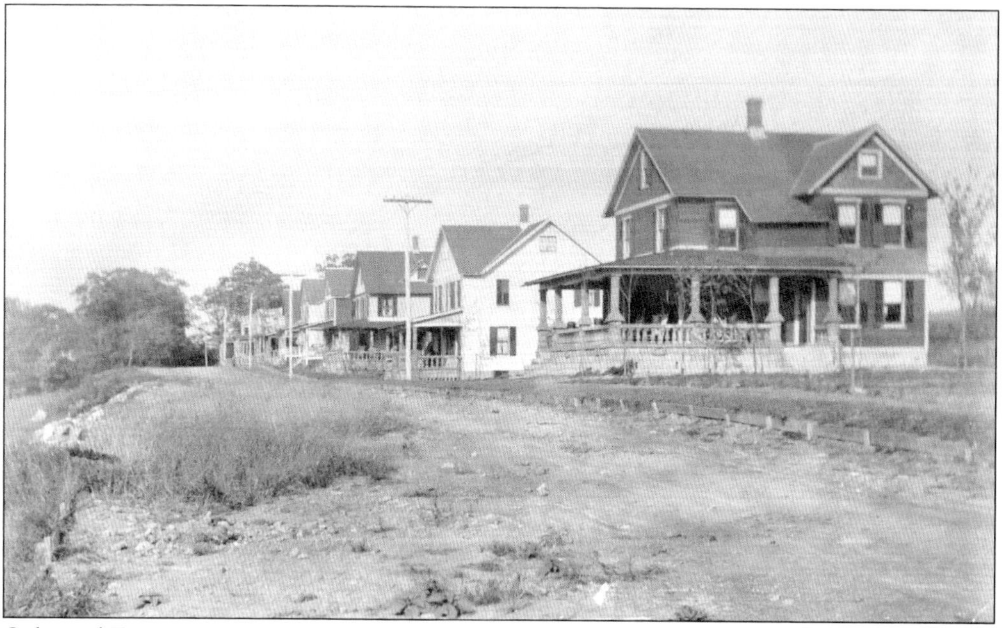

Oakwood Terrace was one of many streets laid out by real estate developer David C. Storr in the early 1900s. D. C. Storr owned a concrete block factory, and many of the houses in his development have concrete stone porches. Two houses, including the one in which he lived, are made entirely of blocks manufactured at his New Paltz factory. The contractor for Storr's development was Henry L. Hasbrouck.

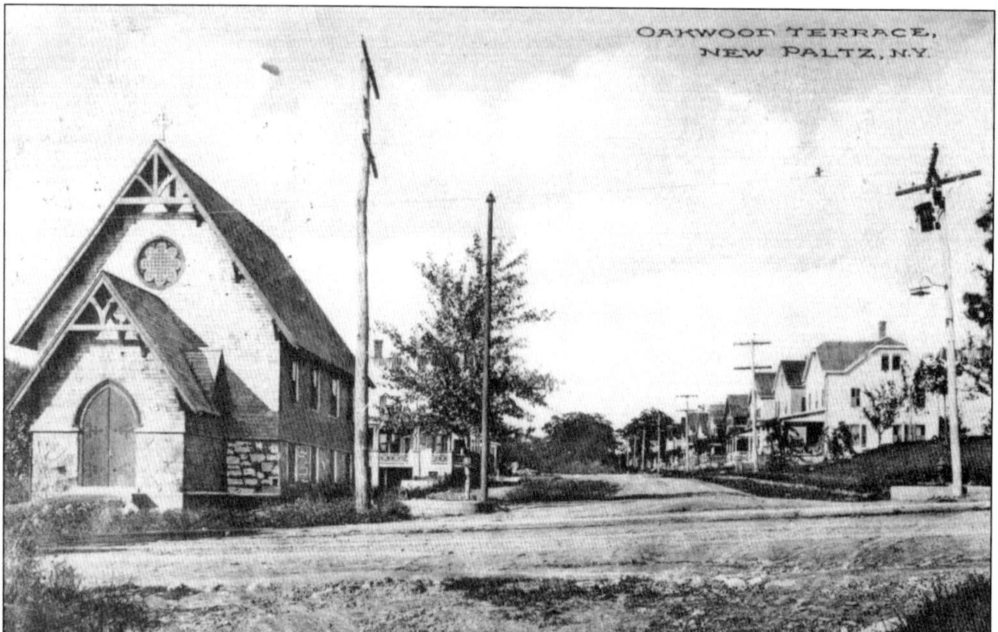

Many of the engineers working on the Catskill Aqueduct needed homes and a place to worship their Episcopalian faith. On land donated by D. C. Storr, architect and Rev. Eli Sutcliffe designed the Episcopal church. The church's cornerstone was laid on St. Andrew's day in 1909.

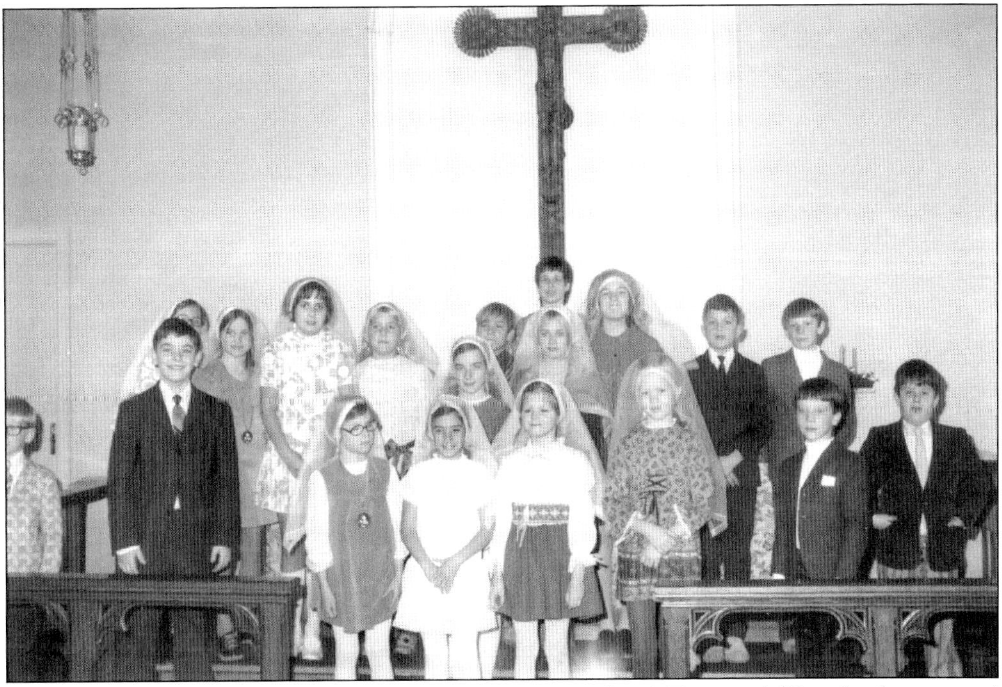

Pictured above are the Sunday school children at St. Andrew's Episcopal Church who received their first communion on December 19, 1974. Among those shown are Paul and Philip DuBois; Allyson, Jennifer, and Lisa Fogg; Donna Gibson; Tori Gordon; David LeMark; Jeffrey and Matthew Logan; Melissa Rosa; Susan Seaholm; Gary, Joseph, and Kim Smith; and Bonnie, Karen, and James Streeter. (Photograph by Joe Smith.)

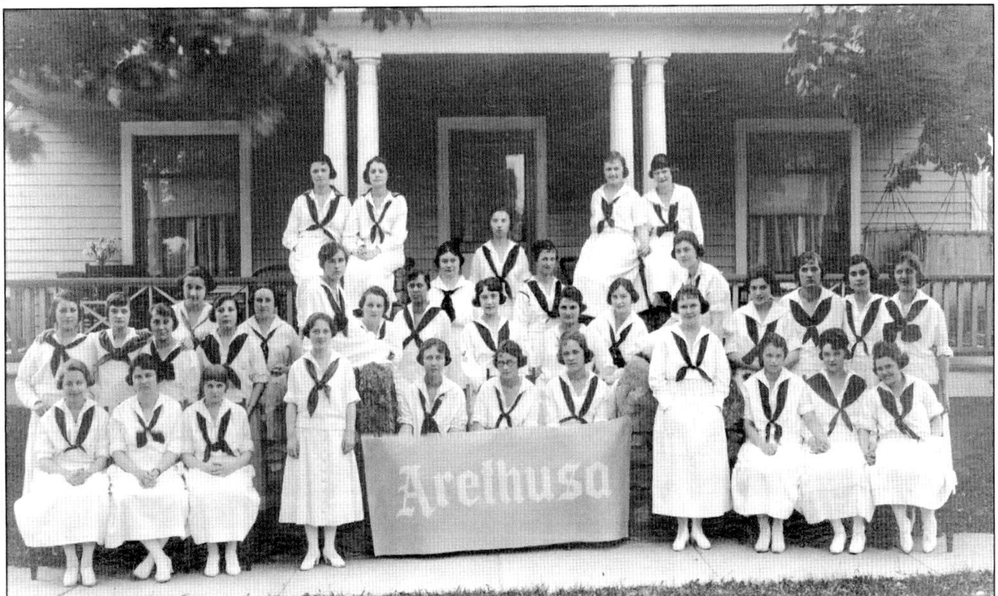

The home at 11 North Oakwood Terrace was built in 1911 by D. C. Storr to house the young ladies of Arethusa Sorority. The home had 13 bedrooms, a reception room, a kitchen, and a dining room. The sorority house is used today as a boardinghouse for students. (Courtesy of Elaine Kniffen.)

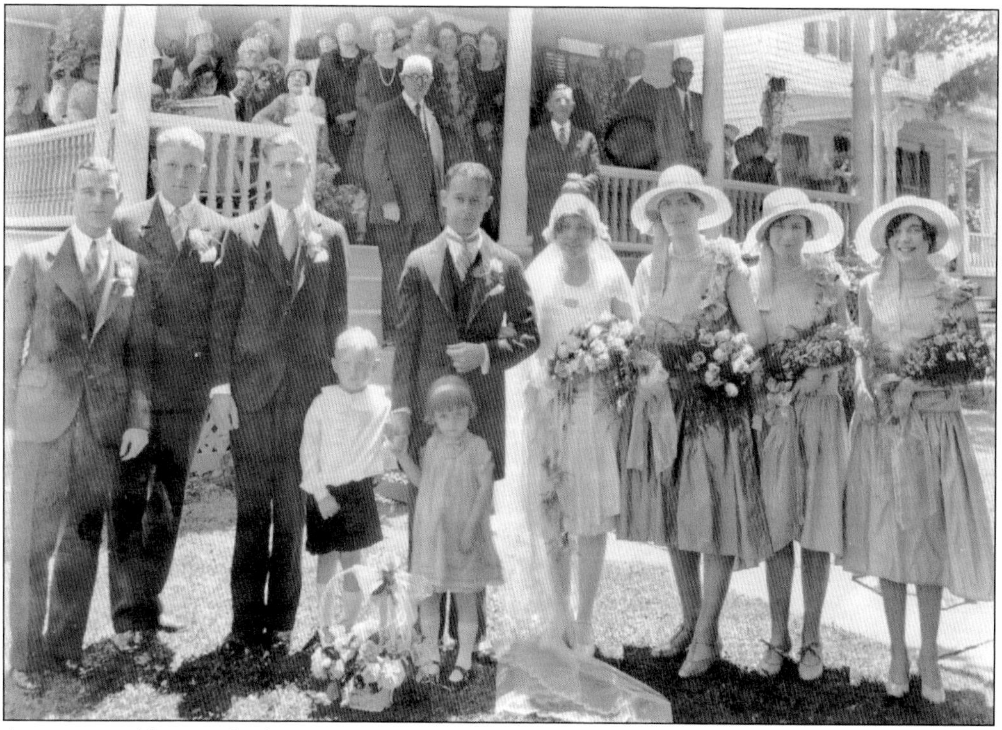

A pretty wedding took place at noon on Thursday, June 28, 1928, when Ethel Silkworth and W. Whitney Miller were married at the home of the bride's parents at 16 Prospect Street. The bride was attired in white satin, wearing a silk embroidered net veil caught with orange blossoms. The bridesmaids were dressed in pastel shades of taffeta. The flower girl wore a dress of peach-colored crepe de chine and carried a basket of garden roses.

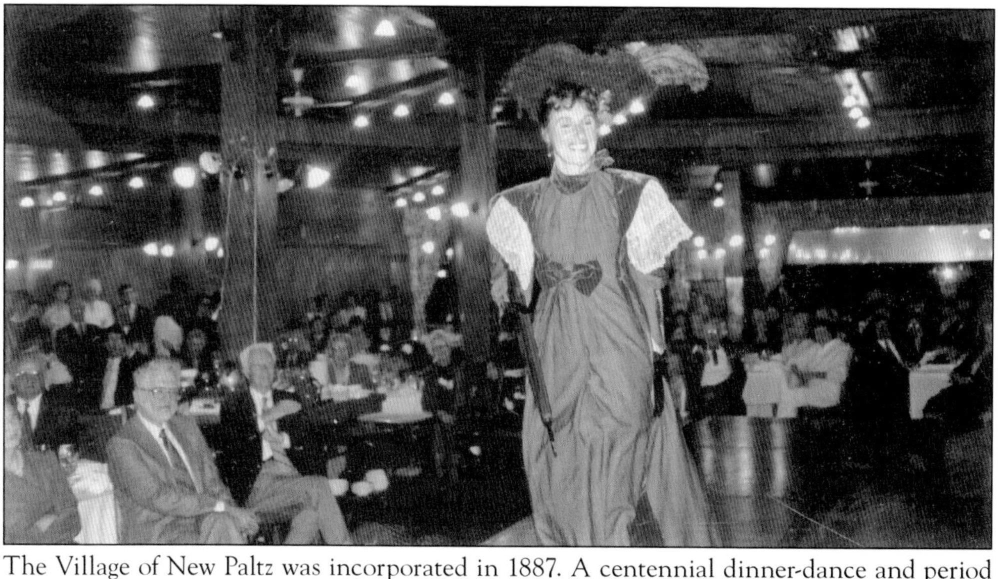

The Village of New Paltz was incorporated in 1887. A centennial dinner-dance and period fashion show at the Mohonk Mountain House was one of several events held to commemorate the village's 100th birthday in 1987. Geri Owens is shown modeling a gown and hat from the 1890s at the occasion.

Four

Education in New Paltz

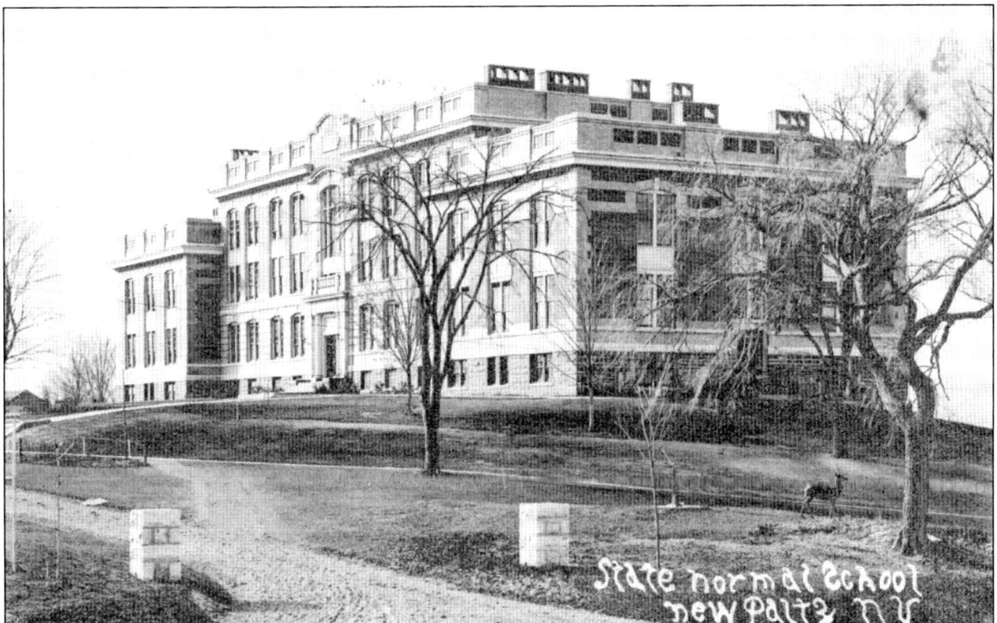

Known today as Old Main, the new normal school building was dedicated in February 1909. The elementary grades were taught on the first floor, the high school classrooms were on the second floor, and the third floor housed the laboratories and lecture rooms for the normal school students. A major renovation of the building began in 2009.

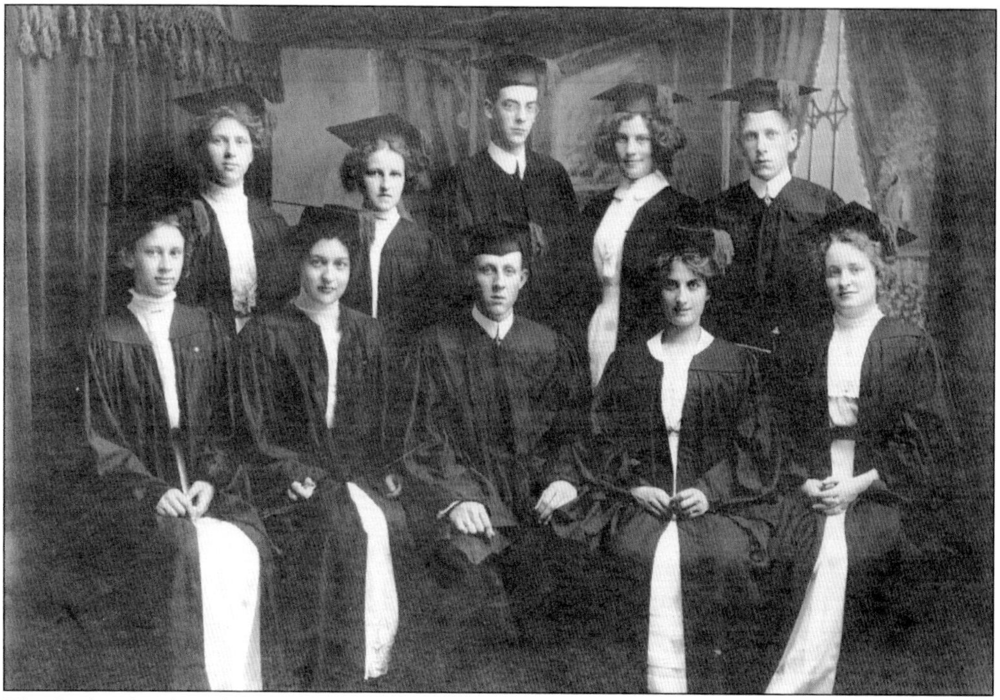

The high school graduates of 1912 were, from left to right, (first row) Ellen DuBois, Gertrude DuBois, Harold Wood, Anna Eltinge, and Dolores Hayden; (second row) Margaret LeFevre, Eleanor Scott, Harold Sutcliffe, Harriet Boller, and Kenneth Snyder. Commencement exercises were held in the New Paltz Normal School gymnasium on Wednesday, June 26, 1912, at 10:30 a.m. (Courtesy of Susanna Lent.)

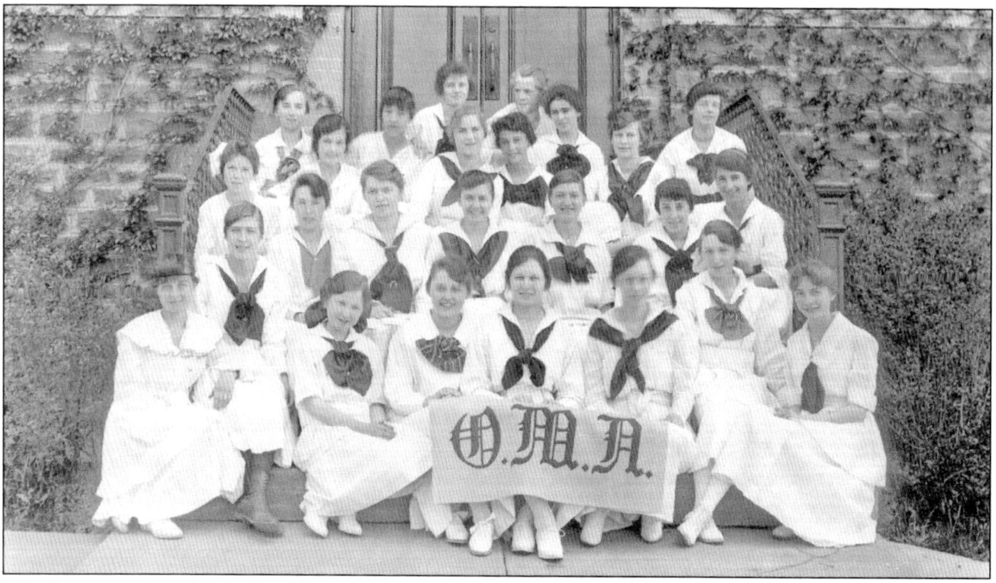

While attending the New Paltz Normal School, sisters Betty and Jane Waring decided that the high school girls needed a sorority. They named it O.M.N., standing for *Omnia Memoria Nostra*, or "all our memories." Marie Jenkins Wiersum recalls having to roll a peanut up Main Street with her nose to join the sorority in the fall of 1937. (Photograph by H. L. Schultz.)

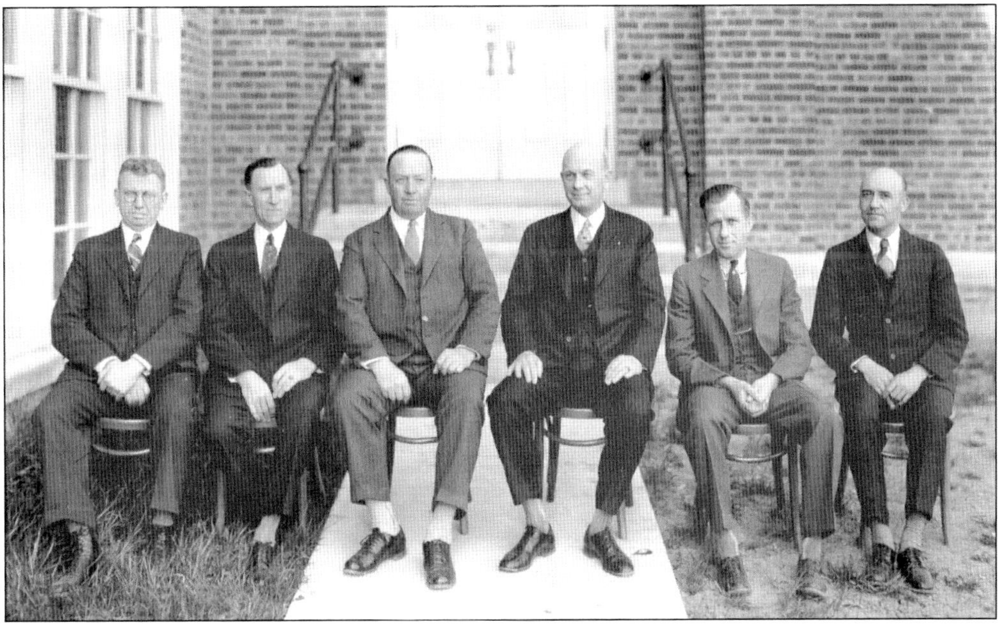

The New York state regents voted to discontinue the academic department of the normal school in 1927. As a result, 12 rural school districts merged with the New Paltz School District to form a consolidated, enlarged, centralized school district. The first board of education was elected, and its members were, from left to right, John Moran, E. C. Elmore, Lester Harvey, Harvey Gregory, Kenneth E. Vanderlyn, and Howard H. Grimm.

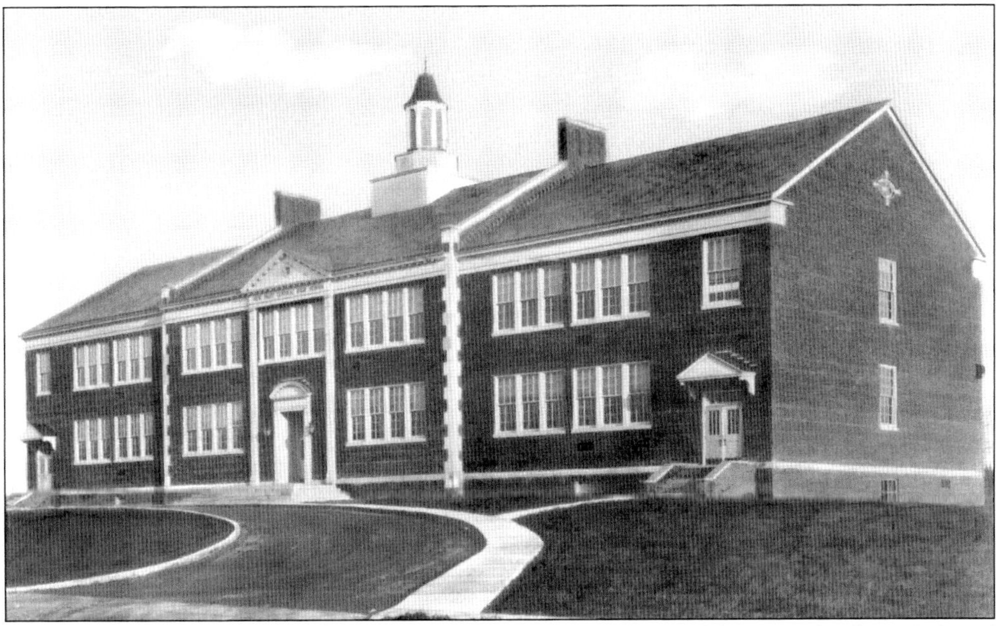

Myron Teller and Harry Halverson, architects from Kingston, designed the new school in a Colonial style. The building contained 15 classrooms, a principal's suite of offices, a teacher's room and health room, a combination gymnasium and auditorium with a large stage, and locker and shower rooms. The cupola atop the slate roof was not only decorative, but also served as an exhaust for classroom vent ducts. (Pennington photograph for Teller and Halverson, Architects.)

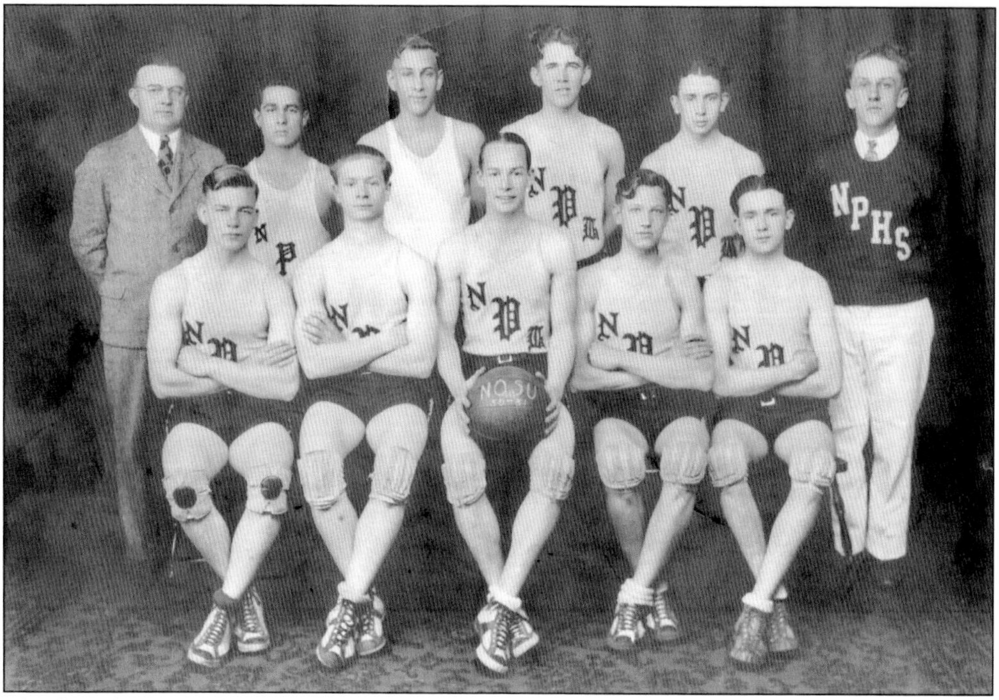

The first championship team of the new school district was coach Ray Cunningham's men's 1930–1931 basketball team. They won the Northern Orange Southern Ulster (NOSU) League with 11 wins and one defeat. Pictured from left to right are (first row) Elting Harp, Willard Barnes, captain Ike Bell, manager Walt Dunham, and Pete Moran; (second row) principal Ray Cunningham, Sam Savago, Donald DuBois, Jim Sherman, Jim Moran, and cheerleader Ray Upright. (Courtesy of Peter Savago.)

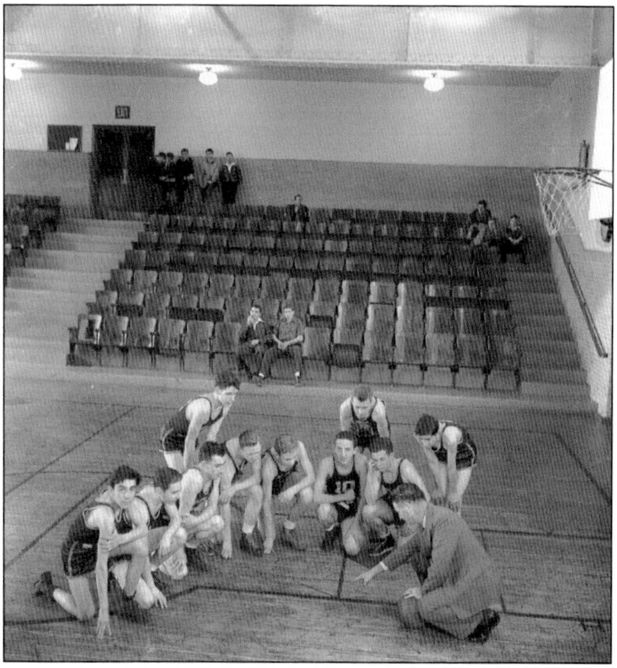

During a practice session in the gym, coach Leonard Wood goes over a play for the 1944 basketball team. Team members included Paul Thompson, Harry Kite, Ernest McCormick, Frank Nadal, Robert Nadal, Alfred Schreiber, and William Yeaple. (Photograph by Erma DeWitt.)

Using the school shop, the Future Farmers of America helped build the high school's rifle club range at the Dodd farm. The War Department loaned the club two army Springfield rifles. The club secured a charter from the National Rifle Association, and the boys participated in several matches. Wesley LeFevre was the president of the club in 1944, with Ernest McCormick as vice president and Richard Weir as treasurer. (Photograph by Erma DeWitt.)

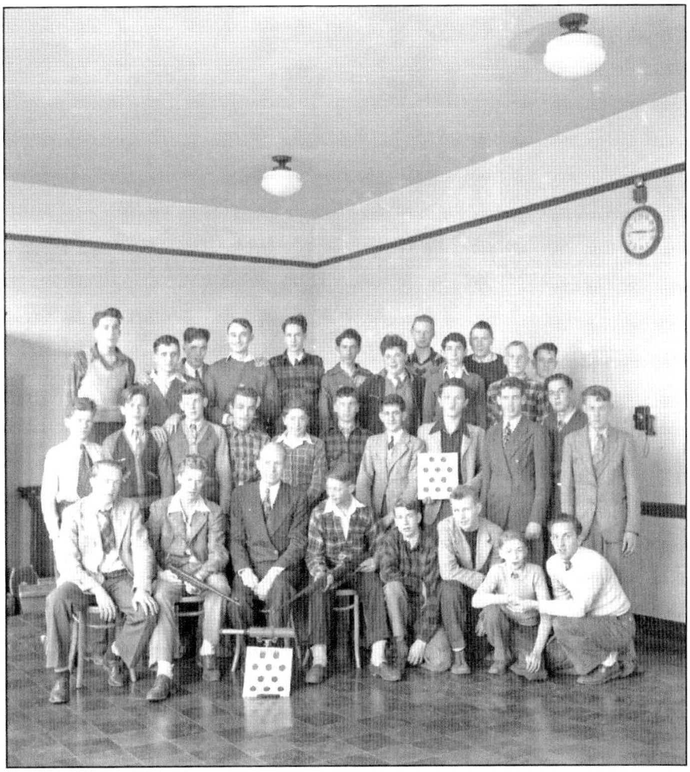

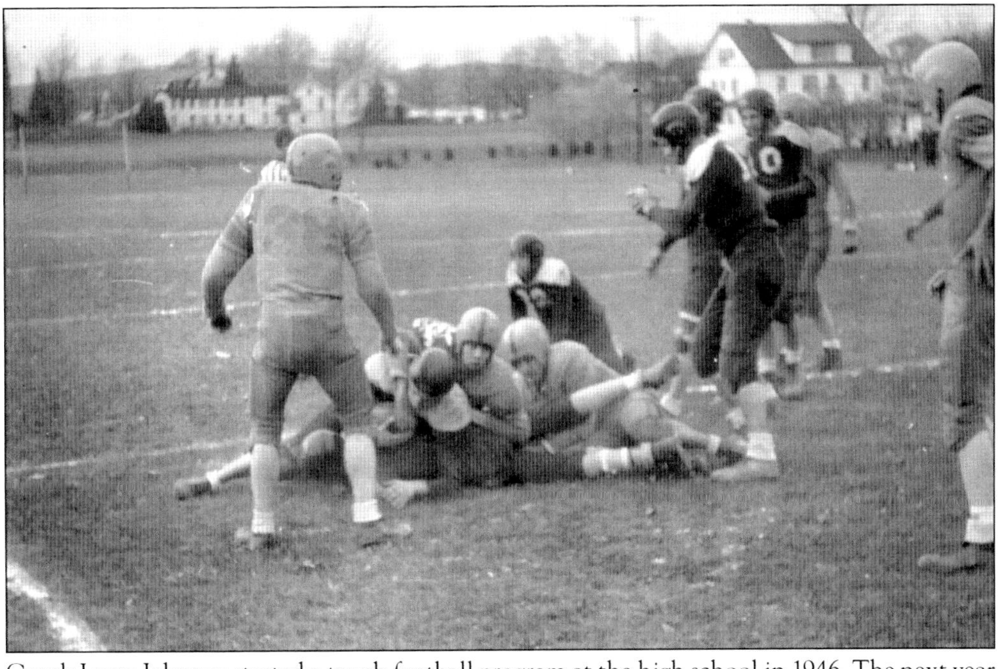

Coach Larry Johnson started a touch football program at the high school in 1946. The next year a six-man football team was added to the varsity program, winning the league championship for the first time in 1948. In this image, a New Paltz player is tackled on the first New Paltz High School football field.

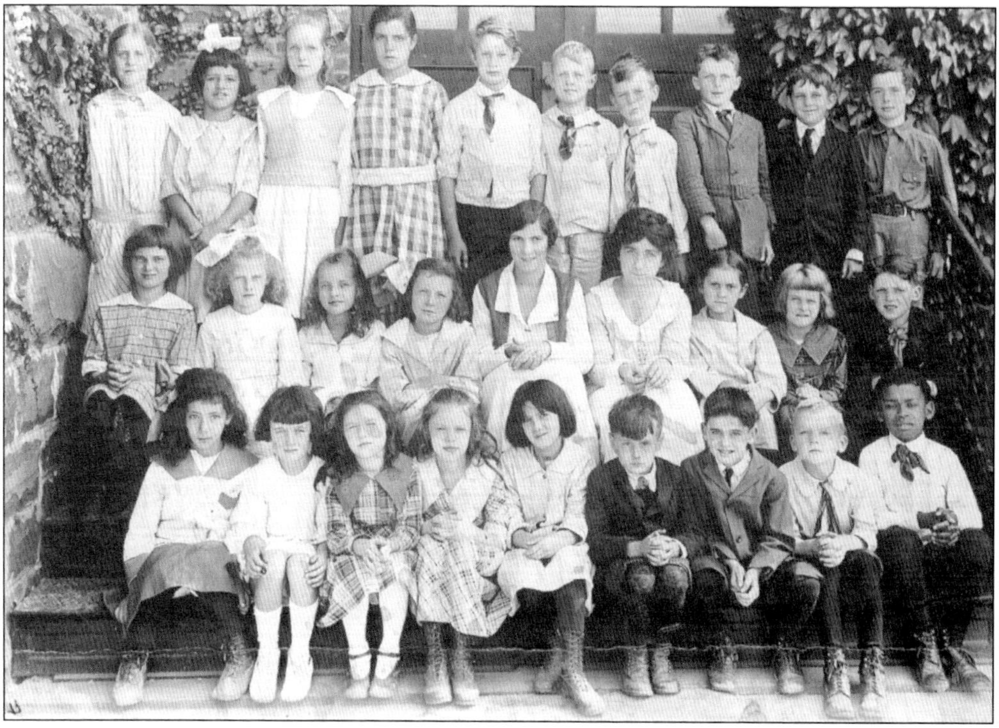

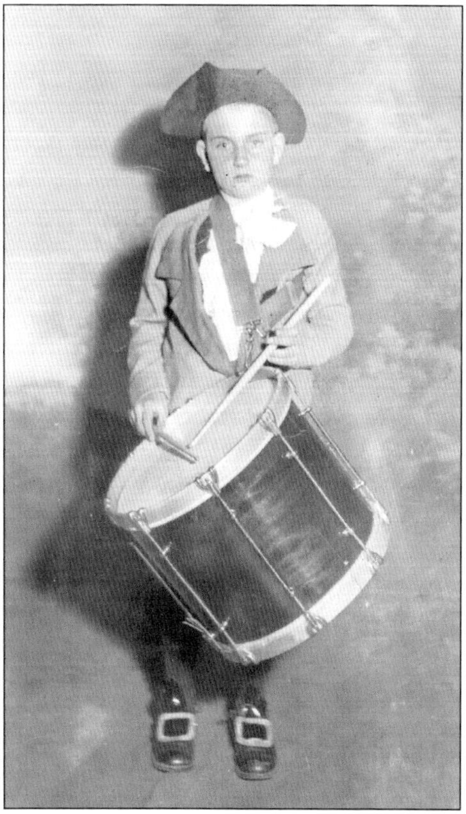

By 1920, schoolchildren from the rural districts started attending the New Paltz Normal School. A scarcity of teachers and rising costs began to force the smaller schools to close. The department of education went to great lengths to have the children transported to a large, centrally located school. A class picture is taken on the steps of Old Main. (Courtesy of Harvey Gregory.)

Don Hoffman portrayed the drummer boy in the February 1932 production of *George Washington's Birthday Party*, commemorating the 200th anniversary of the birth of George Washington. At the end of the year, Don and his schoolmates would carry their own books and supplies down the hill to the new School of Practice, commonly called "The Campus School." (Courtesy of Doris McElhenney.)

Pres. Lawrence H. van den Berg came to New Paltz in 1923, and his accomplishments were many. For the 450 children of the centralized district he built the School of Practice, which opened its doors in September 1932. The building would later be named the van den Berg School of Practice. He died in office only one year after becoming the first president of the State Teachers College in 1942.

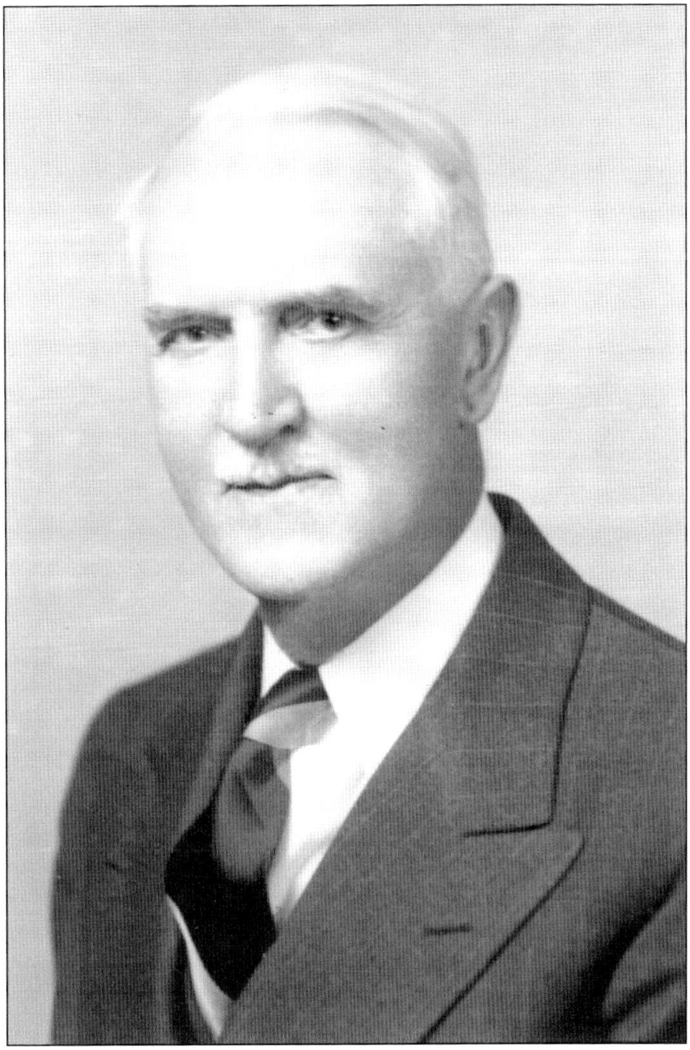

With the opening of the new School of Practice (commonly called the Campus School) came a new kindergarten class. Warren Jewett sits with his back to the camera while he pretends to milk a cow. Warren's kindergarten class is playing in and around a model of his parent's farm on Huguenot Street. (Courtesy of Dave and Mac Jewett.)

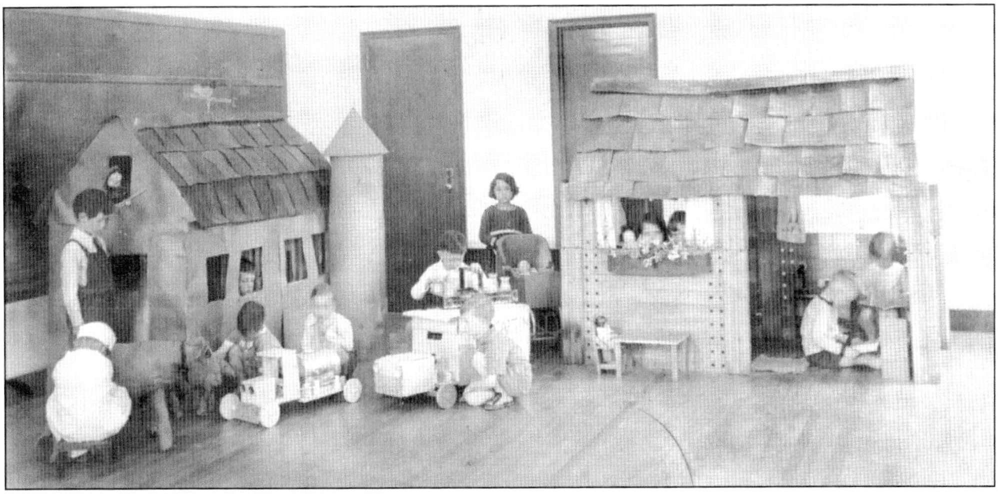

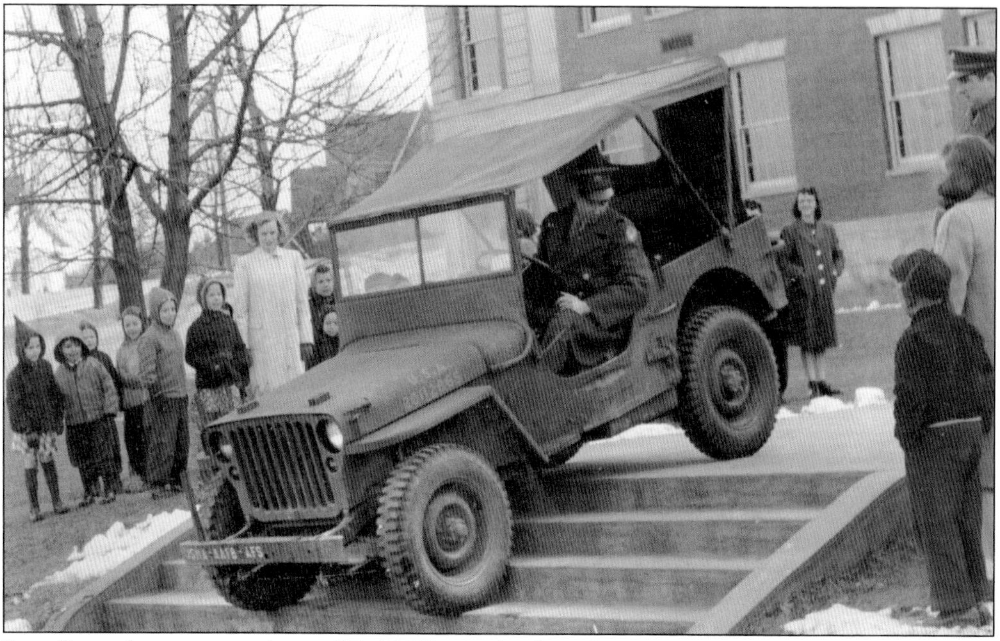

By selling of war stamps during World War II, the first objective of the sixth-grade class was to purchase a $1,200 jeep for the war effort. The second objective was to buy an ambulance and third an airplane. When their first goal was accomplished, the grateful authorities sent a jeep. It spent the day climbing the school steps and giving rides to the hardworking students. (Photograph by Erma DeWitt.)

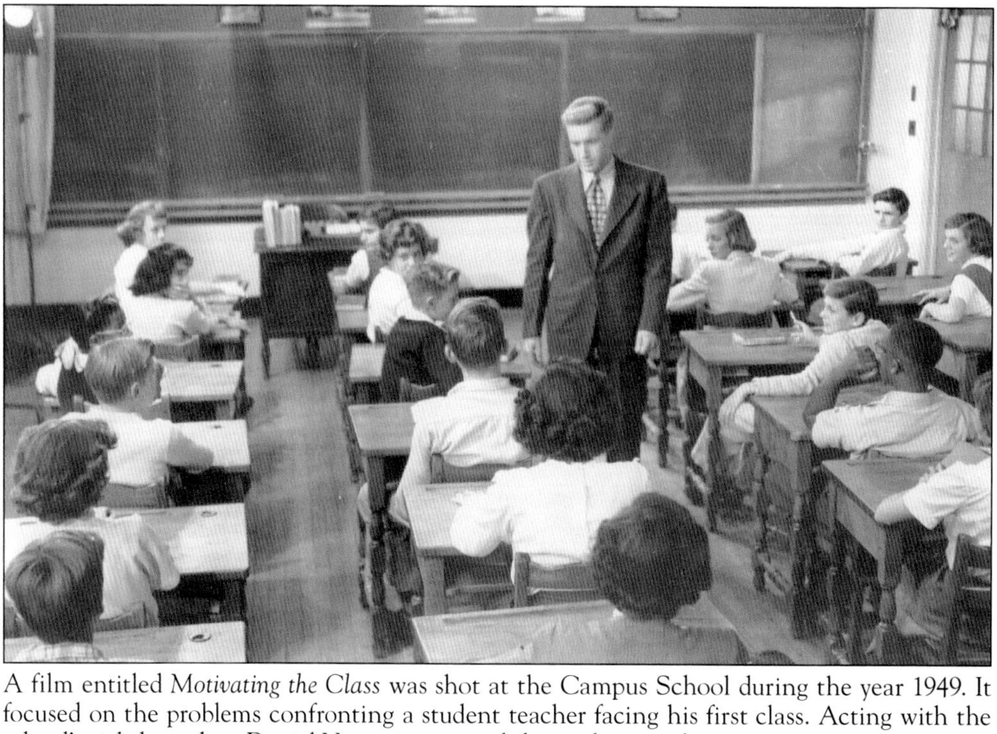

A film entitled *Motivating the Class* was shot at the Campus School during the year 1949. It focused on the problems confronting a student teacher facing his first class. Acting with the school's eighth graders, Daniel Vezzani portrayed the student teacher.

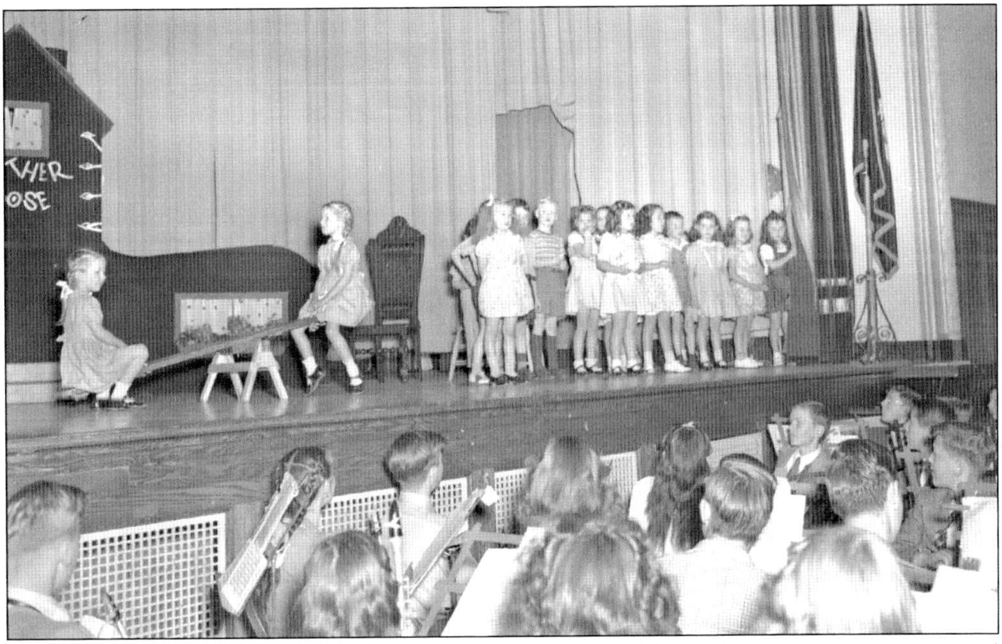

Under the direction of Marion Harding, a music festival with a Mother Goose theme was presented every May. All the children from kindergarten through sixth grade participated. The junior high school glee club sang modern versions of old nursery rhymes while the junior high school band provided the music for the procession and recessional. Above, Janet and Janis Shand are posed on the seesaw while the rest of the class performs in front of a giant shoe made by the seventh-grade boys. Below, Elaine Keator and Dirk DeWitt are dressed as a bride and groom, ready to perform with their classmates in the musical fantasy *A Jack and Jill Wedding.* (Photographs by Erma DeWitt.)

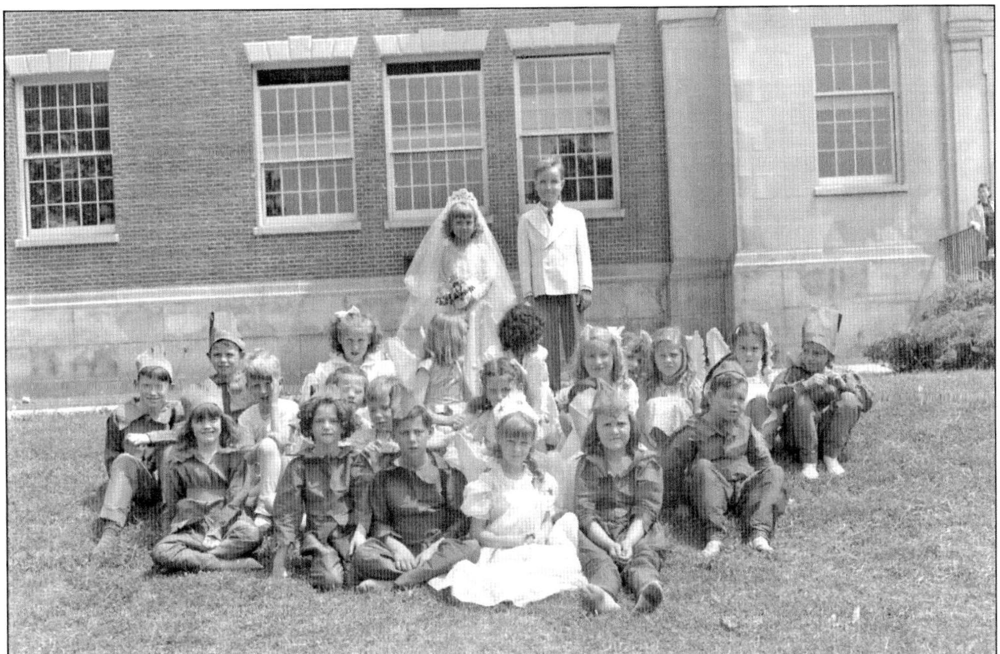

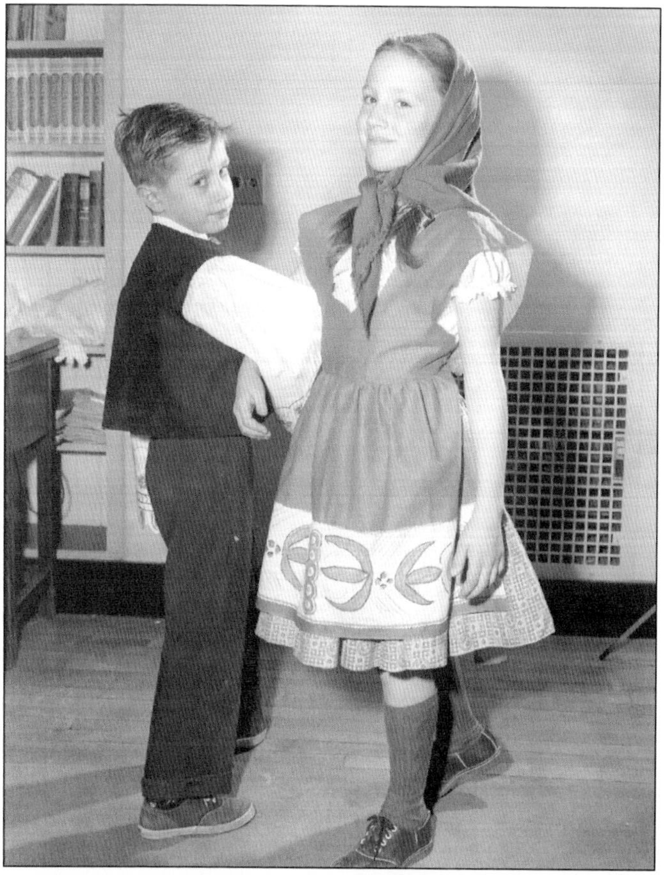

Sponsored by the Parent-Teacher Association, International Night was an evening full of performances by the students of the Campus School. Each class chose a country, and then their curriculum would include information on that country. Physical education teacher Mel Archard taught the children and their teachers the various dances. Many parents made costumes representative of the countries. Shown at left, Andrew Reid and Barbara Allen practice a traditional folk dance. Below, students watch in wonder as the limbo, a traditional dance of Trinidad, is performed.

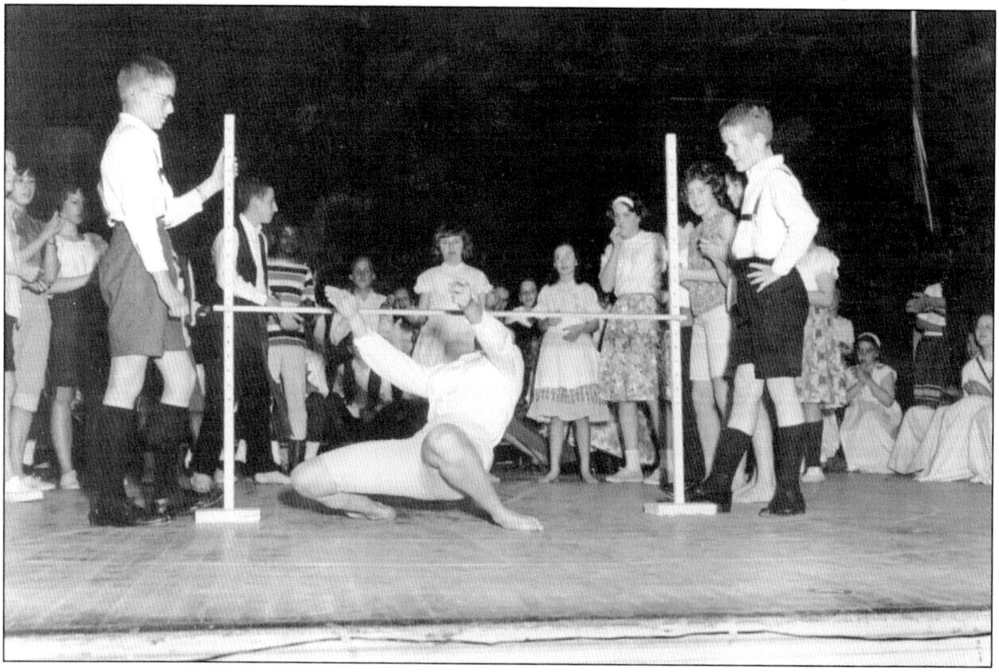

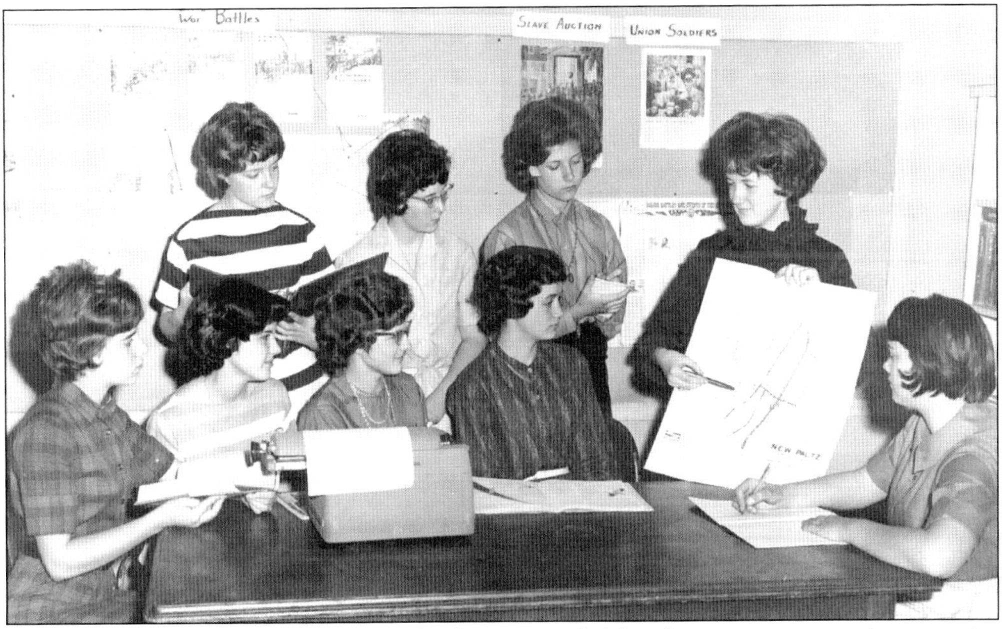

Ninth-grade students at the Campus School were awarded fourth prize in a national community civics contest for high school students in 1962. Their project was a study of the problems of the New Paltz schools. Pictured from left to right are (seated) Laura Buchanan, Ann Fall, Beth Heinze, Victoria Burkhart, and Sharon Roth; (standing) Bonnie Thoben, Betsy White, Georgine Bogert, and Donna Langwick.

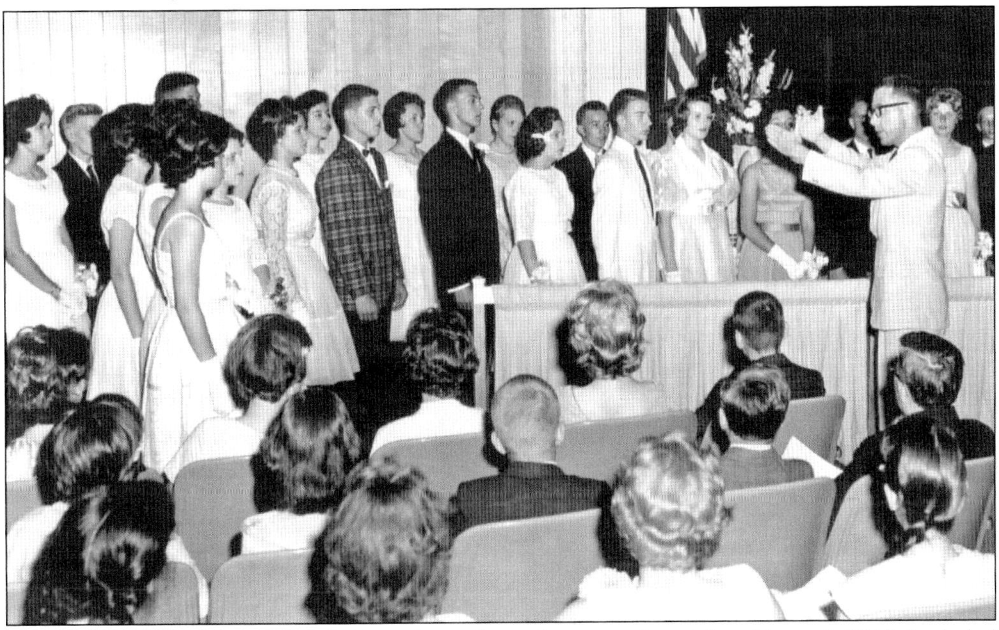

The Campus School graduated 29 ninth-grade students on the night of June 6, 1963. Included in the commencement program was a choral speaking presentation by class members under the direction of Ivan Ferguson. There was a dance for the graduates and their guests following the ceremony. Ninth-grade students stopped attending the Campus School when the new high school on South Putt Corners Road was opened.

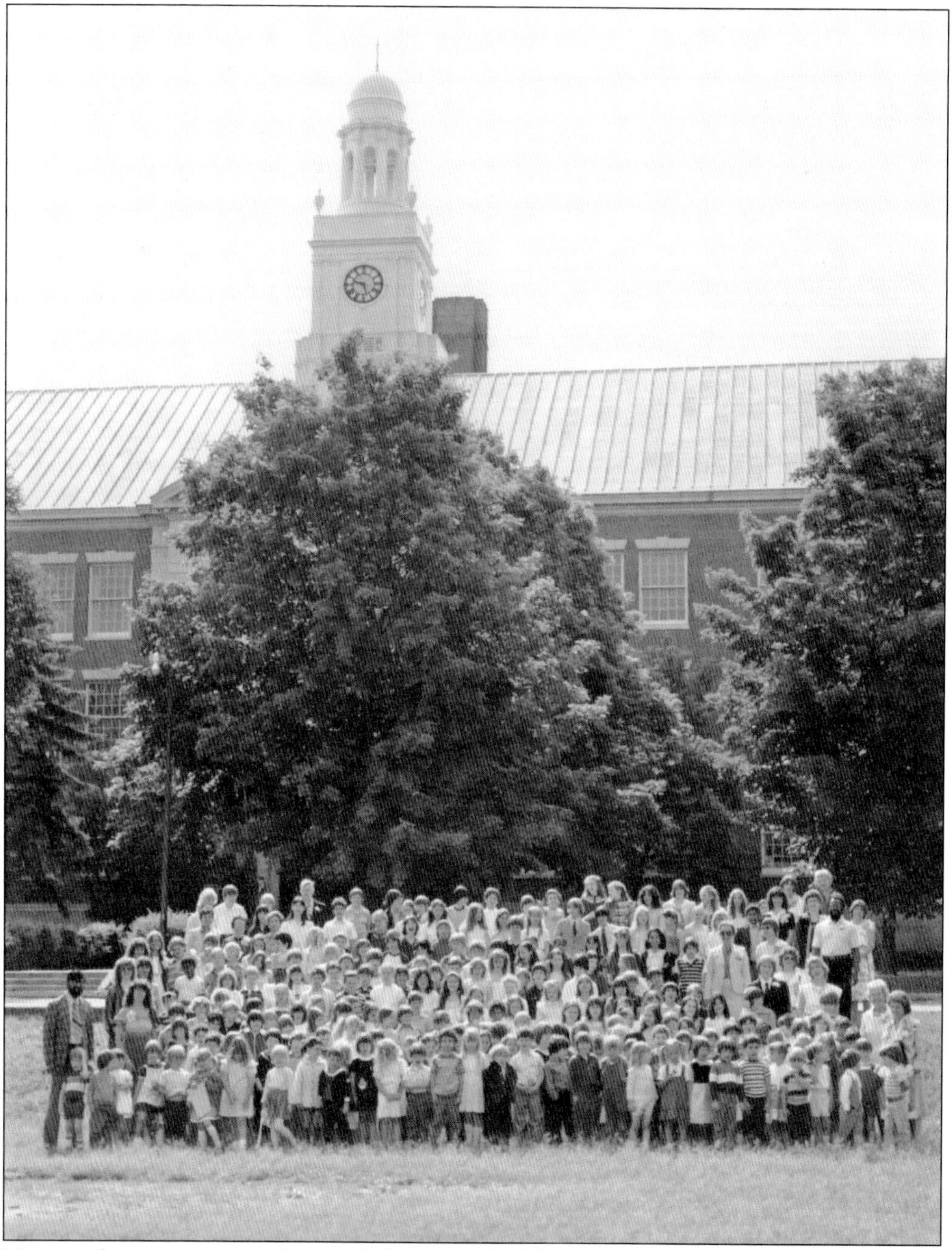

Many students, parents, teachers, and alumni marked the closing of the Campus School in June 1982. Following the ceremony, the crowd picnicked and partook of a large cake shaped in the form of the school. Budgetary cutbacks were behind college president Dr. Alice Chandler's decision to close the school. This image of the children and faculty in front of the school was taken before 1982. (Courtesy of Susan Stegen.)

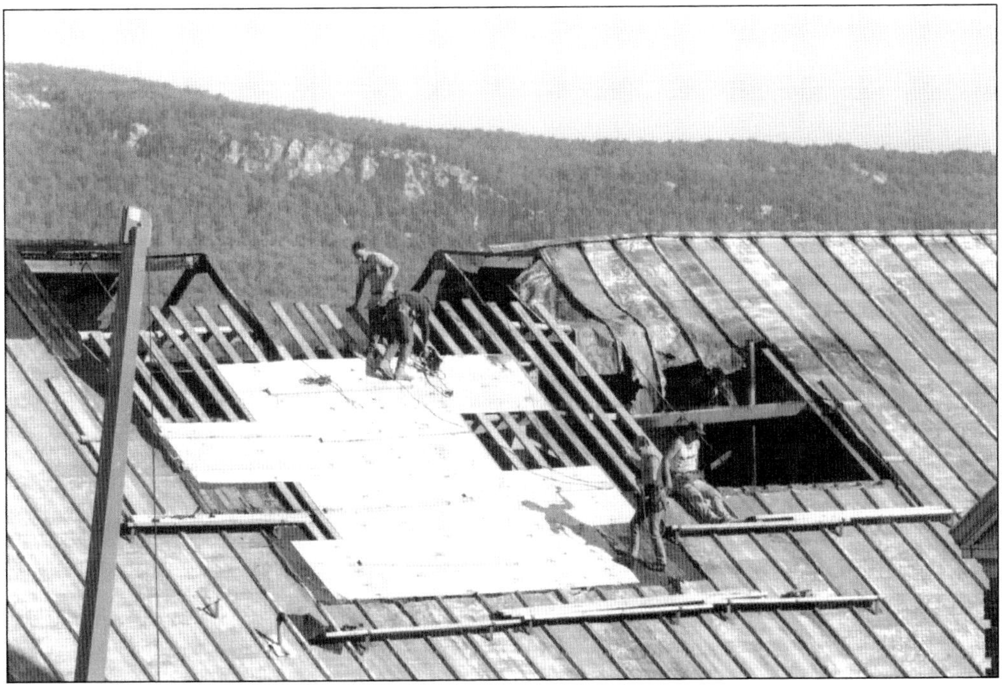

Workers rushed to temporarily repair the roof after a fire destroyed the landmark clock tower atop the van den Berg Learning Center (formerly the Campus School) in May 1990. At the time of the fire, the building housed offices and classrooms for the business administration and nursing programs, the campus psychological counseling center, a day-care center, and the migrant education program. (Photograph by Dennis O'Keefe.)

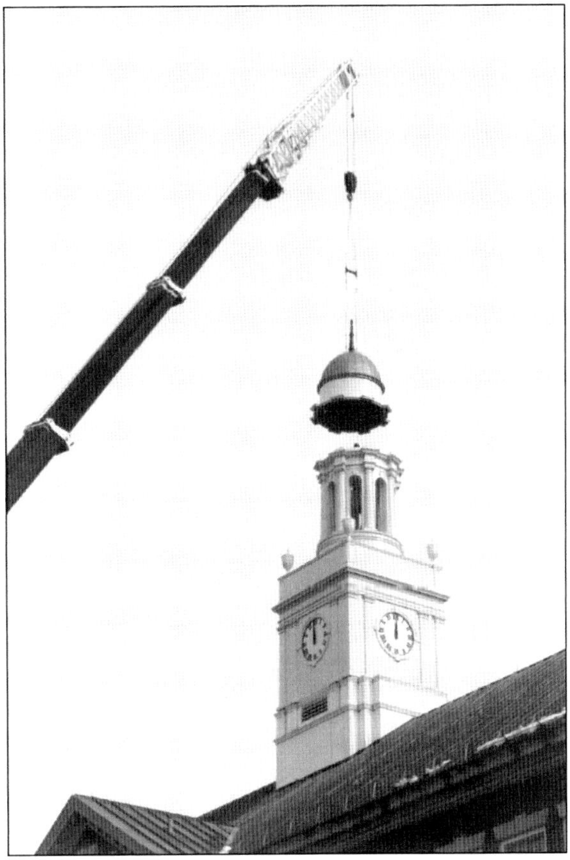

A crane carefully lowers the top of the cupola on the replicated van den Berg clock tower in 2005. The new clock tower was built in Kentucky and includes four working clocks, each 4 feet in diameter on each side. It also features decorative elements, including a spire, cornices, and columns inspired by the original tower. (Photograph by Dennis O'Keefe.)

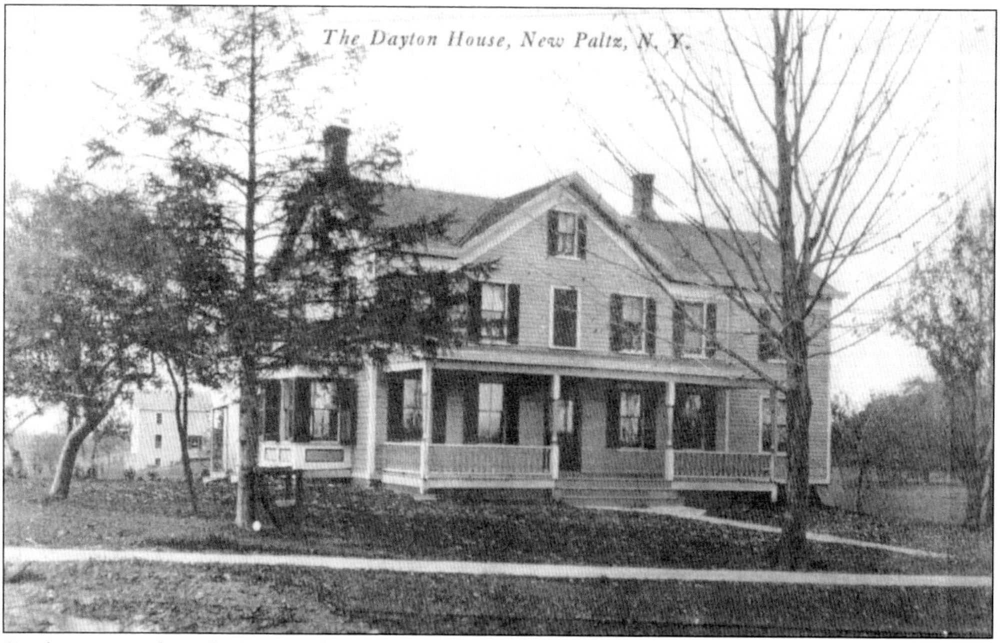

Students attending the New Paltz Normal School boarded in homes throughout the village. This home on Mohonk Avenue was built by A. D. Relyea in 1883 to house summer boarders. Soon after the new school building opened on the hill, Daniel Dayton began boarding students year-round. For several years this was the Theta Phi house. Purchased by the State Teachers College in 1957 to house faculty offices, the building has been torn down. It was replaced by a parking lot.

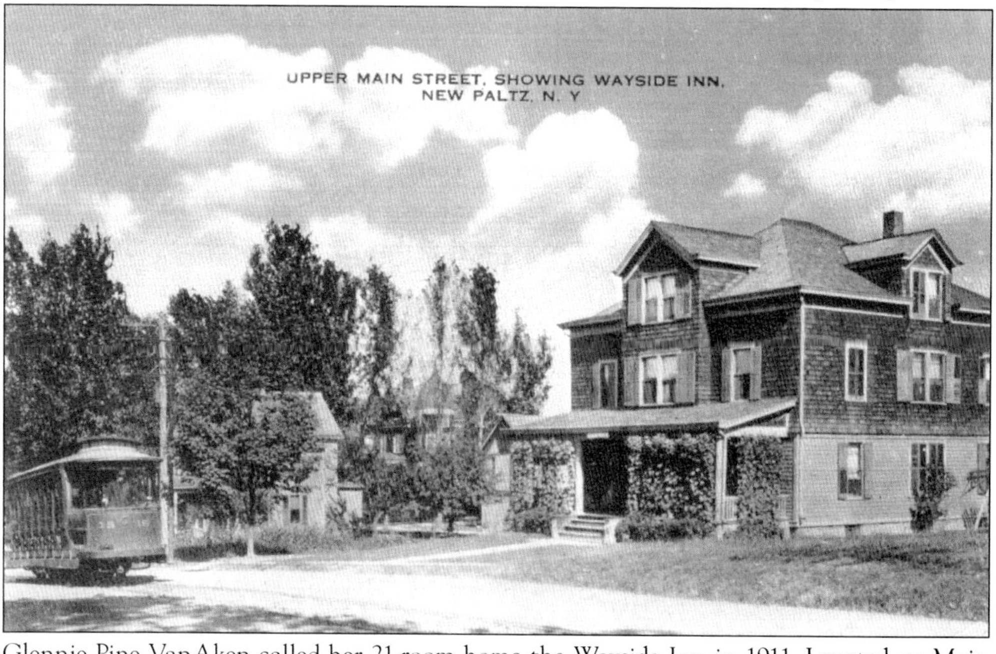

Glennie Pine VanAken called her 21-room home the Wayside Inn in 1911. Located on Main Street between Prospect and Grove Streets, it became the Agonian Sorority house in 1924. Craig Shepherd opened the New Paltz Hostel here in 2001. The trolley can be seen on the left as it makes its way up Main Street toward Highland.

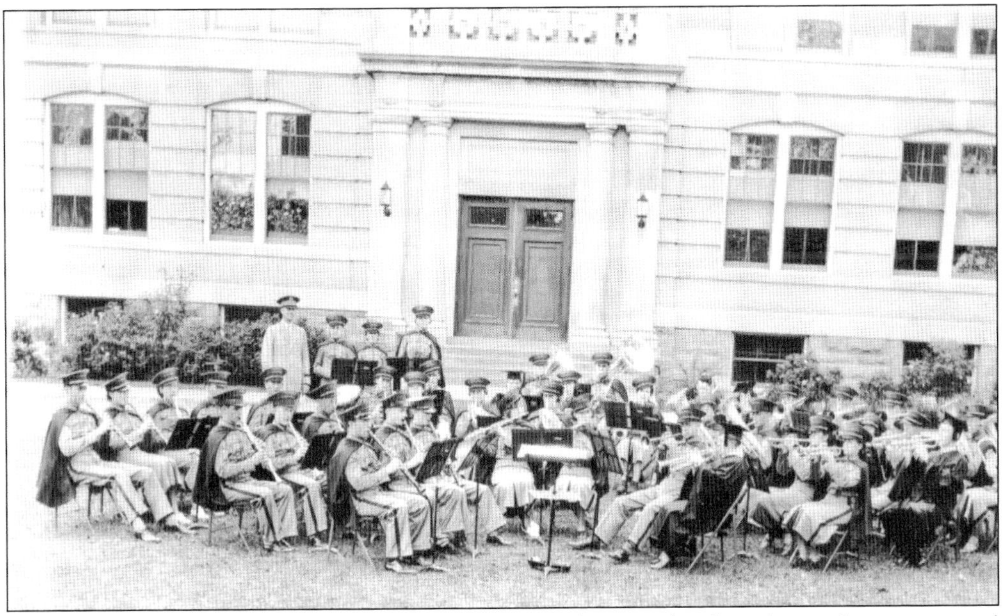

When Marion Harding was added to the faculty in 1928, she immediately took over the instrumental music program at the school. Later she also directed the orchestra and started instrumental music classes at the Practice School. When Howard B. Hoffmann came to the school the instrumental program was further expanded. Operettas, pageants, concerts, band concerts indoors and out, and Christmas caroling continued throughout the years. (Courtesy of Elaine Kniffen.)

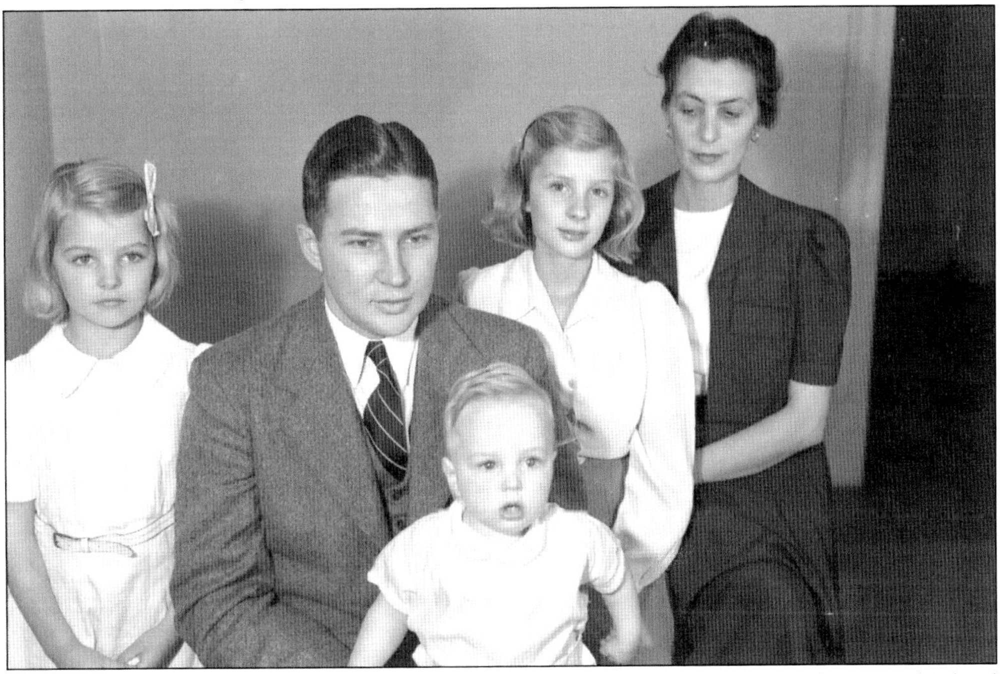

Gov. Herbert Lehman signed a bill in 1942 that changed the name of the New Paltz Normal School to the State Teachers College. After Lawrence H. van den Berg's death in 1943, Dr. William J. Haggerty became the college's second president. The Haggerty family consisted of, from left to right, Sally, William J., James Robert, Susan, and Marjorie Haggerty. (Photograph by Erma DeWitt.)

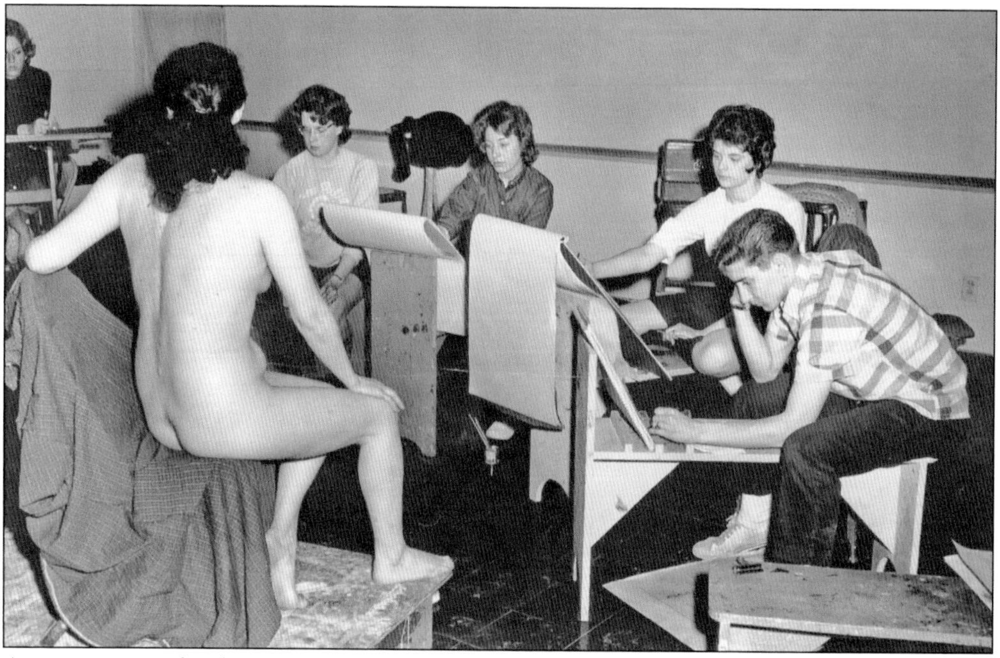

A new program for the preparation of art teachers in 1951 was "the first major change in the offerings of the College since its founding in 1885," announced President Haggerty. For more than 50 years, the art education program at SUNY–New Paltz has prepared students for working with young people in schools and alternative education settings.

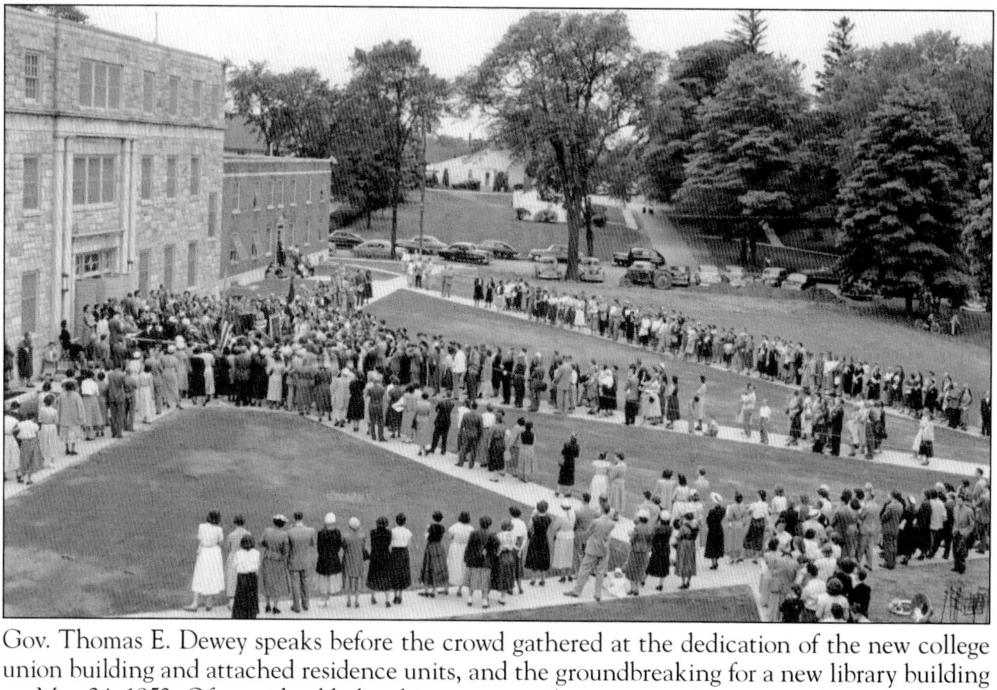

Gov. Thomas E. Dewey speaks before the crowd gathered at the dedication of the new college union building and attached residence units, and the groundbreaking for a new library building on May 24, 1952. Of considerable local interest was the naming of the six residence halls. The names officially proclaimed by Hon. Jay LeFevre, secretary of the board of visitors, were the names of the original New Paltz patentees.

Box after box, containing some 23,000 books in all, came sliding down a chute from the top floor of the Old Main building in the fall of 1954. The books were being moved by approximately 1,000 members of the student body, faculty, and staff from Old Main to the newly built library. A line of students was formed from the end of the chute across the grounds into the new building. (Photograph by Neil Croom.)

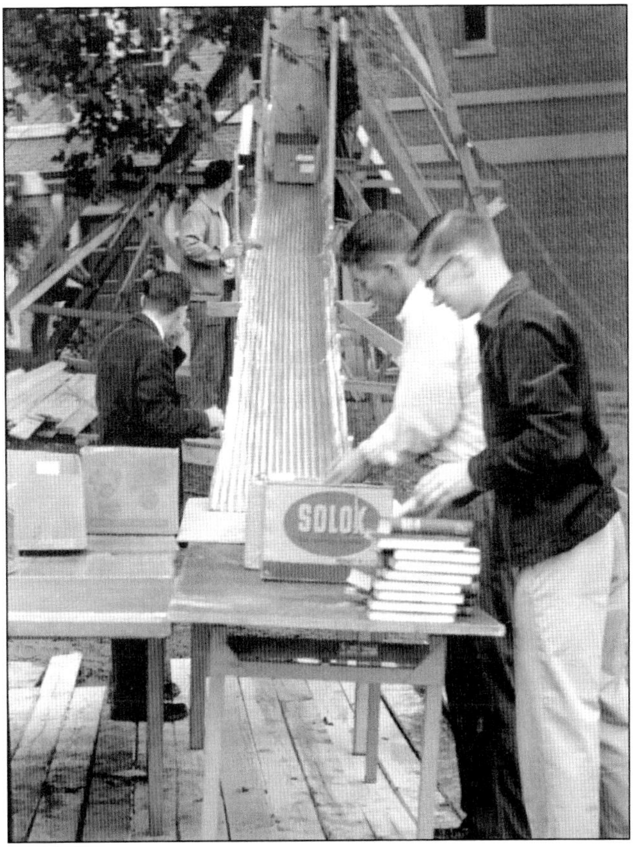

In preparation for further expansion, the state acquired acres of land to the south of the main quad. The first of the new buildings to be completed was Bouton Hall (top left) in the fall of 1958. In July 1959, the name of the college was changed to the State University College of Education at New Paltz.

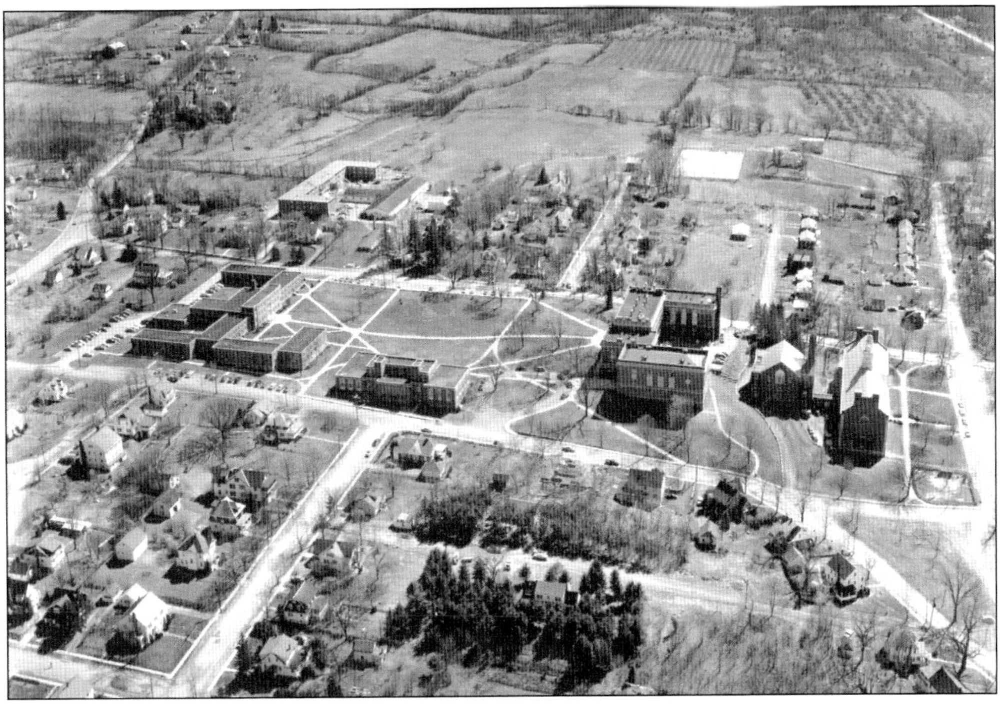

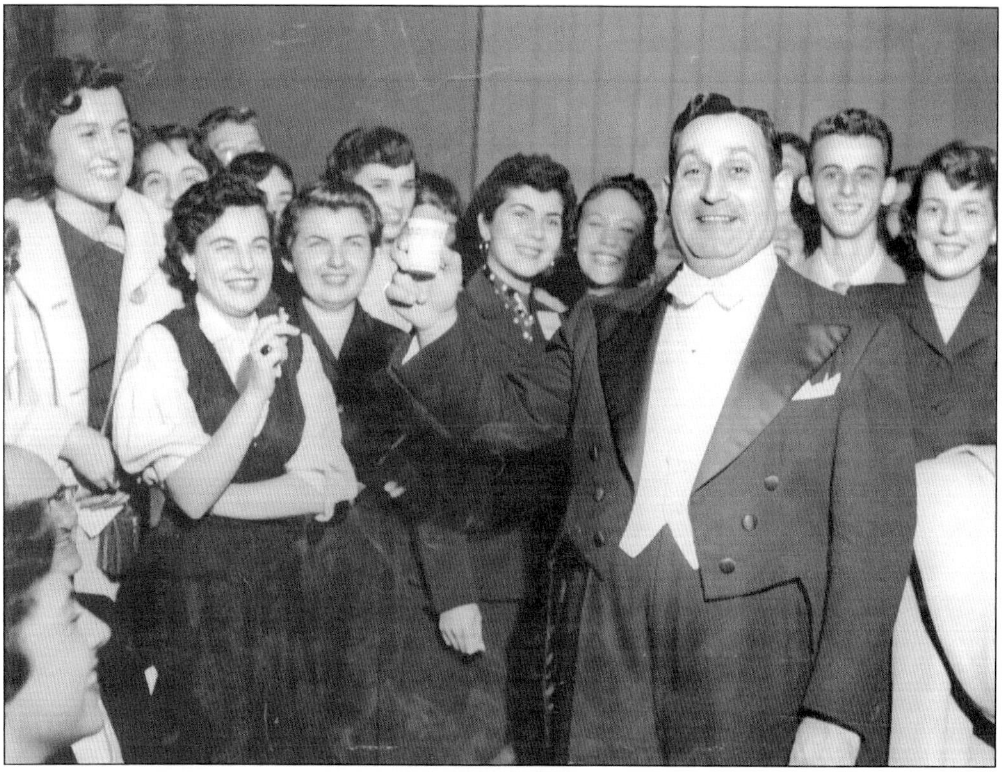

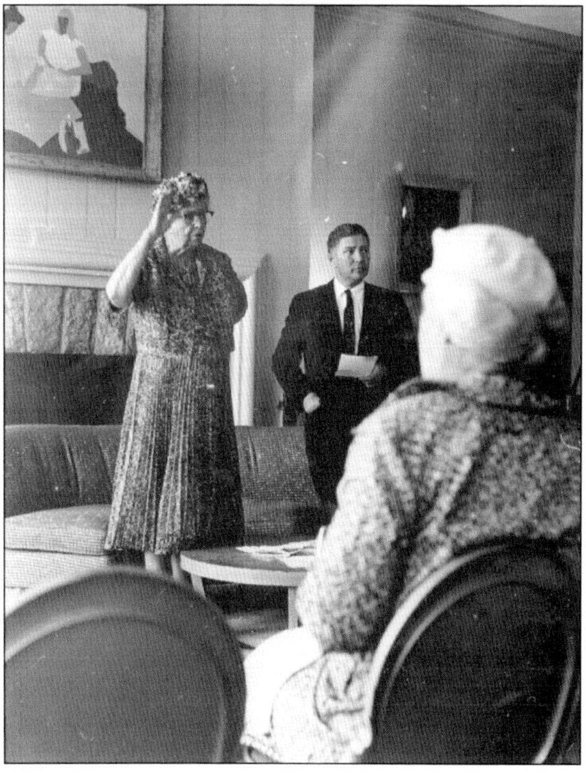

Richard Tucker, considered by many to be one of the world's greatest tenors, appeared in concert at the State Teacher's College as a part of the New Paltz Artist Series in 1953. The artist series had a long history dating back to the Lyceum Lecture Course of the 1890s. Dave Brubeck's jazz quintet, the Vienna Choir Boys, and Jerome Hines were just a few of the many performers who appeared.

Both Franklin Roosevelt and his wife, Eleanor, visited New Paltz many times. Franklin was a descendant of patentee Antoine Crispell. After her husband died in 1945, Eleanor came almost every year to lecture at the college. Young photography student Louis Mosconi took pictures of her during her visit to the college in 1959. She is shown with President Haggerty in College Hall. (Photograph by Louis Mosconi.)

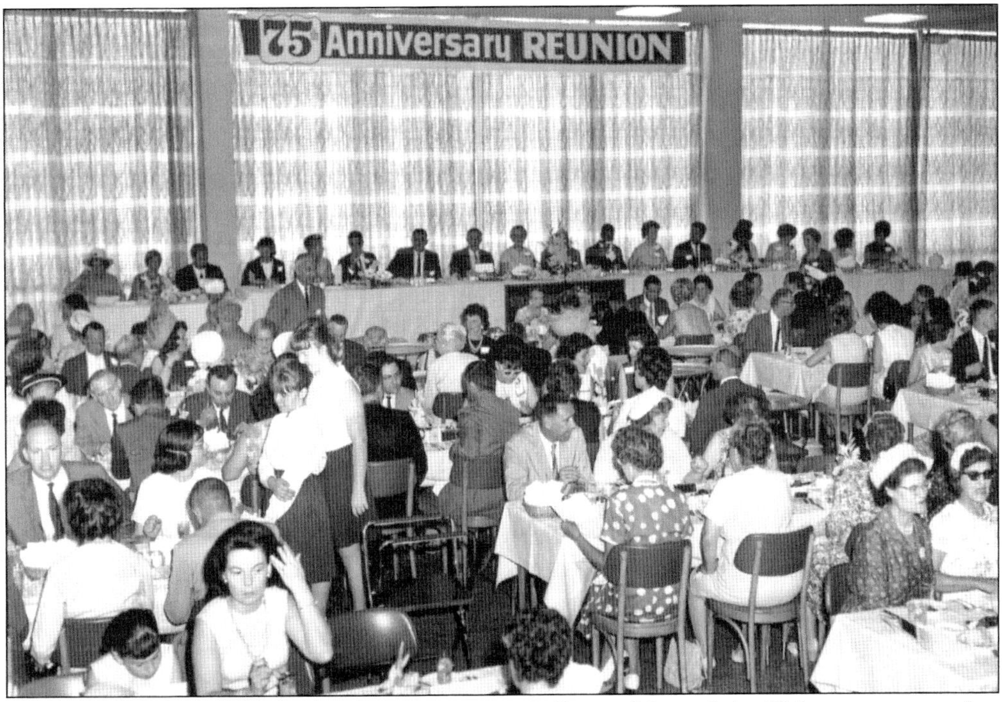

The Alumni Association of the State University College celebrated the 75th anniversary of its founding on June 12, 1965, with a luncheon in Parker Dining Hall. The dining hall was named for Alton Brooks Parker, a former normal school trustee who ran for president of the United States in 1904. Ray Kurdt and Frank Kraat converted the dining hall into a theater in the early 1970s.

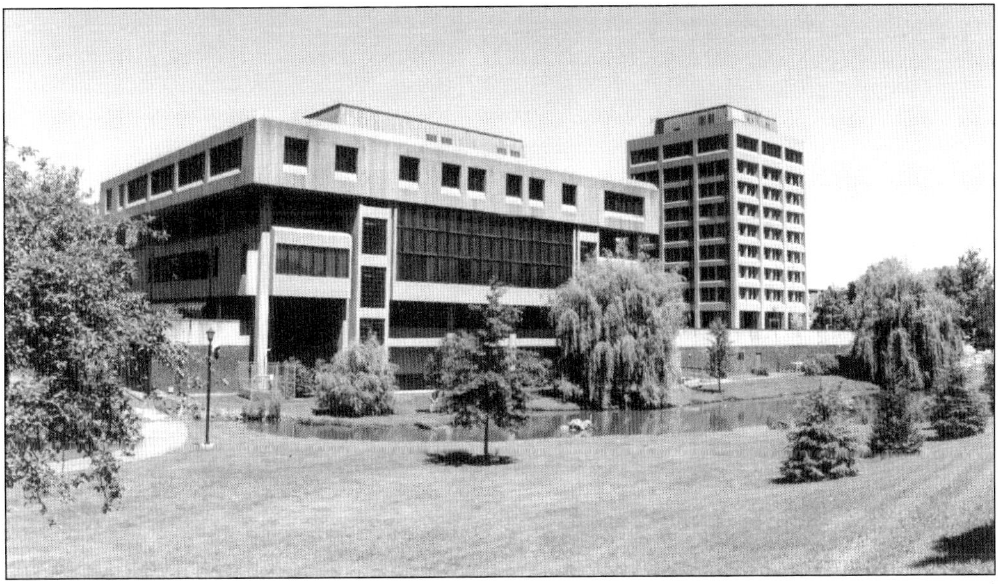

The campus was renamed SUNY College of Arts and Science, New Paltz, in 1961. It was renamed again in 1994 to the State University of New York at New Paltz. Pictured here are the student union building (left) and the Haggerty Administration Tower (right), both constructed in 1970. The administration building is named for William J. Haggerty, who held the post of college president at New Paltz from 1944 to 1966. (Photograph by Dennis O'Keefe.)

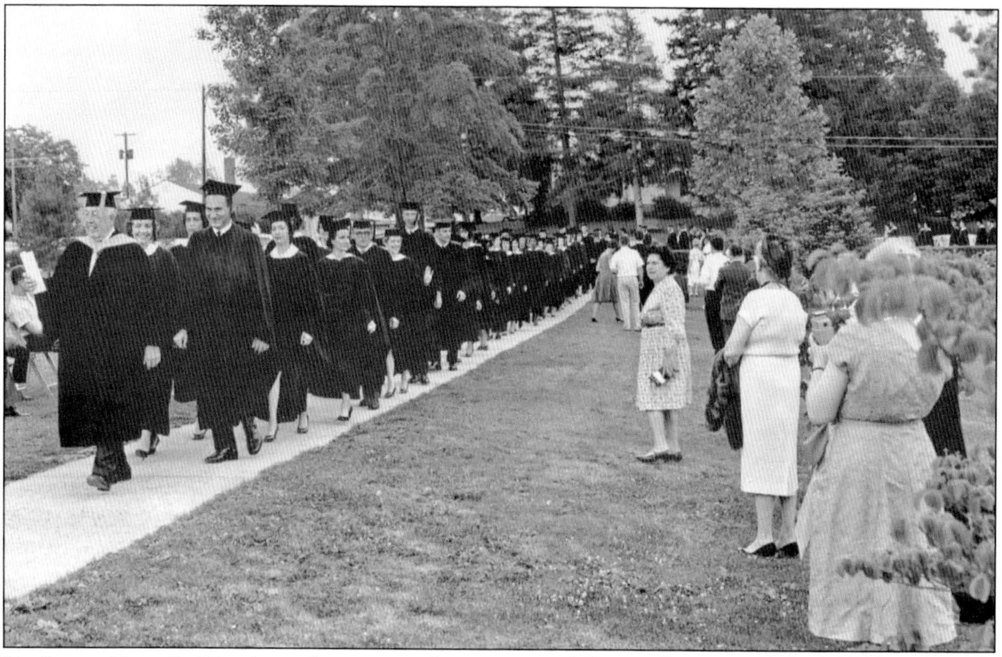

Dr. Loren Campbell leads graduates into the main quad during the processional of the June 1962 graduation ceremonies. The commencement exercises were held under a large tent that covered approximately 3,000 people. Presiding over the ceremony was college president Dr. William Haggerty. College graduations continue to be held on the main quad to this day.

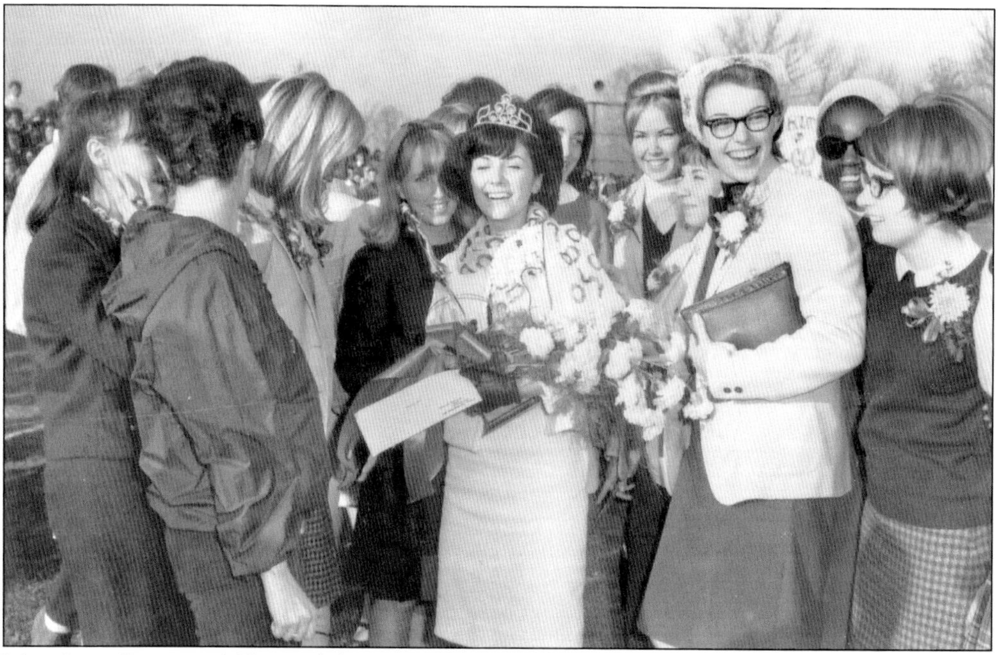

Mary Jane Capozzi of Clintondale, a member of the Clioian Sorority, was elected homecoming queen in the fall of 1965. The selection of homecoming queen was just one of the day's events that marked the first homecoming celebration at the college. Other events included a soccer game, open houses at the new campus buildings, and a parade.

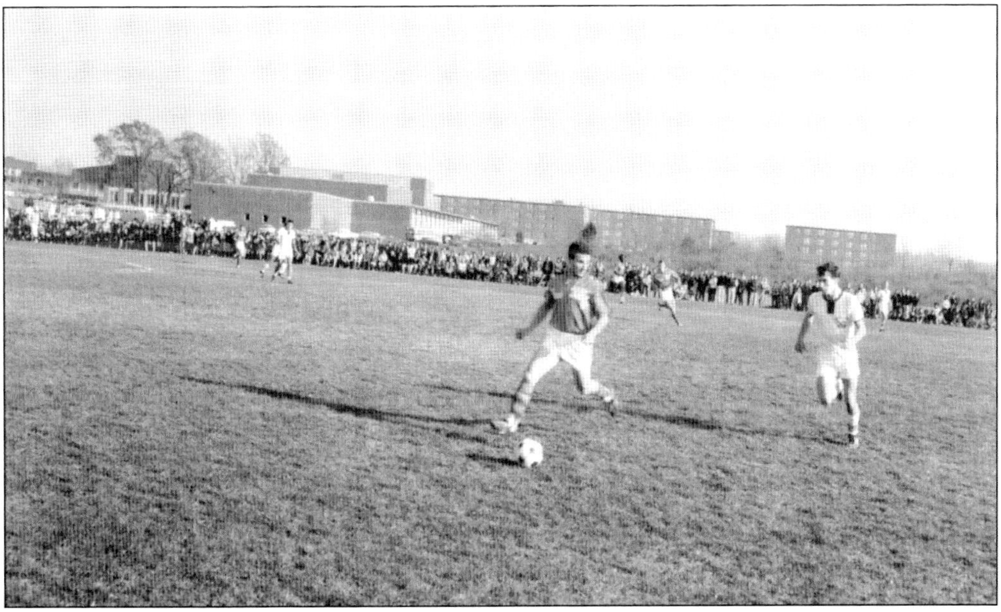

Eugene "Gino" Ventriglia tracks the ball down during the 1965 homecoming soccer game against Oneonta. For four seasons he was named All-SUNY and All-State. He was a three time All-American, and as a senior he was selected Player of the Year as the best college player in the country. He was selected as a member of the U.S. Olympic soccer team in 1968.

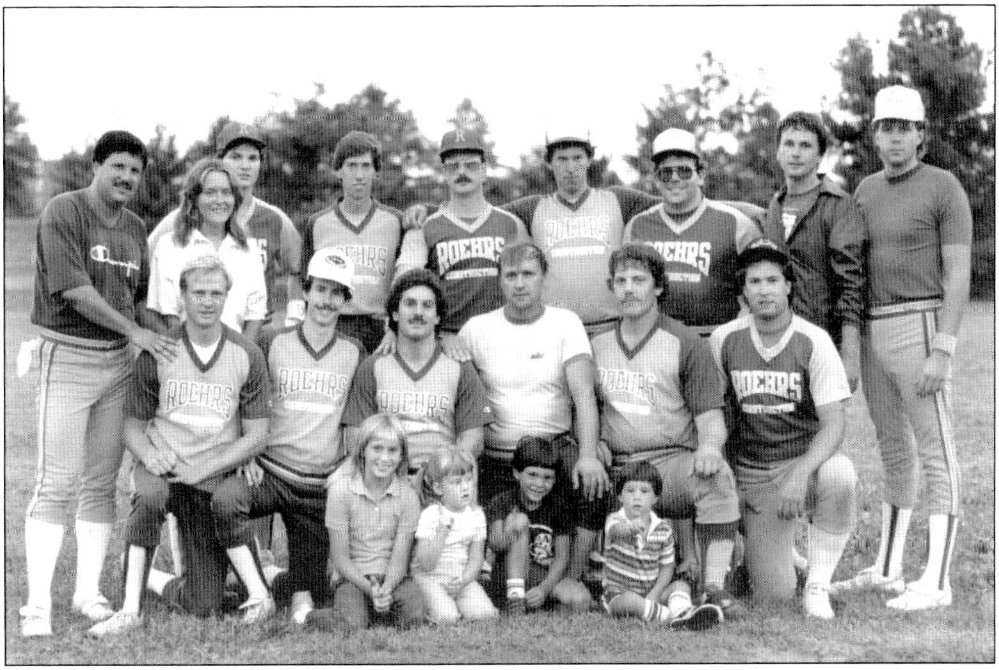

For years, the men's and women's softball leagues would play their games on the college athletic fields. Sponsored by local bars and businesses, eight teams could play at once on the four diamonds laid out on the college's expansive fields while their friends and families watched from the sidelines. Pictured is the 1985 championship team sponsored by Roehrs Construction. (Courtesy of Bob Geller.)

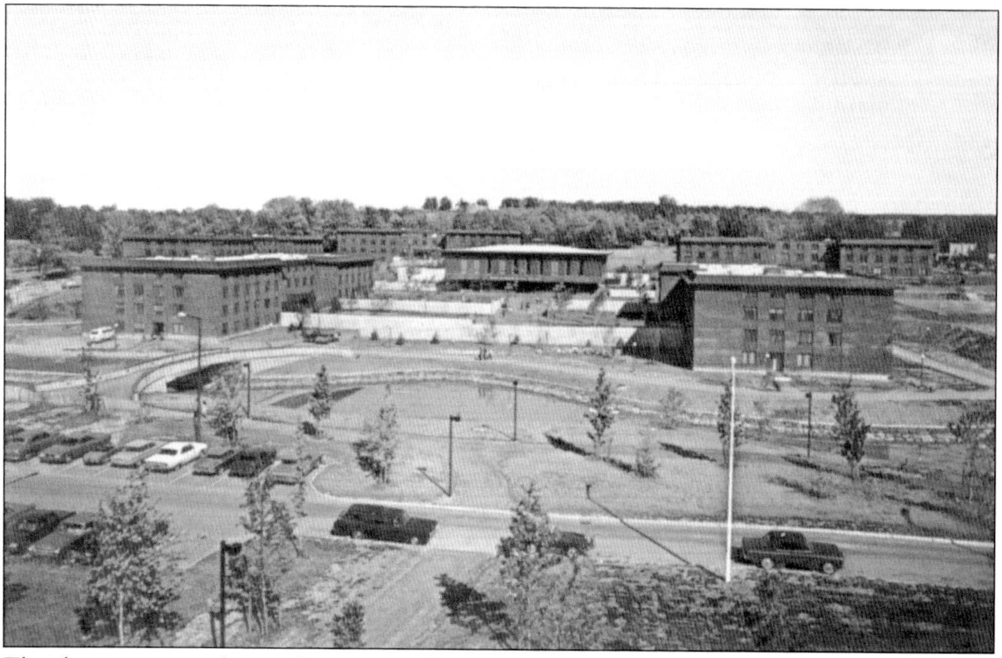

This dormitory complex on the eastern edge of the SUNY campus is anchored by the Hasbrouck dining hall. The dining hall is surrounded by Bevier, Crispell, Deyo, DuBois, and LeFevre Halls—all named in honor of the New Paltz patentee families. A 250,000-volume library, a second science building, and a communications/lecture center were also opened in the fall of 1968.

The back of Elting Gymnasium, with its accompanying tennis courts, looks far different today than when it was constructed. Built in 1963, the tennis courts were initially replaced by a sports bubble in 1986. In 2006, a new 57,000-square-foot athletic and wellness center opened on the spot of the original tennis courts.

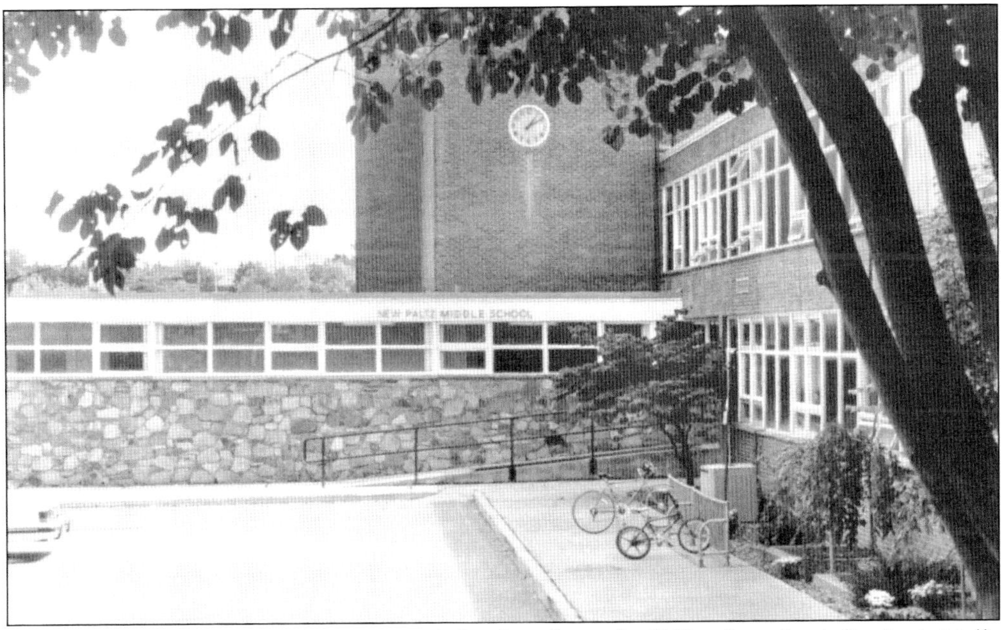

To relieve overcrowding in the Campus School in the early 1950s, the school district initially held classes in nearby buildings. Then an addition designed by local architect Jedd Reisner was constructed at the school on South Manheim Boulevard. In September 1956, the school opened to all grade levels with a new elementary wing, a gymnasium and cafeteria below, locker rooms, offices, and storage rooms. It became the New Paltz Middle School in 1968.

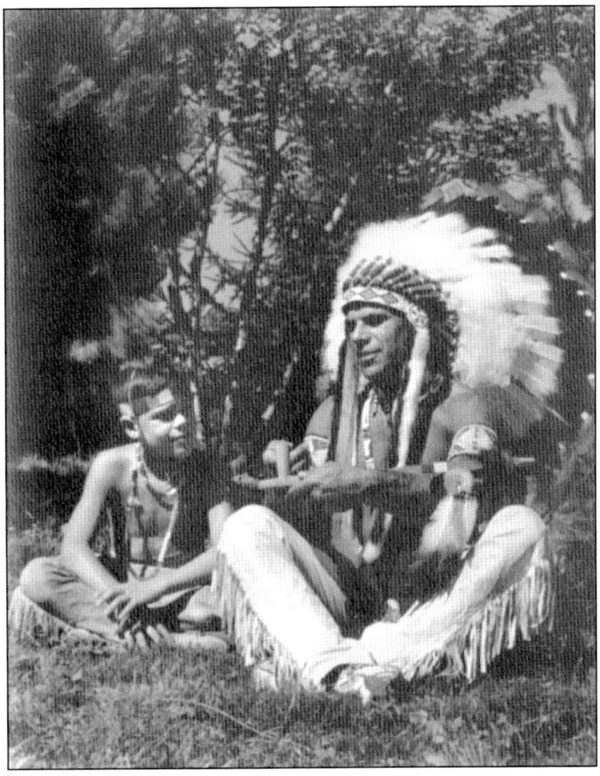

When he had spare time from his sixth-grade teaching duties, Alfred Douglas studied Native American lore and often performed ceremonial dances to illustrate his culture. A Cherokee called "Thunder Boy," Al is shown here teaching his son, Ross, about a pipe. The Douglas family lived in the Freer House on Huguenot Street and performed at several Stone House Days. (Photograph by Erma DeWitt.)

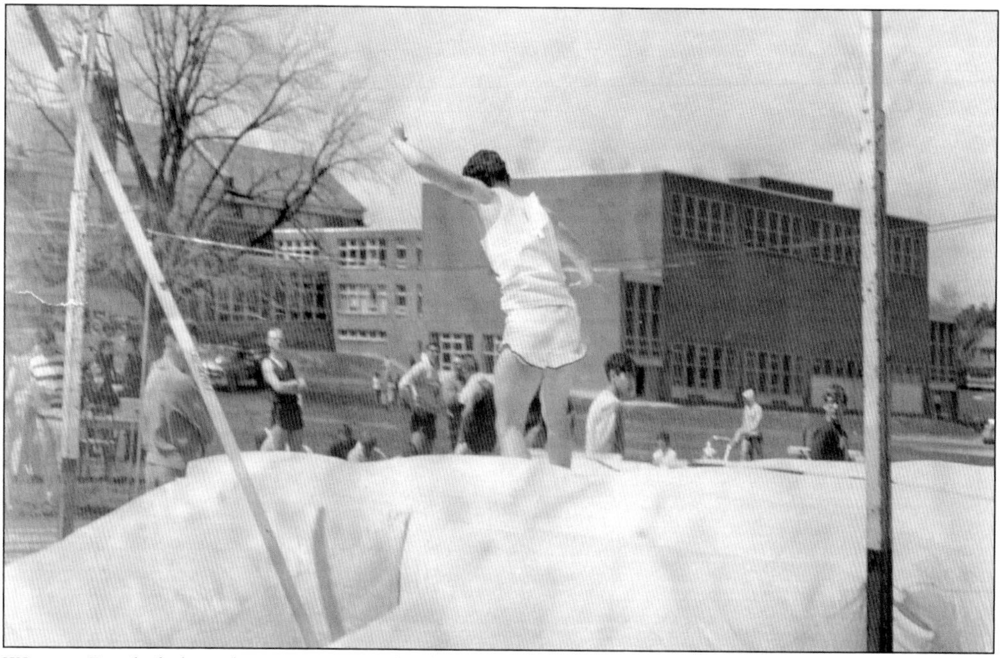

Warren Ronk fails in his attempt at the high jump during a track meet at the New Paltz High School. From 1954 to 1967, the school played host to the Hudson Valley Relays to raise money for the school's clubs and teams. The money was used to buy equipment such as the "cloud nine" shown here, which was used to soften a jumper's landing. (Photograph by John H. Kruh.)

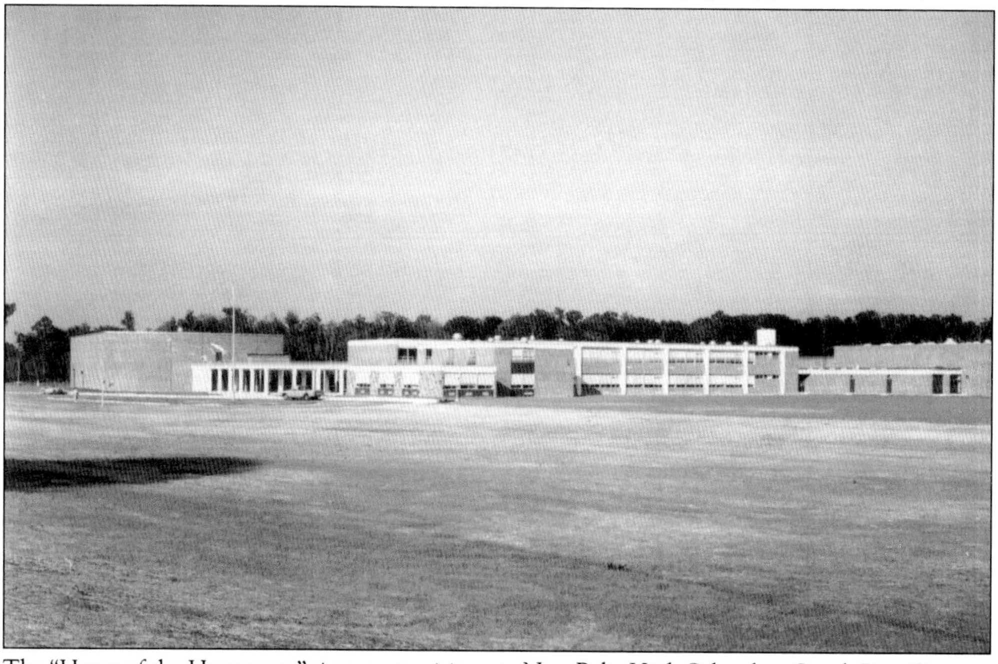

The "Home of the Huguenots" sign greets visitors to New Paltz High School on South Putt Corners Road. The south side of the school complex looks quite different since it was dedicated in October 1968. An expansion project in 2004 added eight classrooms, four labs, and a gymnasium. New athletic fields have also changed the school's original appearance.

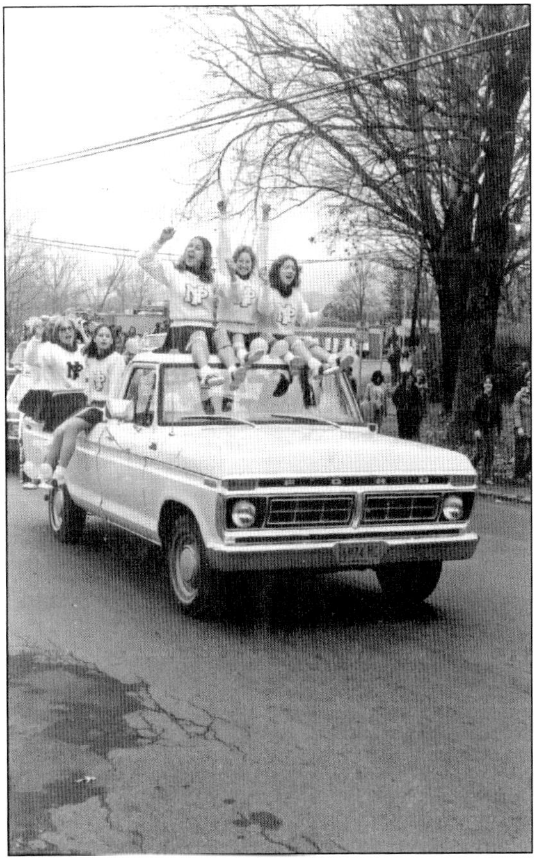

"Here we go, Hugies," chant the New Paltz High School cheerleaders perched atop a pickup truck during a homecoming parade up Plattekill Avenue. They are on their way to the middle school football field. Each year homecoming week marked the crowning of a homecoming king and queen who reigned over the football game and other events throughout the school year.

The New Paltz Middle School's Huguenot band marches down Main Street in a cold St. Patrick's Day parade. On March 17, 1986, an intoxicated man from Port Jervis drove a stolen car into the parade and struck two small children and an adult, injuring all three. Police immediately pounced on the car and arrested the man, but this St. Patrick's Day tragedy ended what had been a beloved 14-year New Paltz tradition.

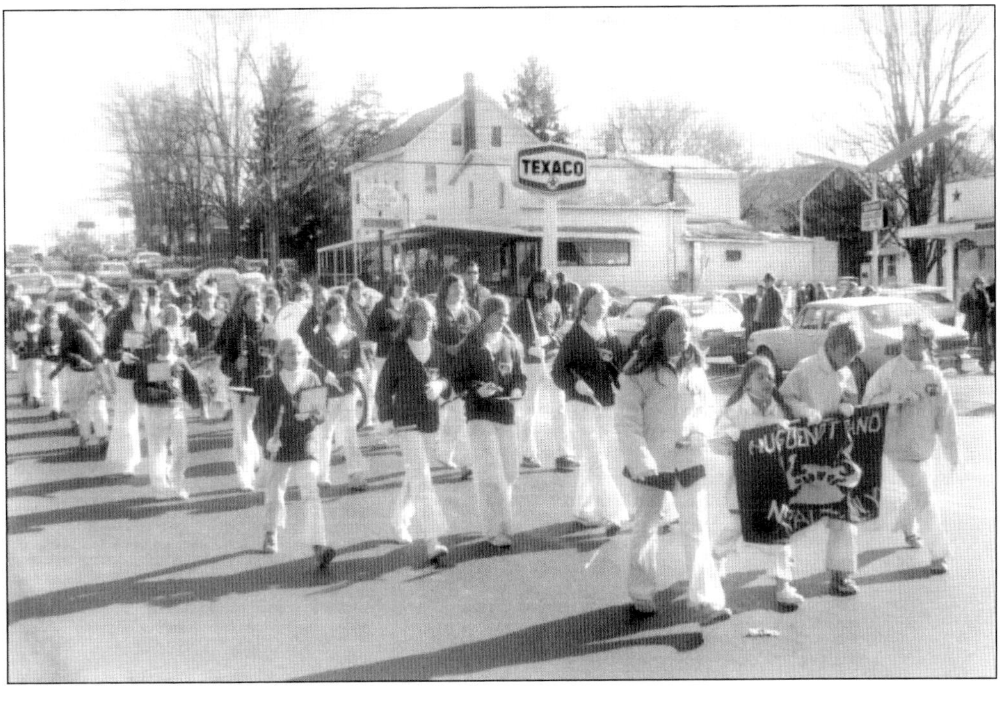

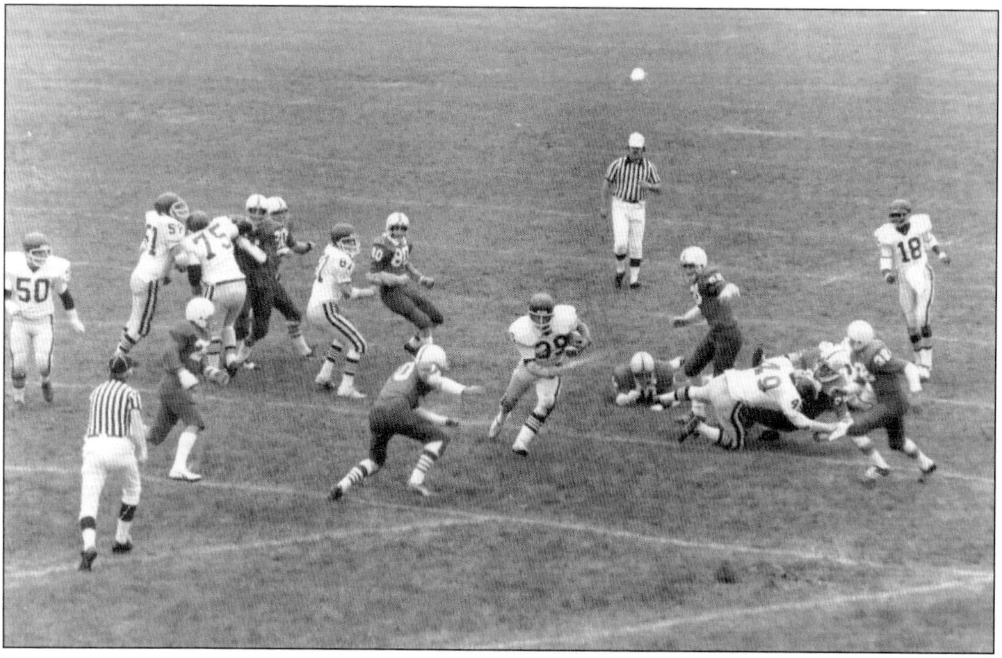

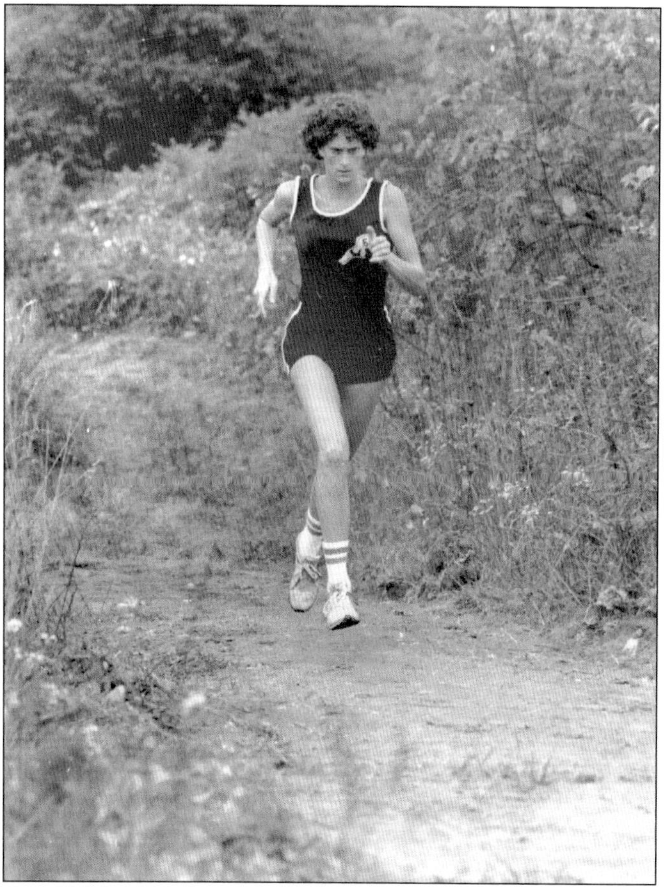

Quarterback Charles Davis (No. 18, in white) led the Huguenot football team to the Mid-Hudson Athletic League Championship in 1980. He went on to star as a defensive back at the University of Tennessee and tried out for the Dallas Cowboys. He is now a broadcaster for Fox and the NFL network.

Kim Ryan won the state Class B intersectional girls' cross-country championship on a 5-kilometer course in the fall of 1982. It was the first time anyone in New Paltz or the Mid-Hudson Athletic League had won a state title. She also excelled in track and Nordic skiing. Kim also was the first athlete to win gold medals in both the summer and winter Empire State Games. (Photograph by Marion Ryan.)

From left to right, Denise Edebohls, Jennifer Ackert, and Erin Quinn learned how to make candied apples with their third-grade teacher, Betty Taylor. Local farmers have allowed generations of New Paltz nursery and elementary school students to visit their apple orchards and pumpkin patches. Many class lessons have resulted from this generosity. (Courtesy of Betty Taylor.)

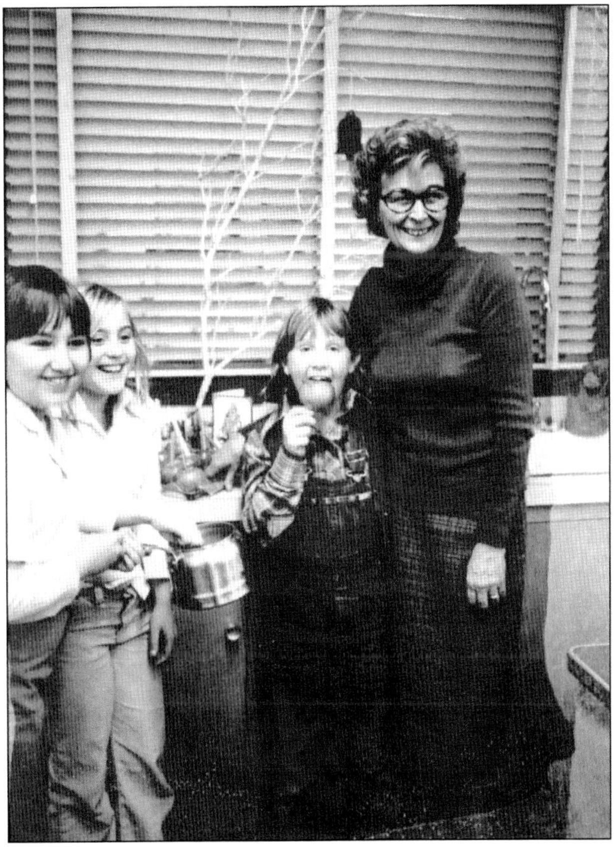

Pictured below from left to right, Keelin Smith, Melissa Kraus, Roseanne Ricci, Carlos DeRosa, and Glenn LaPolt proudly display their handmade marionettes before performing in front of their invited guests at Duzine School. For years Betty Taylor's third-grade class would put on an annual marionette or puppet show; this one seems to have a winter theme. (Courtesy of Betty Taylor.)

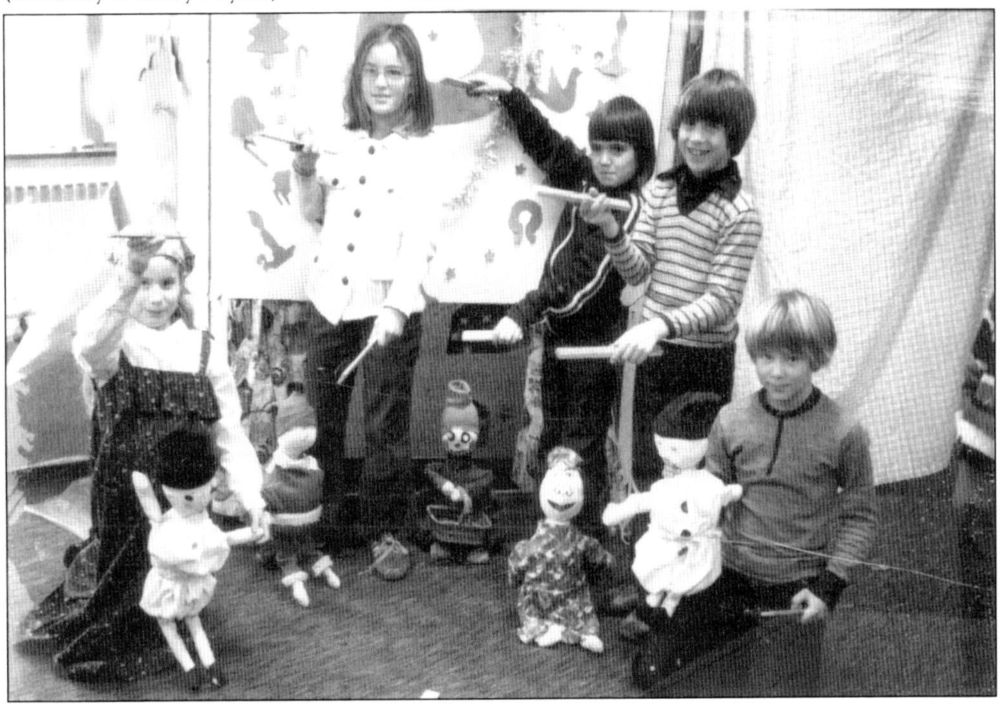

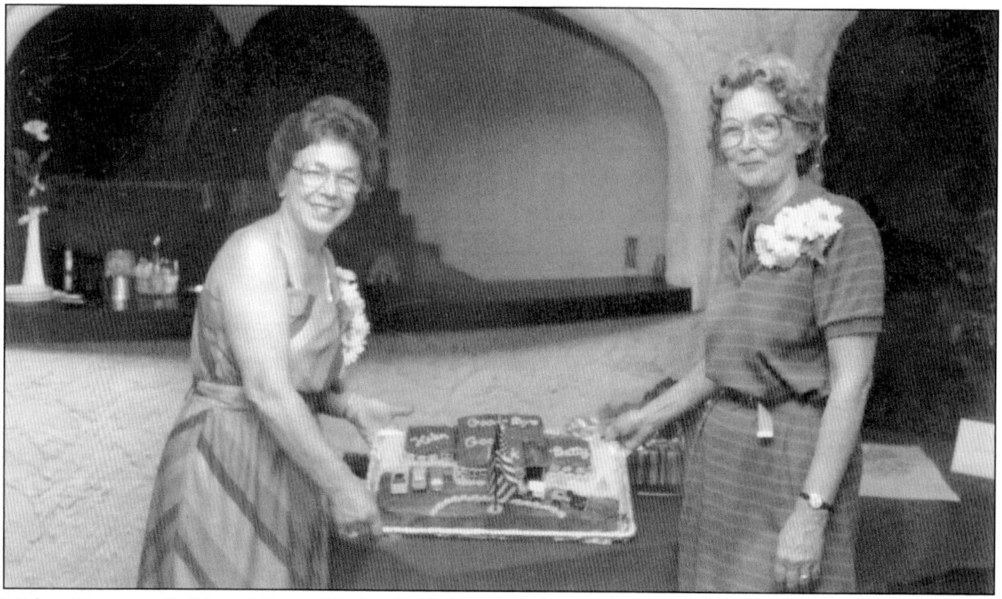

Helen Coutant (left) and Betty Taylor (right) had both been teaching for years by the time Duzine Elementary School was built in 1963. Coutant began teaching kindergarten in 1953, and Taylor started teaching in 1954. Due to the overcrowded conditions at the Campus School at that time, their classrooms were located in the Stanley Hasbrouck House, which was later used as the district office. Both retired in 1983. (Courtesy of Betty Taylor.)

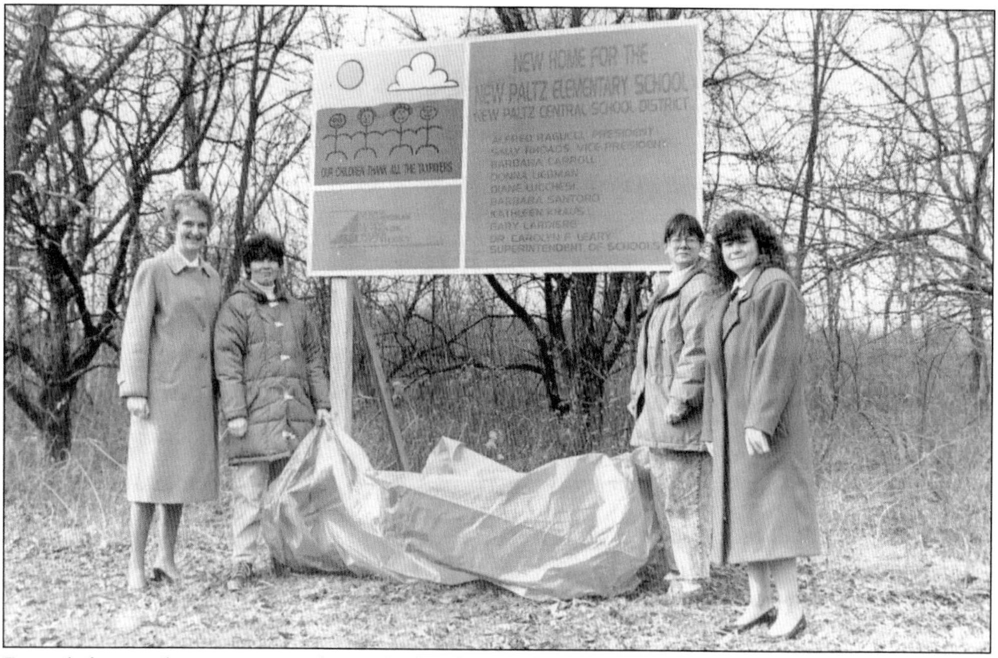

From left to right, superintendent of schools Carolyn Leary and school board members Sally Rhoads, Barbara Carroll, and Kathy Kraus unveil a sign on the site of the future elementary school in January 1990. Barbara Carroll's daughter, Kate, suggested naming the school "Lenape" in honor of the Native Americans who lived in the area when the Huguenots arrived in 1678. Lenape Elementary School opened in September 1992.

Five

Social Life in New Paltz

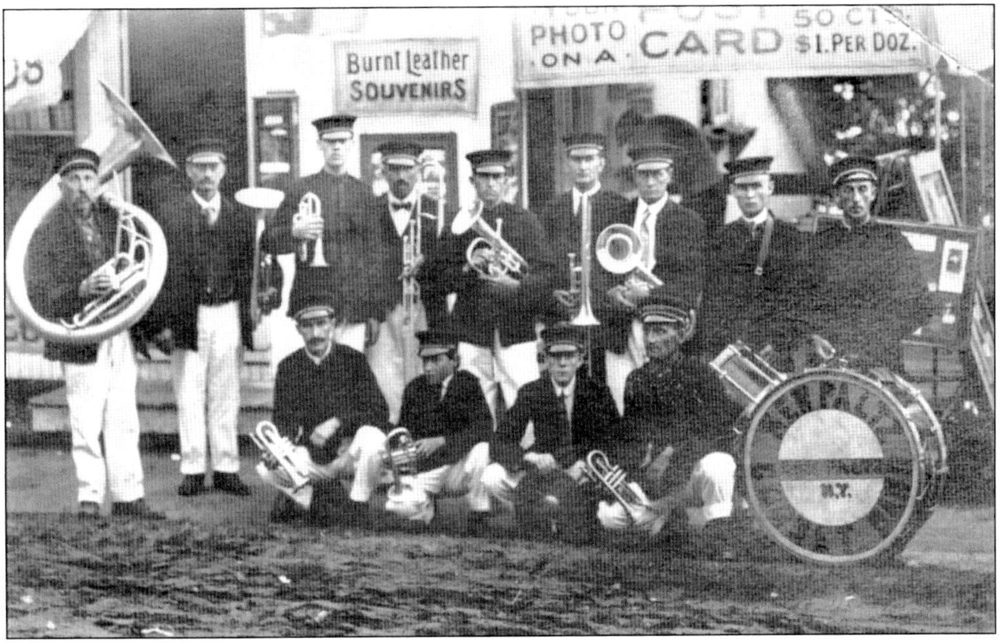

The New Paltz Cornet Band marched in parades, furnished music for the reunions of the Civil War soldiers, gave dances and chicken suppers in the Opera House, and performed in an annual concert. At the February 1914 performance, there were selections by the full band, duets, violin selections by Prof. George Rudolph, and a vocal solo, "Last Night was the End of the World," by George F. Ackert. (Courtesy of Diana Seigman.)

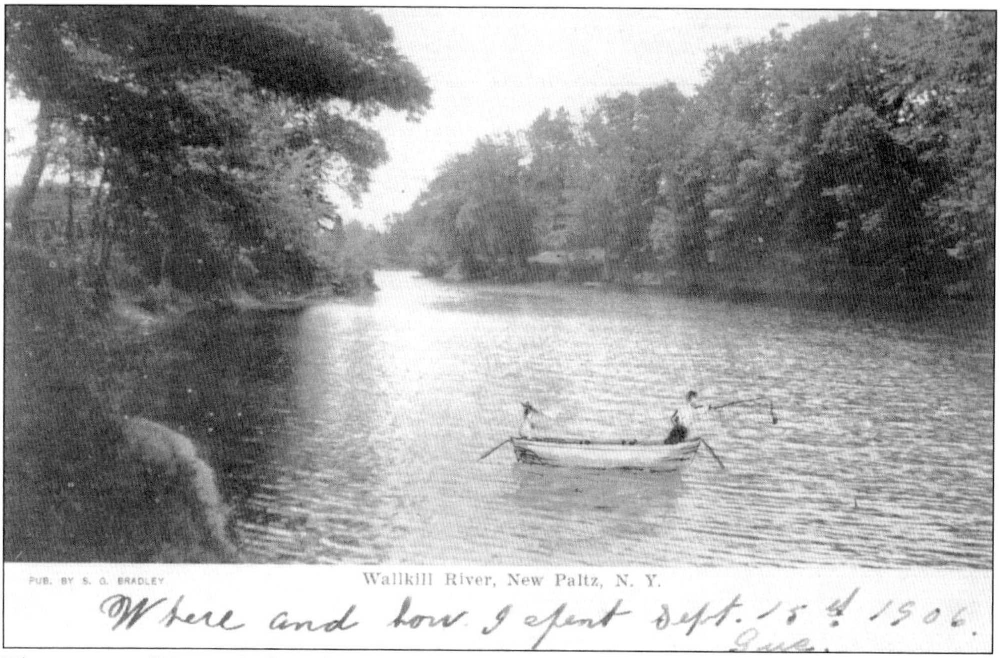

The citizens of New Paltz have boated and fished on the Wallkill River for more than 300 years. It was a great pastime for students at the New Paltz Normal School. On this postcard, "Gus" has drawn a boat with two occupants on the river. He captioned this card, "Where and how I spent Sept. 15th, 1906." (Courtesy of Gordon Kreth.)

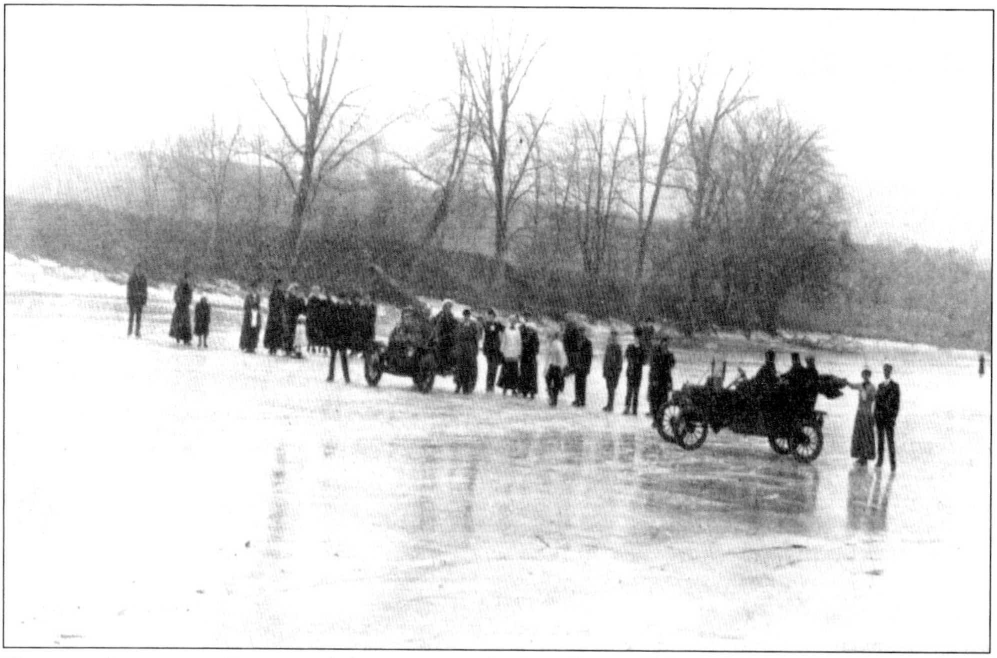

Car races between early automobile owners took place during the winter on the Wallkill River's ice. Skaters would also attach themselves to a car driving on the ice and get towed as far as the Springtown bridge and back again. The car on the left in this photograph was owned by Joseph H. Vanderlyn. George Johnston was the owner of the Ford on the right.

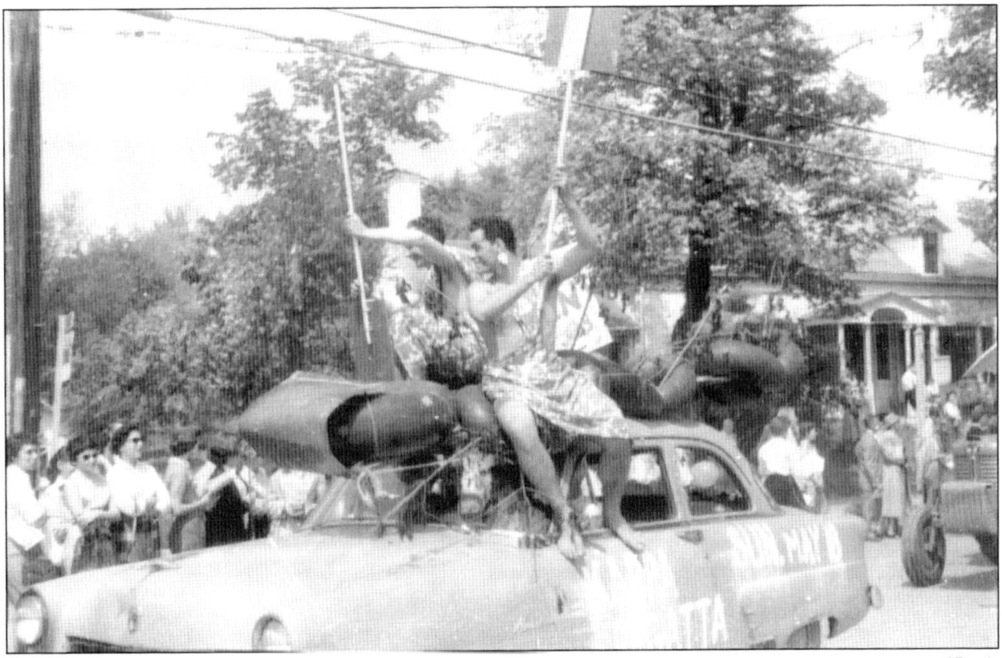

The Delta Kappa Fraternity organized the inaugural Wallkill River Regatta in May 1955. A massive parade down Main Street preceded the spectacle in the water. All of the strange craft to be entered in the race were carried atop automobiles. Bob Pellegrini (left) and Sam Mungo rode atop a car in front of the Elting Memorial Library in 1958. (Courtesy of Louis Mosconi.)

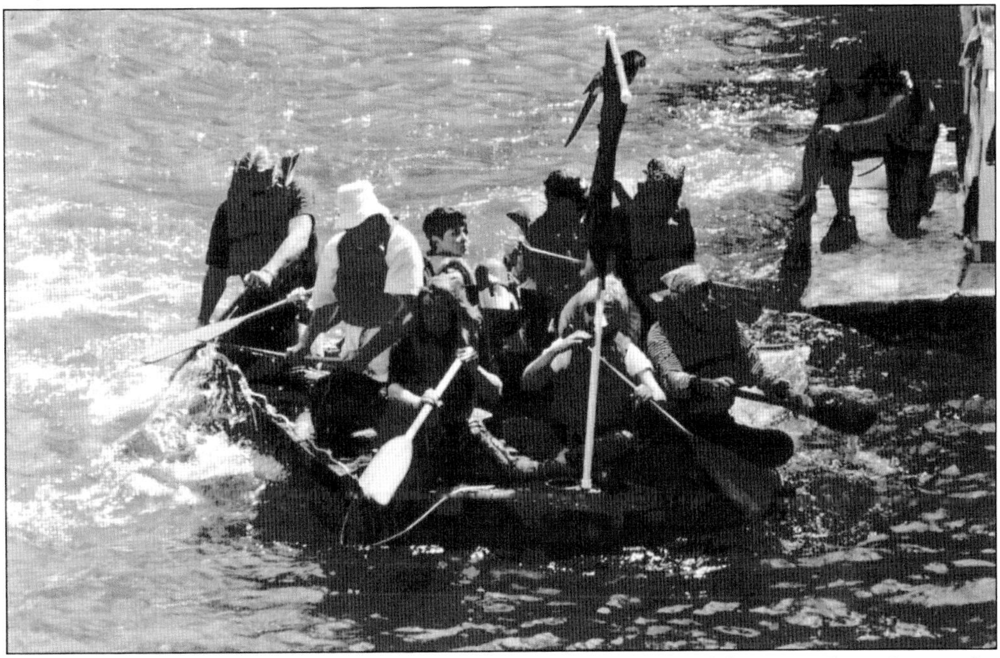

The *Village Victors* craft came close to colliding with the *Spirit of the Sixties* boat during the 2001 Wallkill River Regatta. Sponsored by the town, village, Downtown Business Association, SUNY–New Paltz, and the New Paltz Chamber of Commerce, the regatta also featured kayak and canoe races. (Photograph by John Bennett.)

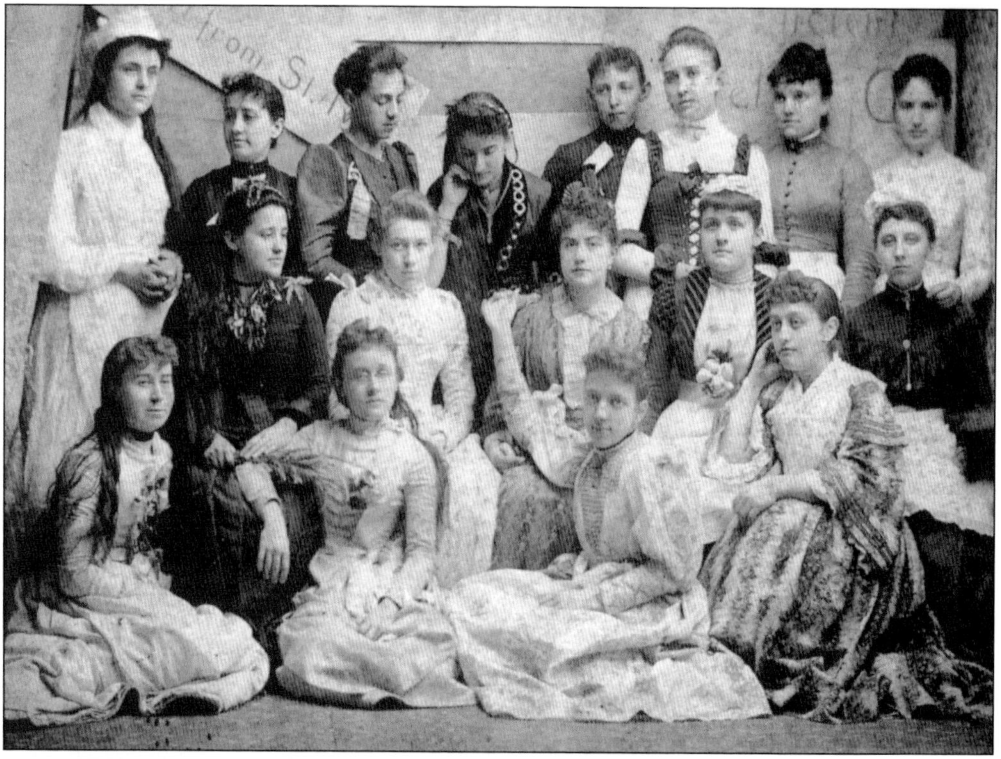

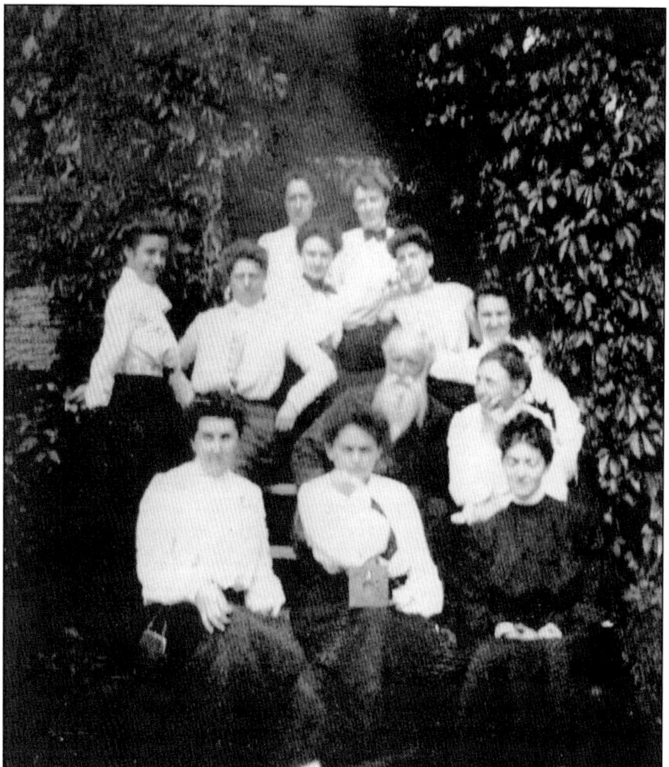

The Ne savez vous? ("Don't you know?") was an early women's club. The women would meet at each other's homes, embroider, discuss current events, and share recipes. They would also stage plays and take day trips to local historical and scenic sites. Helena Smedes, Katy Hasbrouck, Lanetta DuBois, Sara Deyo, Emma LeFevre, Maggie Hayden, Jennie Hasbrouck, and Gertrude Brodhead were some of the members when the above picture was taken in 1900. One day trip they took was to visit John Burroughs (shown at left, center) at his home, Slabsides, in West Park. Burroughs (1937–1921) was a naturalist and writer who was influential in the evolution of the American conservation movement.

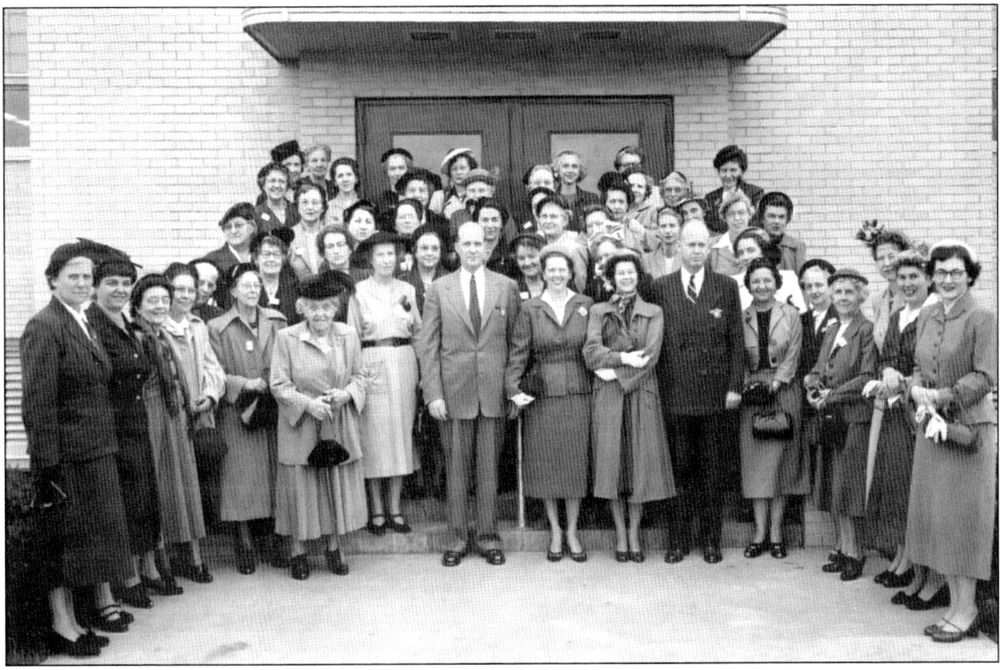

The New Paltz Study Club was founded in 1907 to bring women together to learn more about their world. Club members visited the IBM plant No. 2 in October 1952. A Mr. Wolfe welcomed the group and introduced Paul VanNess, who gave the history of IBM and explained its corporate setup. Guides then showed the study club members the plant, explaining its operations and machinery.

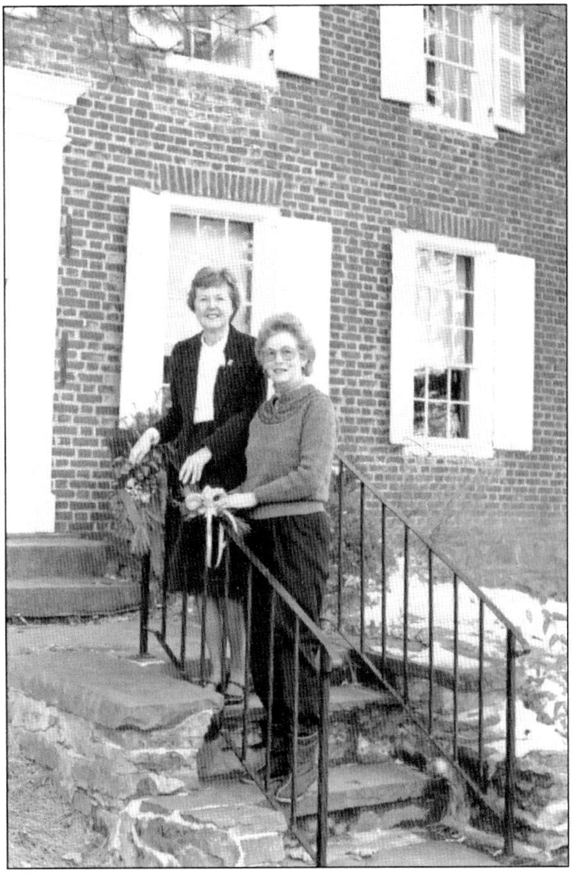

New Paltz Garden Club members Miriam Clough (left) and Irene Martin are shown decorating the entrance to the LeFevre house for a Saint Nicholas Day celebration on Sunday, December 7, 1986. The garden club was initially started by the New Paltz Study Club in 1946. It became a separate organization in 1950 in order to allow both men and women to join. Only women are permitted membership in the New Paltz Study Club.

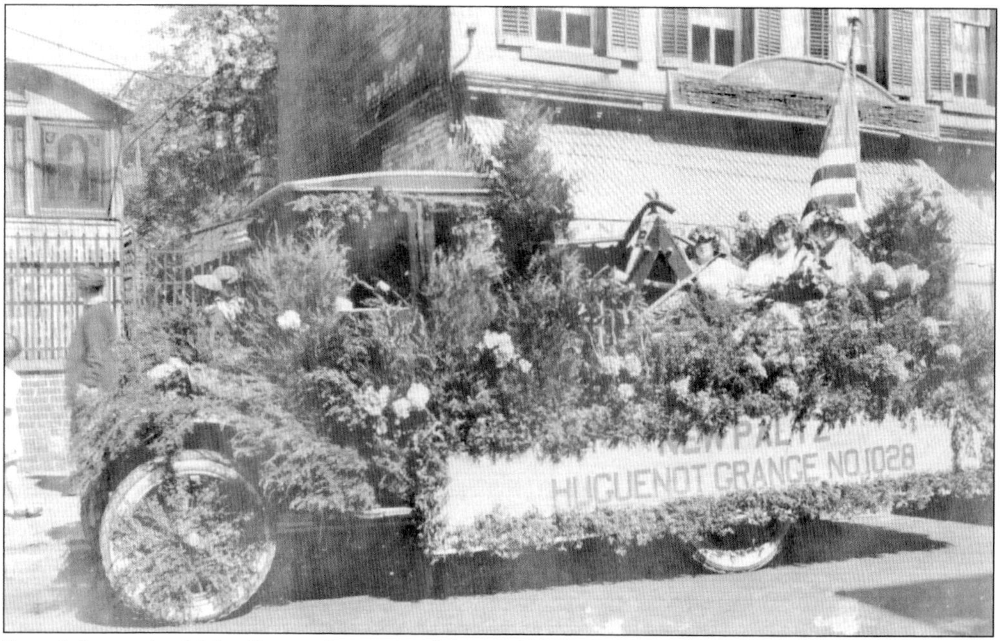

From left to right, Helen Beatty, Lucie Gardner, and Alice DuBois are seen riding on the Huguenot Grange float in an out-of-town parade. Huguenot Grange, No. 1028, Patrons of Husbandry, was organized in New Paltz on January 23, 1905, with 22 charter members. The Grange Hall in New Paltz was located at 10 North Chestnut Street and was torn down in 1968. (Courtesy of Rosalie Nelson.)

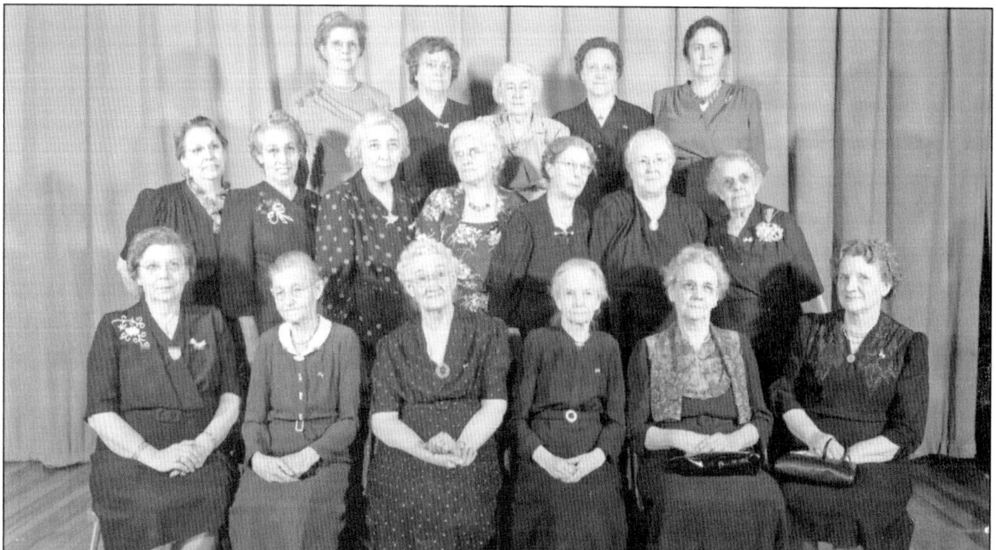

These ladies were some of the members of the Woman's Christian Temperance Union in 1949. Pictured from left to right are (first row) Leola Palmer, Elizabeth Roosa, Ida Stephens, Emma Roosa, Olive Waldron, and Lois Betz; (second row) Ruby VanKeuren, Mabel Ingraham, Mrs. T. Swift, Grace Hasbrouck, Laura Dwight, Eliza VanVliet, and Bertha Metcalf; (third row) Mrs. Albert Wright, Daisy Tighe, Annie Decker, Lola Kniffen, and Mayella Clearwater. (Photograph by George Parker.)

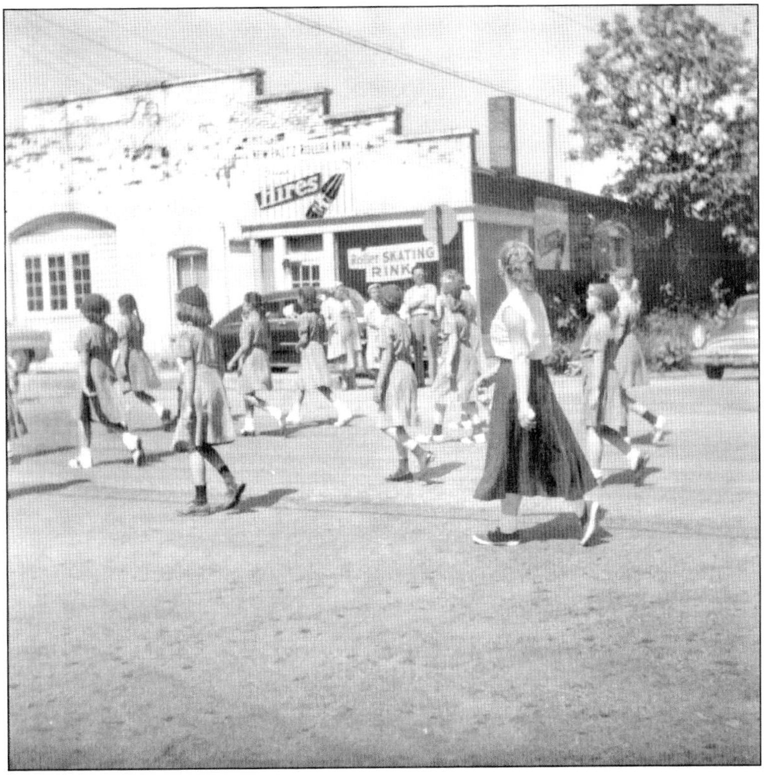

A Girl Scout troop marches past the New Paltz Roller Rink in the 1957 Memorial Day parade. Built as an automobile repair shop by Vernon and Lester DuBois in 1916, this building has housed various tenants. Since 1916 it has been a garage, a ladies underwear factory, a roller rink, an office building, a disco, a candle factory, an antique shop, and a carpet store, among other commercial enterprises. (Courtesy of Dede Smith.)

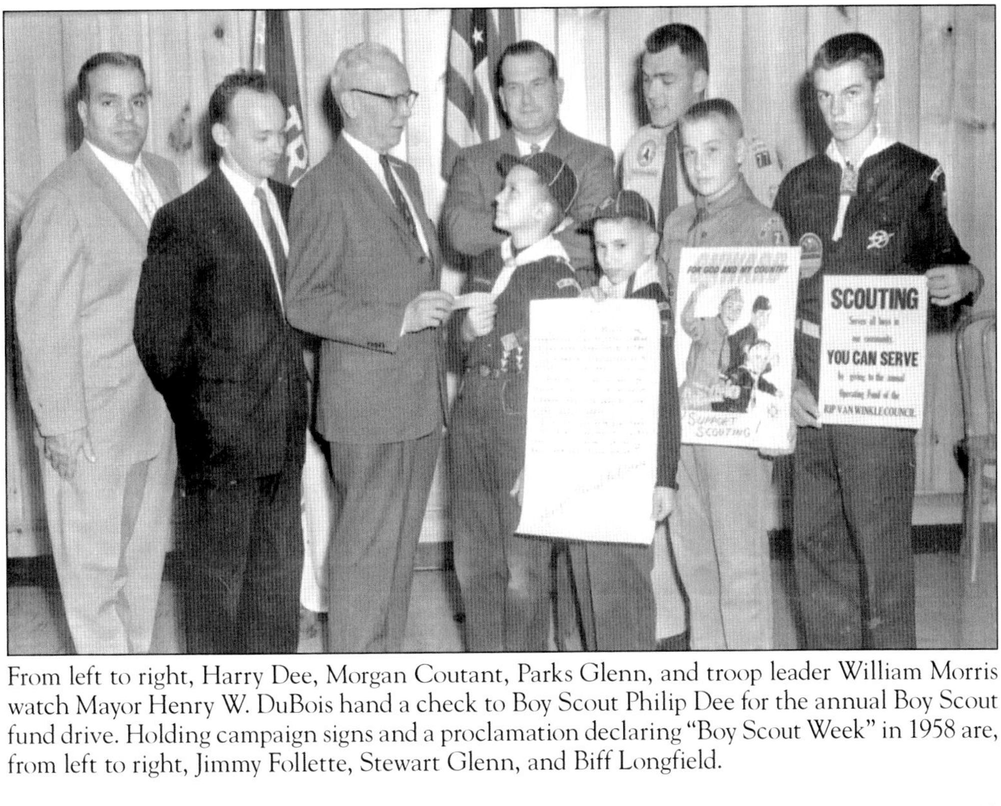

From left to right, Harry Dee, Morgan Coutant, Parks Glenn, and troop leader William Morris watch Mayor Henry W. DuBois hand a check to Boy Scout Philip Dee for the annual Boy Scout fund drive. Holding campaign signs and a proclamation declaring "Boy Scout Week" in 1958 are, from left to right, Jimmy Follette, Stewart Glenn, and Biff Longfield.

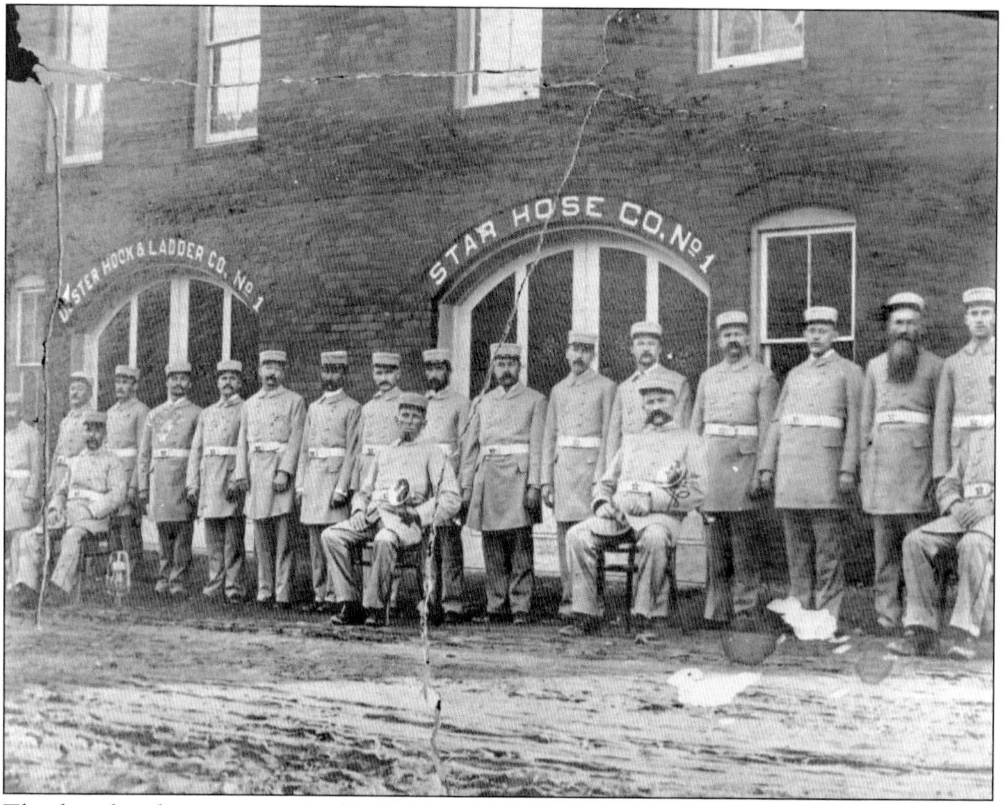

The first fire department was the Huguenot Engine Company No. 1, founded in 1861 and discontinued in 1868. The Ulster Hook and Ladder Company No. 1 organized as a bucket company in 1889. When the waterworks were completed in 1892, the Star Hose Company was formed. These two companies merged in 1918 to form the New Paltz Fire Department.

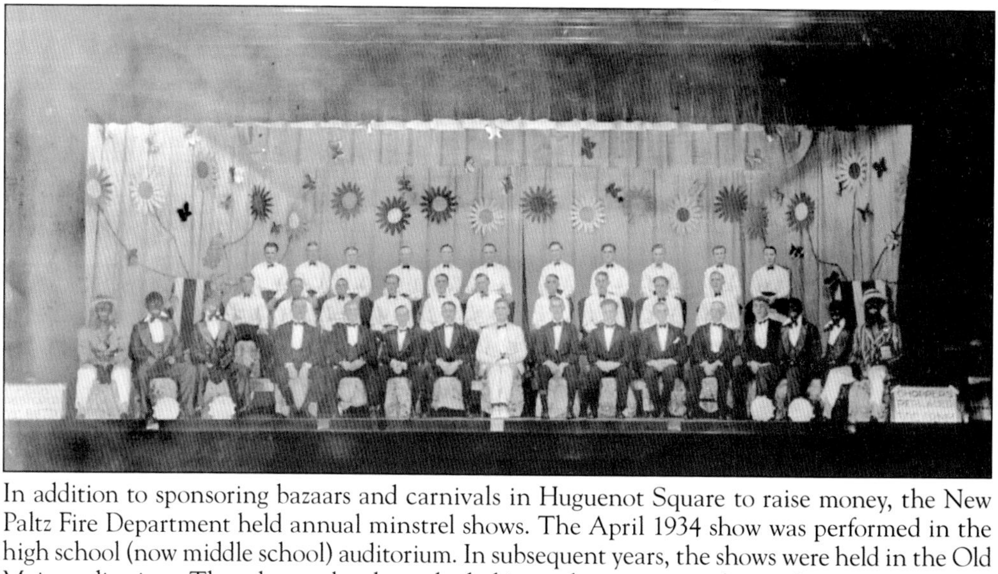

In addition to sponsoring bazaars and carnivals in Huguenot Square to raise money, the New Paltz Fire Department held annual minstrel shows. The April 1934 show was performed in the high school (now middle school) auditorium. In subsequent years, the shows were held in the Old Main auditorium. Though popular then, the habits and viewpoints of an earlier generation can be troubling, embarrassing, and offensive in modern times.

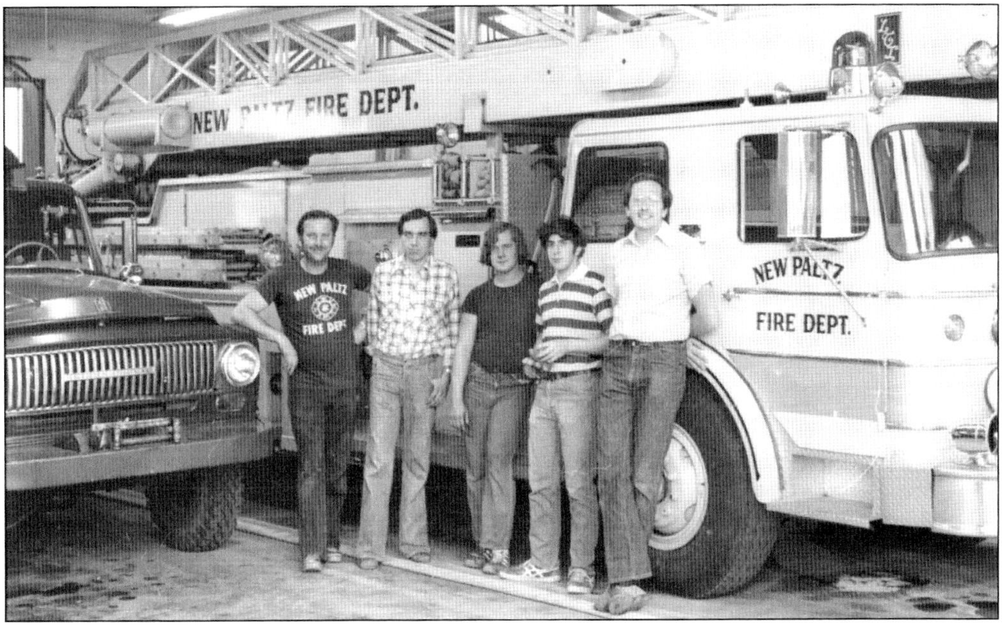

From left to right, firemen Robert Dammier, William DuBois, Richard Natoli, Michael Benenati, and Dennis O'Keefe are standing beside the New Paltz Fire Department's yellow ladder truck in May 1978. For several years, the New Paltz Fire Department had yellow fire trucks. Neighboring Tillson Fire Department had a green fire truck that would participate in the annual St. Patrick's Day parade. (Photograph by Bob Fagan.)

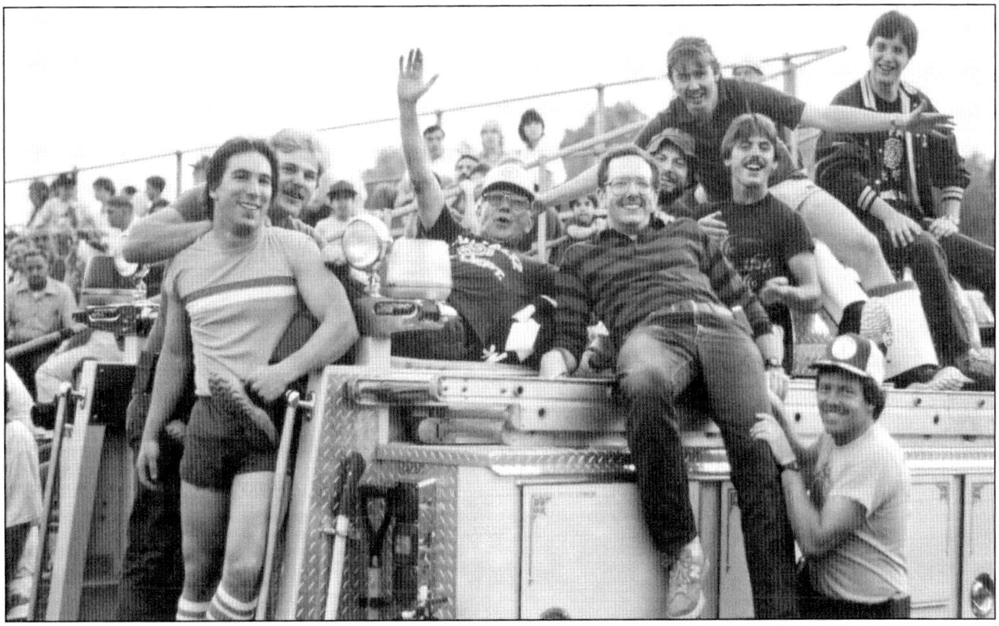

For many years fireworks were held around the Fourth of July on the back fields of the SUNY–New Paltz campus. The fire department was always standing by in case one of the fireworks went astray. From left to right, firemen Dan Ale, Rick Drosdowich, Bob Clark, Dennis O'Keefe, Bob Krajicek, Scott Woebse, Ed Grainger, Garry Kniffen, and Greg Burton are shown enjoying the festivities on July 5, 1985.

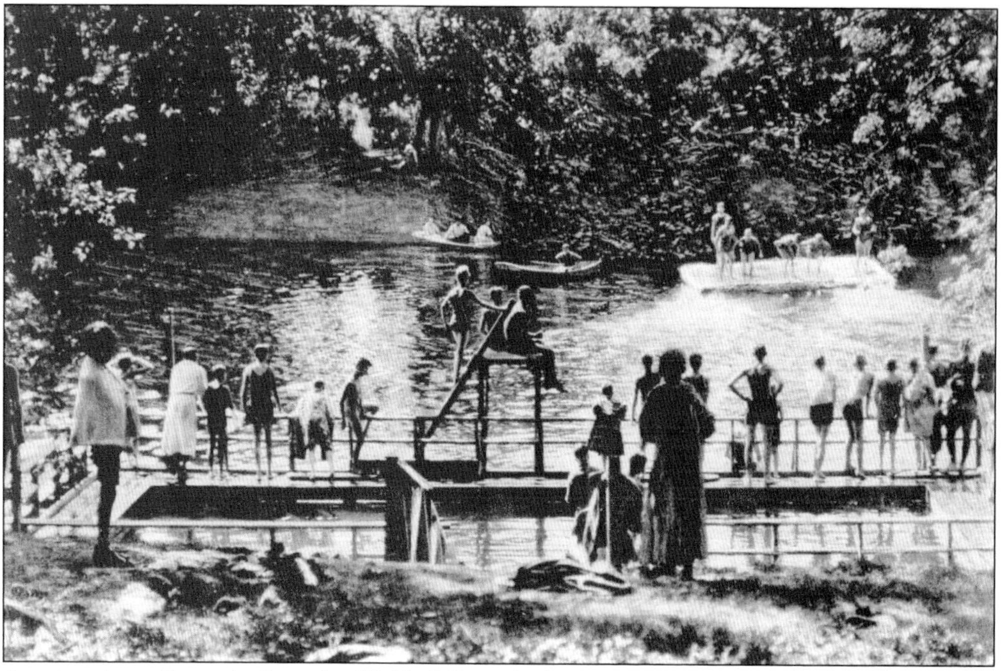

A swimming crib was built in the Wallkill River for beginner swimmers at Camp Wallkill. This boys' camp was located about 3 miles north of New Paltz from 1922 to 1925. The facility included a diving tower and springboards built for diving into the river. The camp's water sports program also included water polo, canoeing, and fishing. Camp Wallkill was bought by St. Agnes Church of New York City in 1925, and the name was changed to Camp St. Agnes. More than 100 boys from New York City attended the summer camp. The Catholic Diocese of New York later changed the name to Camp Dineen.

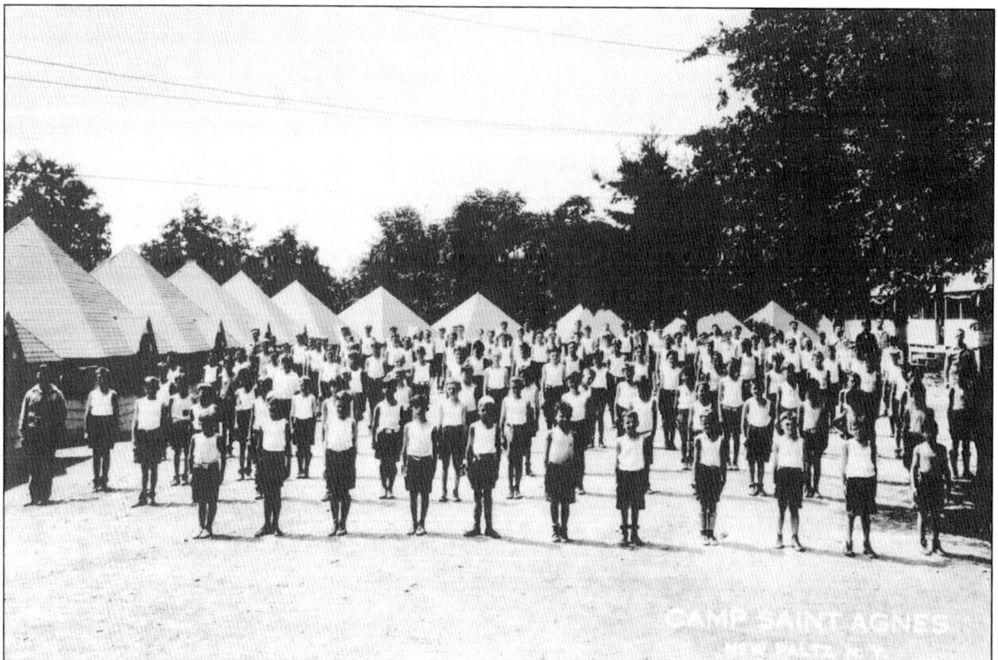

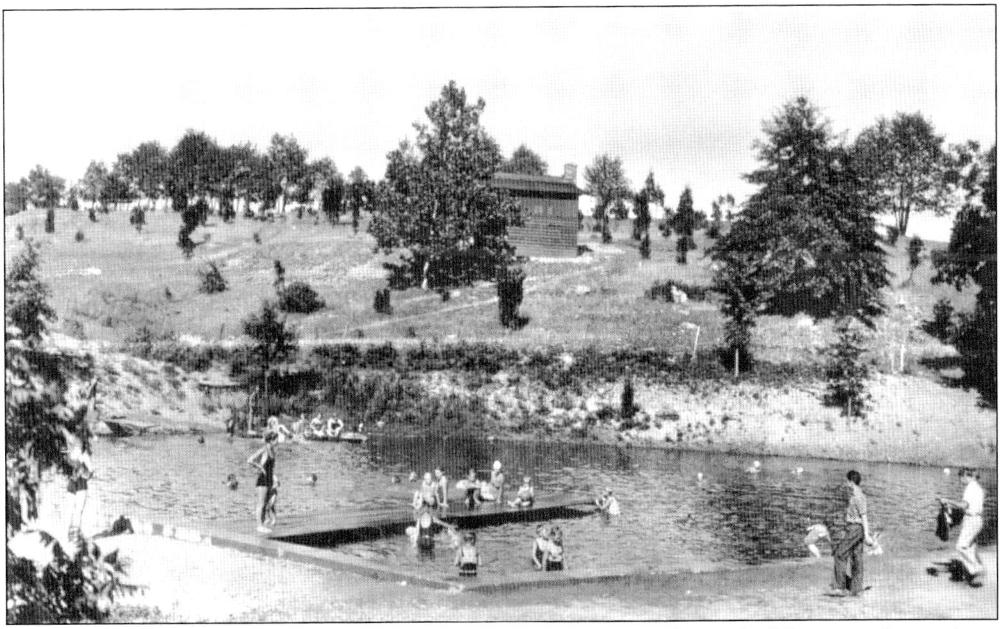

Dan Shaw owned the historic William E. DuBois property at the end of Prospect Street from 1932 to 1933. During that year, he built a swimming pool by damming the Mill Brook. Josef and Julia Bruckmayer bought the 88-acre Millbrook Farm and developed it into a bustling summer resort.

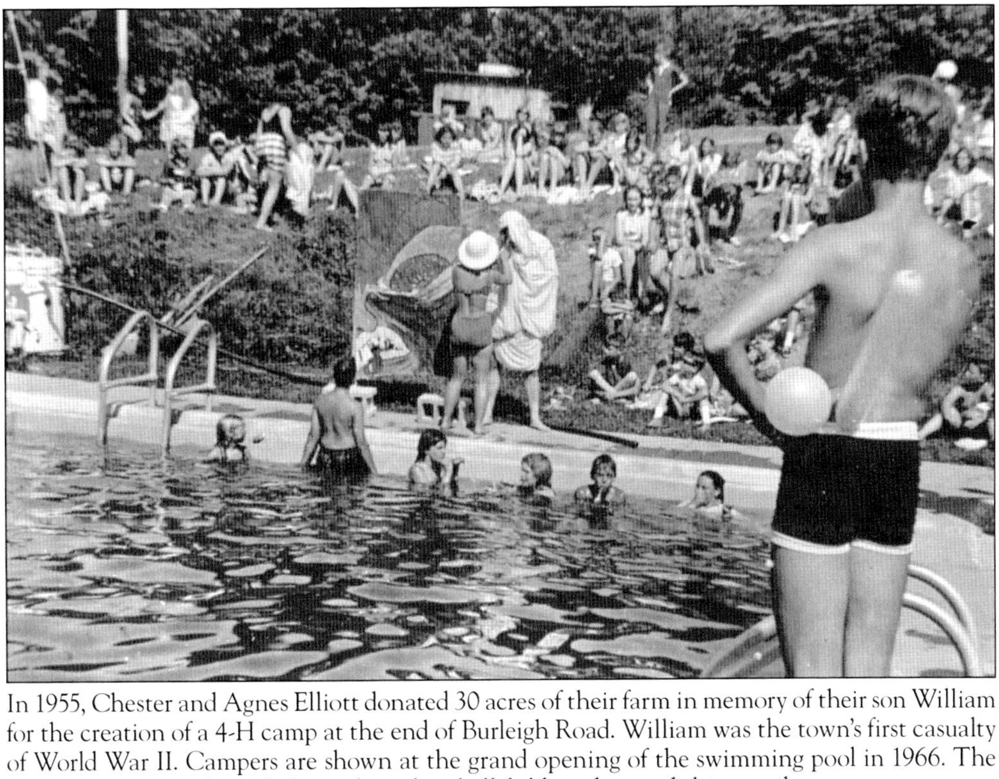

In 1955, Chester and Agnes Elliott donated 30 acres of their farm in memory of their son William for the creation of a 4-H camp at the end of Burleigh Road. William was the town's first casualty of World War II. Campers are shown at the grand opening of the swimming pool in 1966. The camp also consisted of a lodge, cabins, baseball field, and many hiking trails.

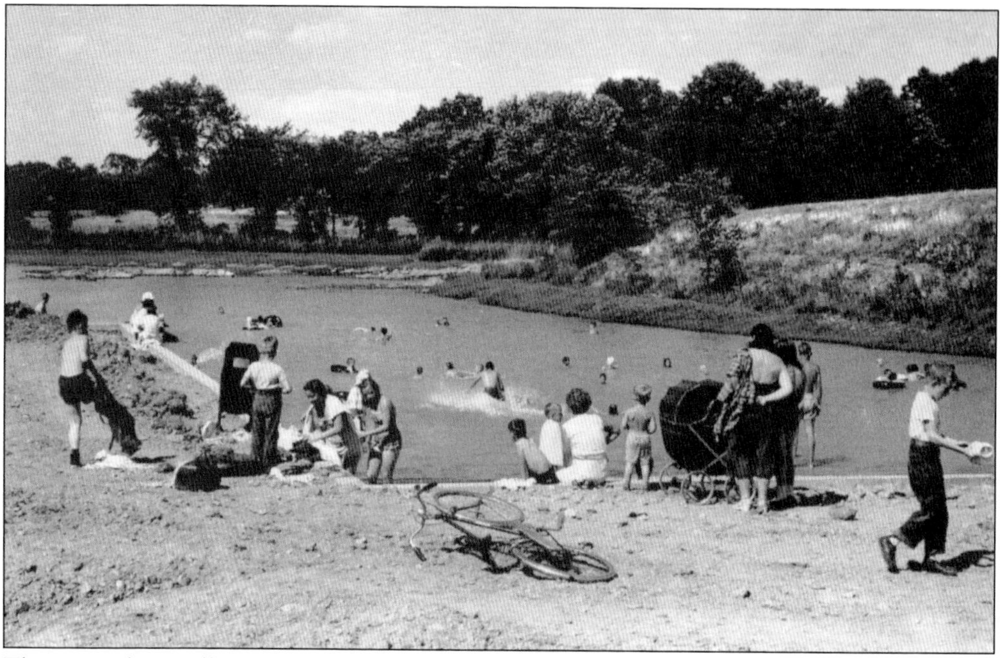

The original Moriello Pool officially opened on July 4, 1956. The pool was only three-sided, with the deep end open to the site's 3-acre pond. The park was named for local fruit farmer Michael Moriello, who had been killed when his airplane crashed on the Frank LoCicero farm in April 1955. Owned and operated by the New Paltz Park and Recreation Association, the pool was enclosed three years later, and a filtration system was added to clear the sediment and purify water. In winters past, Patentee's Pond was harvested for ice, and an icehouse was located near it to supply ice to the creamery. A gristmill was built on the site by patentee Abraham Hasbrouck or his son Daniel, making it the first manufacturing industry established in Ulster County.

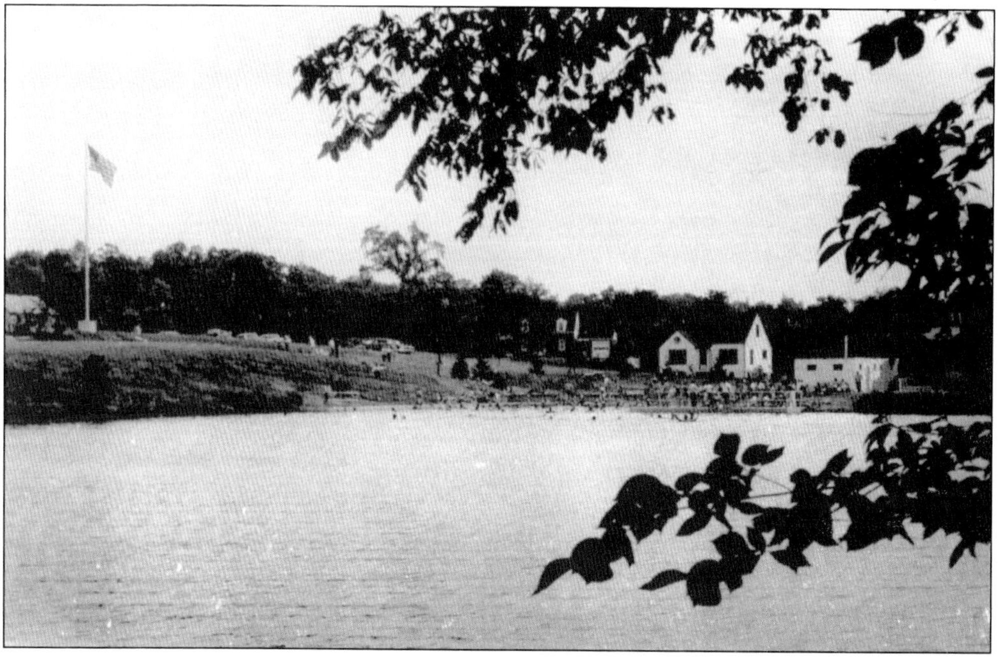

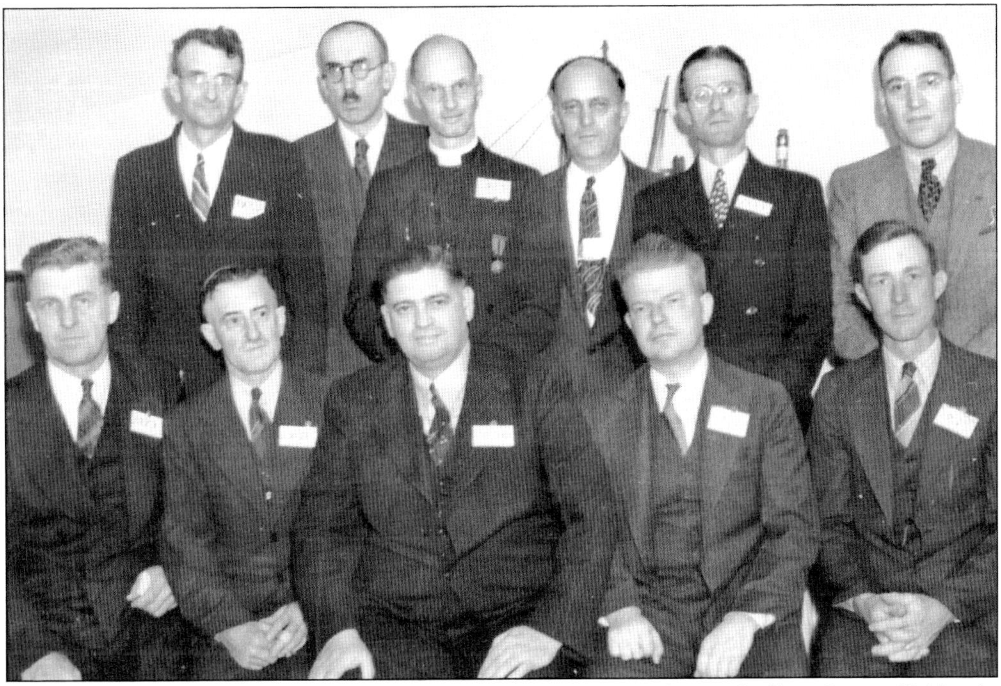

Adjacent to Moriello Park, the American Legion built a new legion hall on Route 32 North. The legion hall was bought by the Town of New Paltz in 1974, and it is now the town hall. Early commanders of the American Legion were, from left to right (first row) Albert Koch, Charles Parker, Edward Curtis, Peter Harp, and Raymond Miller; (second row) Elting Clearwater, Louis LeFevre, Rev. Frank Wilson, Louis Vandermark, Harold Miller, and John Thomas.

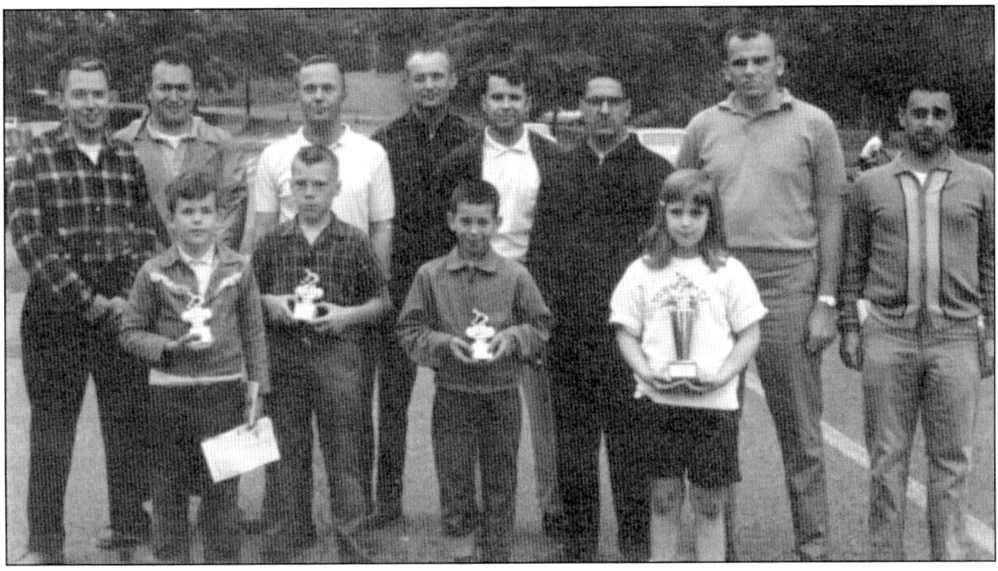

Winners of the Jaycee Bike Rodeo in 1964 were, from left to right, (first row) Bruce Hathaway, David Cassano, Bobby Ashton, and Judy Carter; (second row) Jaycees members Gordon Connally, Peter Bronson, Phil Carter, Hal Powell, Herb Peterson, Tom Benenati, Dick Schleiter, and Bob Doucette. The Jaycees also sponsored the annual Easter egg hunt, Special Olympics, Snowmobile Field Day, and a ski meet at the Bonticou Ski Hill.

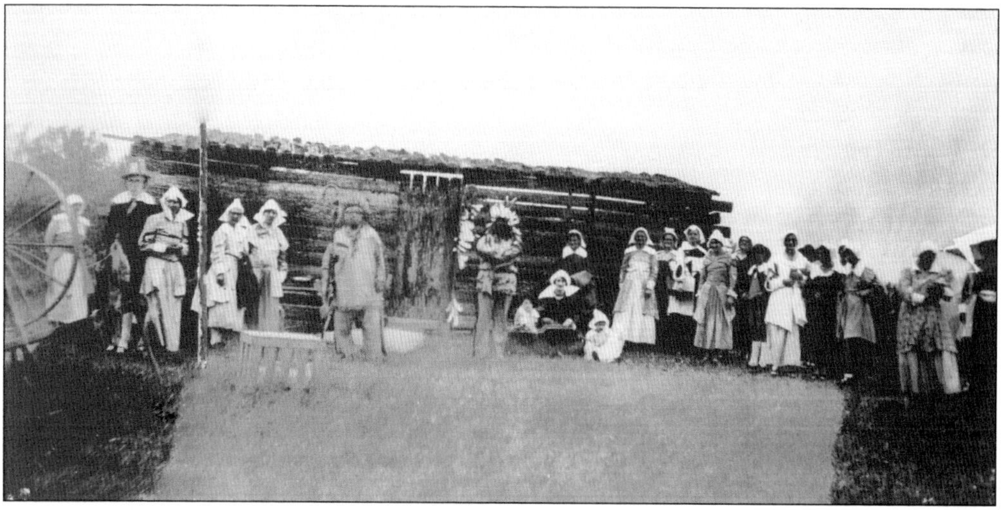

As a part of the Huguenot-Walloon Tercentennial, a historical pageant depicting the events leading up to the settling of New Paltz was performed on the lowlands to the west of the Reformed church on June 3, 1924. More than 6,000 people attended the performance, including the French ambassador, the prime minister of Belgium, and Burgomaster Adolphe Max of Brussels. More than 400 people were in the cast of characters, and the chorus of 150 voices was accompanied by Scofield's 21st Regiment Band. Pictured from left to right below performing the "Dance of the Iris" during the 1924 pageant are (first row) Donald DeWitt, Leroy Juckett, and Forrest Hasbrouck dressed as bees; (second row) Margaret Dunham, Ethel Hart, and Margaret Wicks dressed as butterflies.

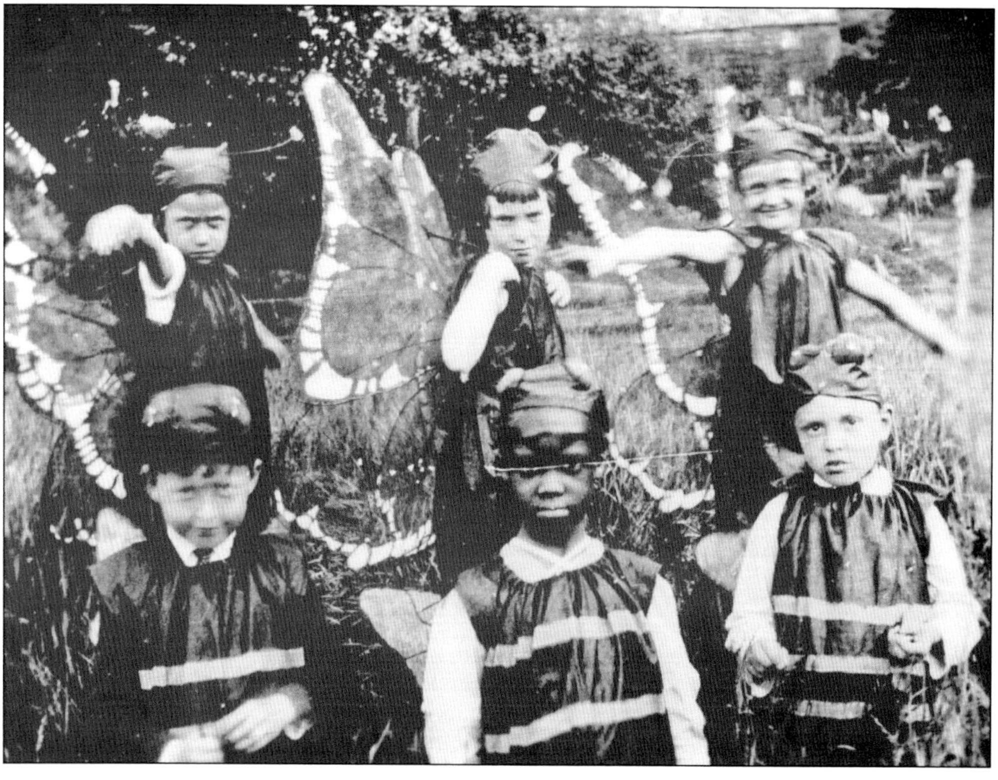

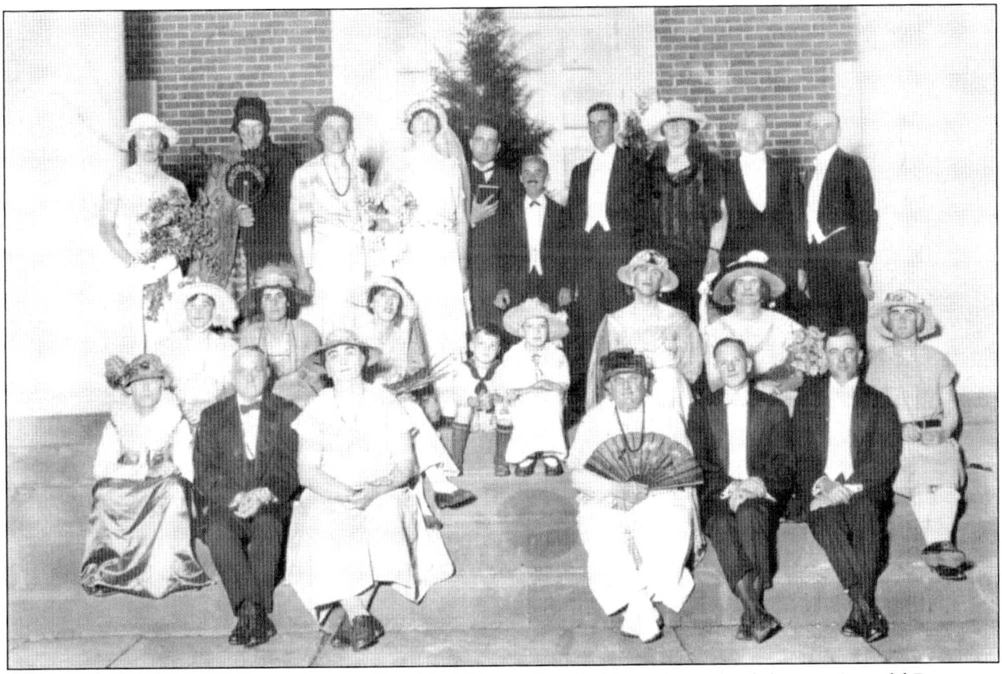

Sponsored by the Dutch Guild in 1924, *The Womanless Bride* had a colorful cast. Arnold Petersen portrayed the bride, I. Gottam Atlas, and S. Gardner portrayed the groom, Mr. E. Z. Mark. Other characters were the maid of honor, Miss Hope Imnex, played by Raymond Jenkins; the best man, I. M. Freer, played by Solomon VanOrden; the minister, Fuller Prunz, played by Joe LeFevre; and bridesmaids Narry A. Chance and U. R. Faded, portrayed by Kenneth Snyder and Fred Coulter.

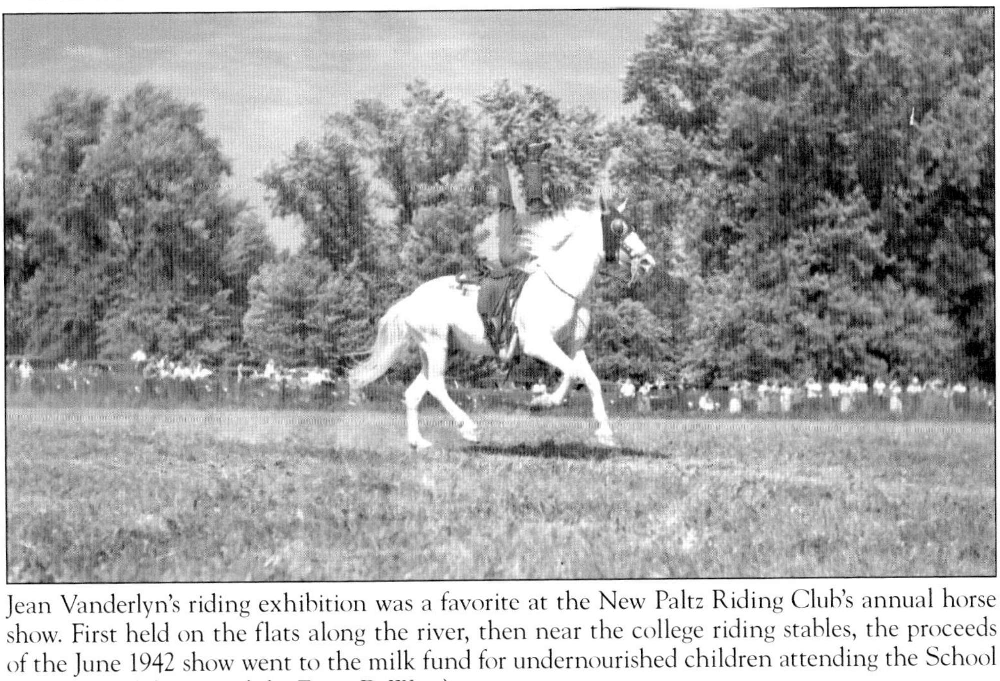

Jean Vanderlyn's riding exhibition was a favorite at the New Paltz Riding Club's annual horse show. First held on the flats along the river, then near the college riding stables, the proceeds of the June 1942 show went to the milk fund for undernourished children attending the School of Practice. (Photograph by Erma DeWitt.)

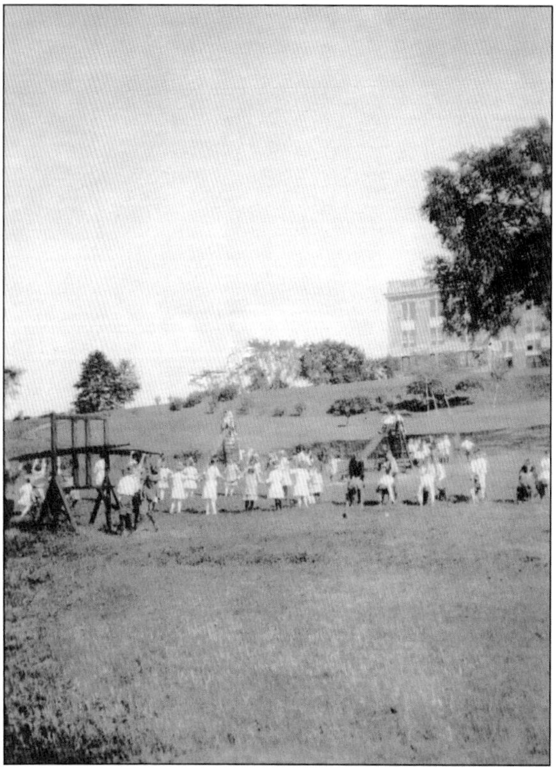

Jean Hasbrouck Memorial Park was a gift to the community in 1923 from Laura Hasbrouck Varick. During the Depression, the park could not be maintained by the village, and it was leased to the State of New York. The state used it as playground for the young children at the Campus School until the school closed in 1981. The park was rededicated by the village during its centennial celebration in 1987.

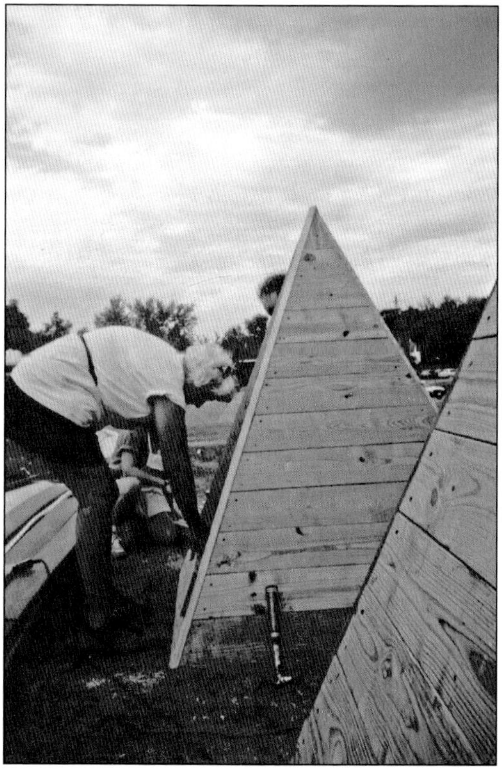

Hasbrouck Park was enhanced by the building of a community playground in 1995. Spearheaded by Mary Strothenke and Patti Wilcek, the playground was built by volunteer labor and more than $75,000 in donations. Volunteer Carol Roper is shown assembling one of the turrets during the construction of the new playground. (Photograph by Fawn Tantillo.)

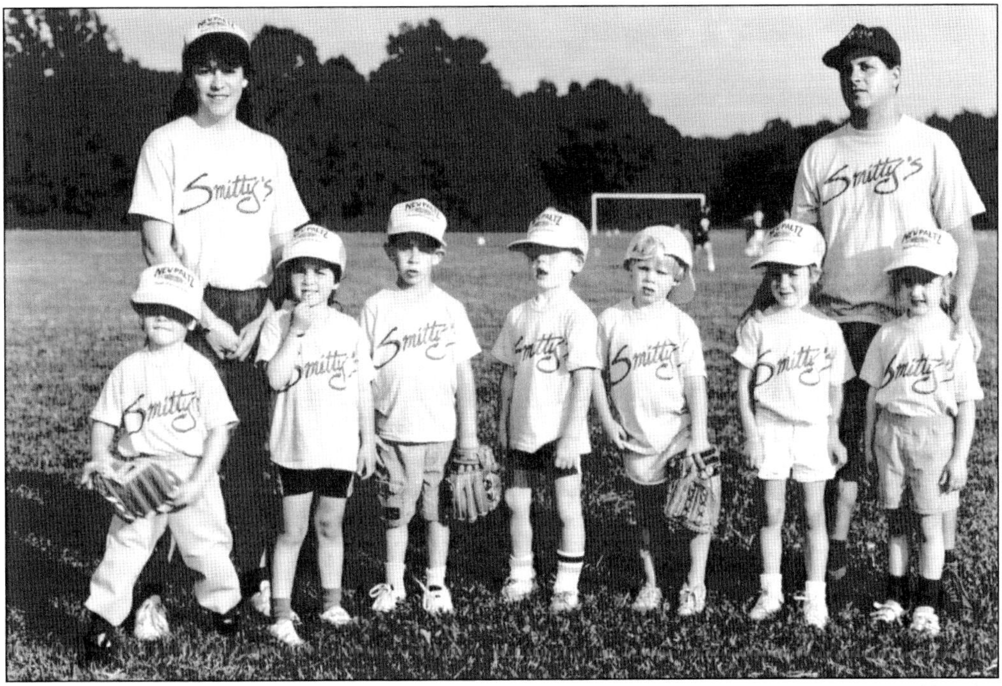

Home of the New Paltz Little League for many years, the baseball field was constructed by the Works Projects Administration in 1936. The Little League began in 1952 with four teams. The first champions were the Giants, coached by Warren McDowell. At the end of the season, all players, managers, coaches, umpires, and scorekeepers were treated by the league to a game at the Polo Grounds to watch the New York Giants play the Philadelphia Phillies. The New Paltz Baseball Association has grown to include girls' and boys' teams from ages 5 to 15, all-star teams, and travel teams. Pictured on the field are a pee wee league team (above), and a girls' Little League team (below). (Above, courtesy of Kip Ruger; below, courtesy of the Powers family.)

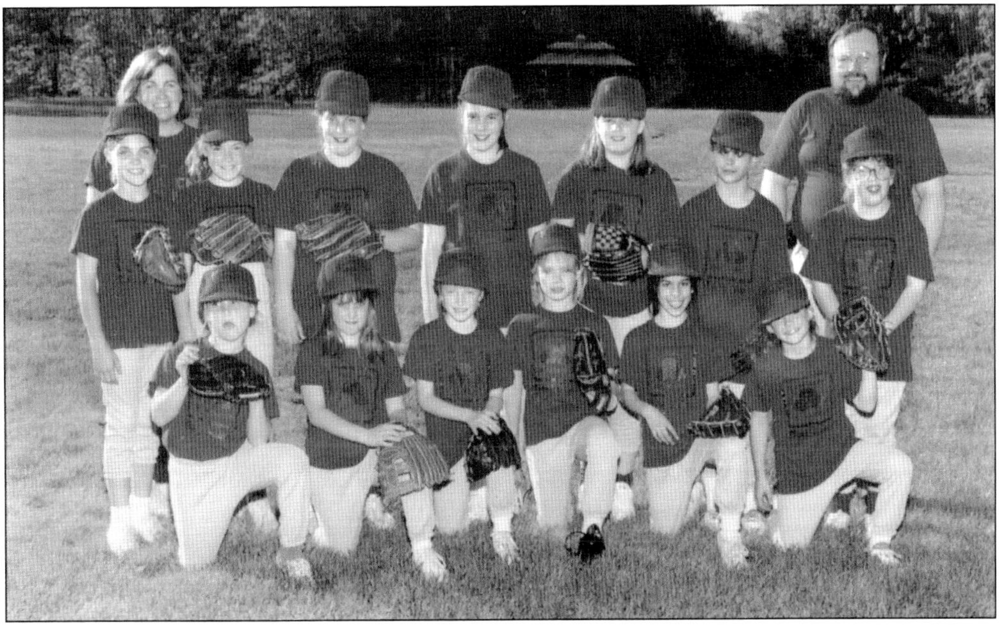

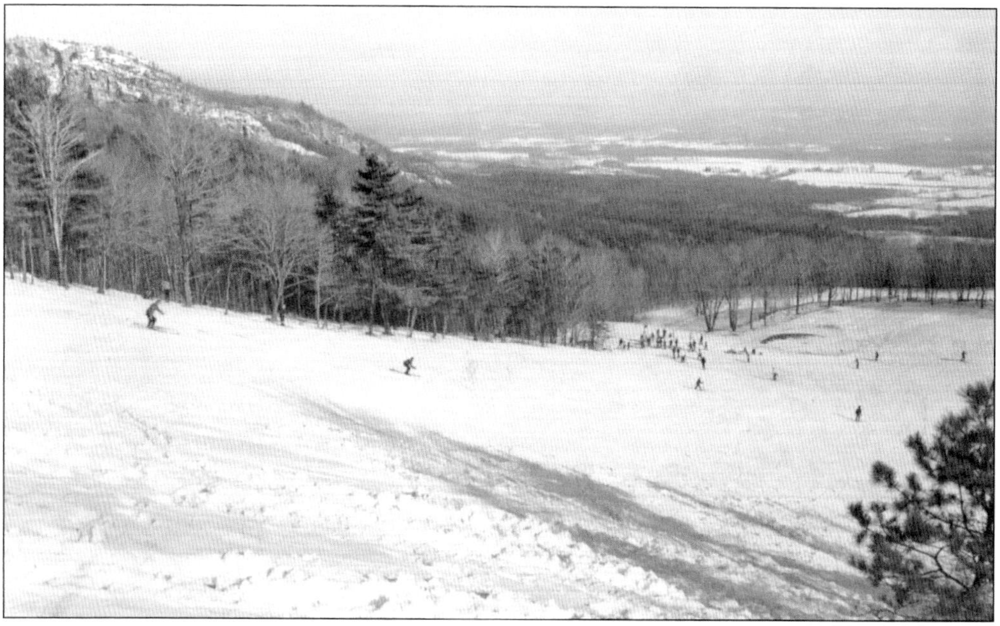

Skiers enjoyed the Bonticou Ski Hill for several years. This photograph shows Bonticou Crag to the left and the Wallkill Valley to the right. The citizens of the town of New Paltz hired Aaron Burr as their attorney and won a lawsuit against the Town of Marbletown over disputed lands around the crag after the Revolutionary War. (Photograph by Leo Spies.)

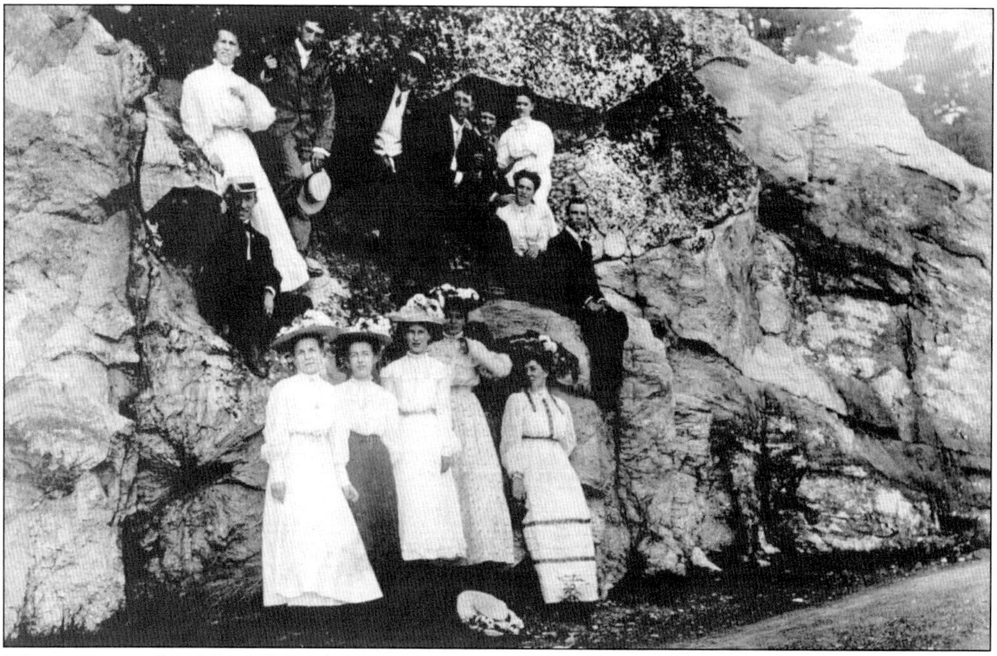

The scenic trails of the Mohonk Mountain House and Mohonk Preserve have attracted hikers and climbers for generations. The preserve has more than 100 miles of carriage roads and trails for hiking, running, mountain biking, horseback riding, and cross-country skiing. After using the old Bonticou ski lodge as a visitor center, the Mohonk Preserve opened a new visitor center in the town of Gardiner in 1998.

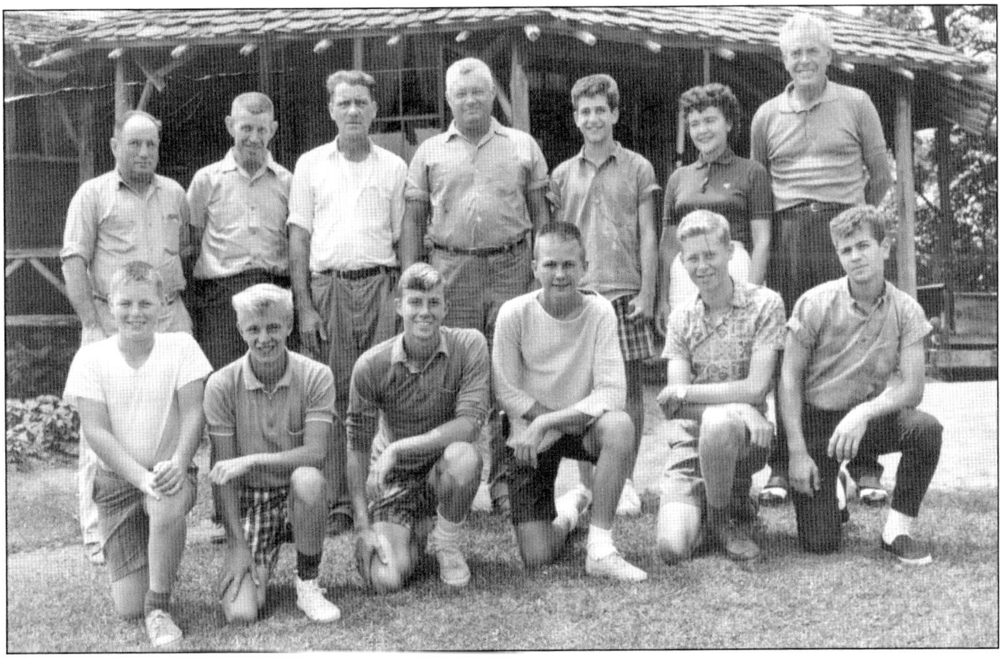

The Mohonk Golf Course, located on Mountain Rest Road, was laid out in 1898. Stages were run regularly from the Mountain House to the golf course. Caddying for hotel guests was a great summer job for many local boys. Here are the caddies and staff of the golf shop from the summer of 1960. (Courtesy of Jeff Ackert.)

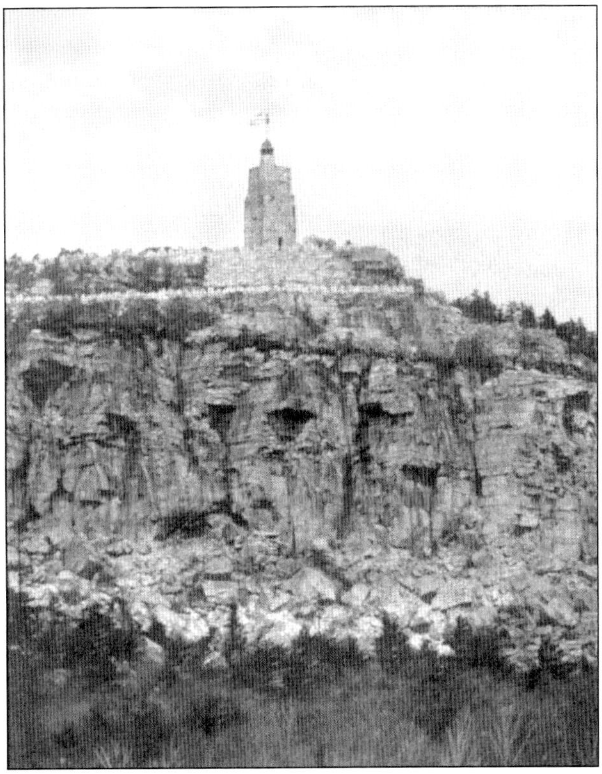

Hikers head for Sky Top Tower and climb to the 60-foot-high observation platform. A New Paltz landmark, the tower was built as a memorial to Albert Smiley in 1923. Constructed using stone from a quarry near its base, that quarry is now used as a reservoir for the Mountain House. For many years, the cupola was manned by a ranger watching for forest fires. (Courtesy of Vivian Wadlin.)

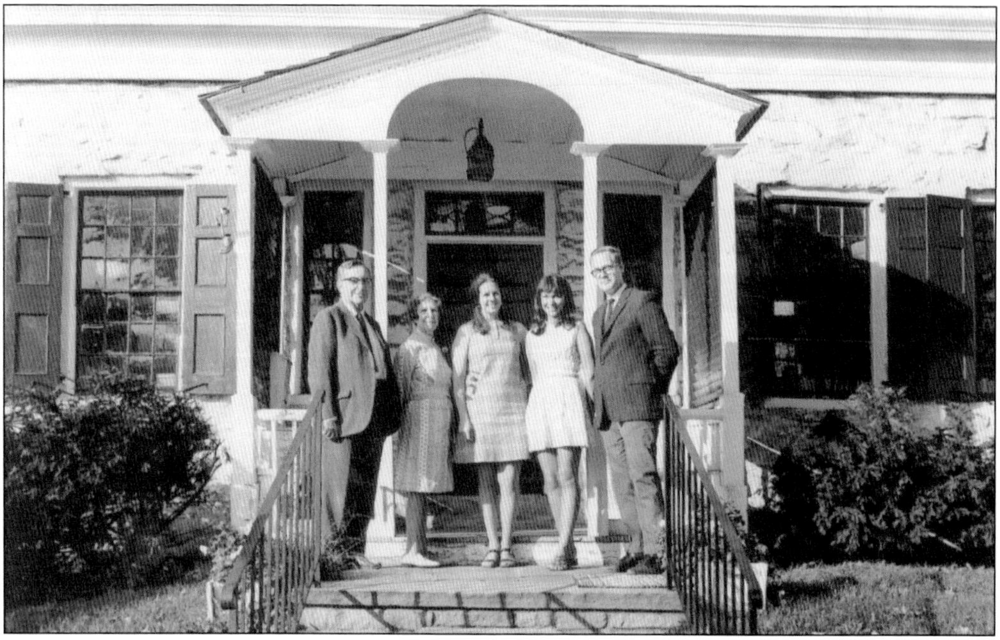

Former board and staff members of the Elting Memorial Library are standing in front of the old Solomon Elting homestead at 93 Main Street. Purchased by Philip LeFevre Elting in 1920 to house the New Paltz Free Library, the name of the library was changed to the Elting Memorial Library at his request. Founded in 1909, the library celebrated its centennial in 2009.

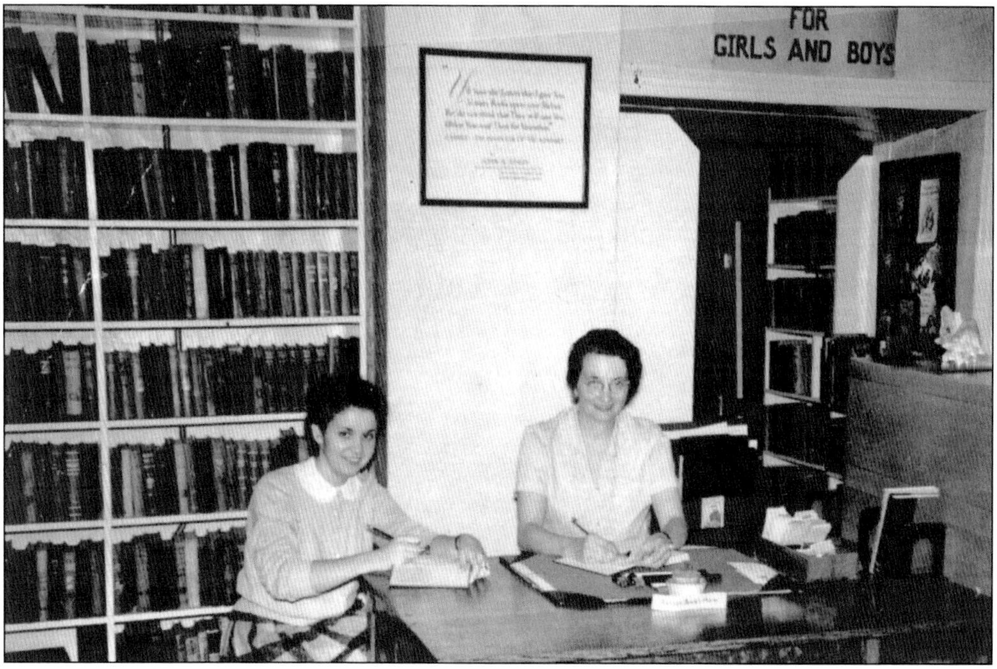

Initially only the two rooms on the west side of the building were used for the library, but shelves were added to the center hall and east room a few years later. The Fireplace Room was refurnished in 1949 and was used as a children's room. For many years a sign over its entry read, "For girls and boys." Pictured are Eleanor Collins (left) and Janet Bracken at work in the library in 1961.

With only one letter of appeal to the New Paltz community, some newspaper publicity, and a few personal contacts, more than $25,000 was raised by the building committee of the library to construct a new youth center in 1962. A 46-by-19-foot wing was added to the original stone building. The youth center at the Elting Memorial Library was formally dedicated on July 7, 1962, during the annual library fair. (Photograph by A. E. Woolley.)

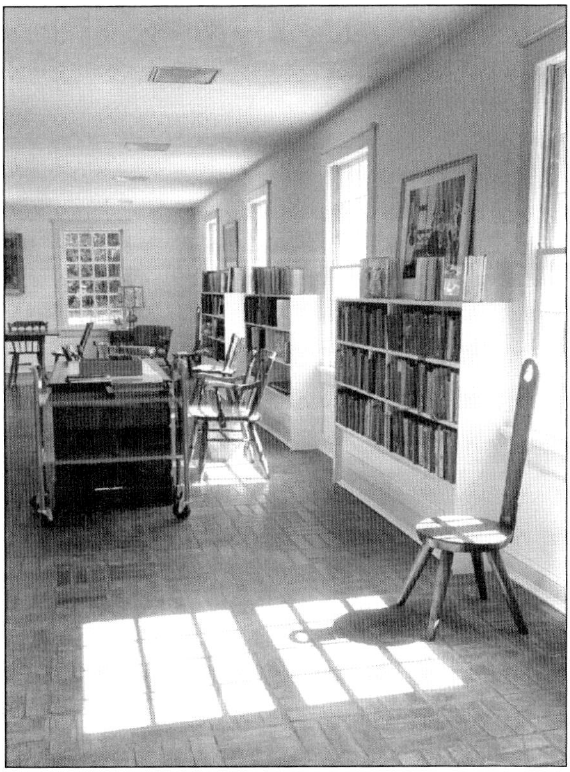

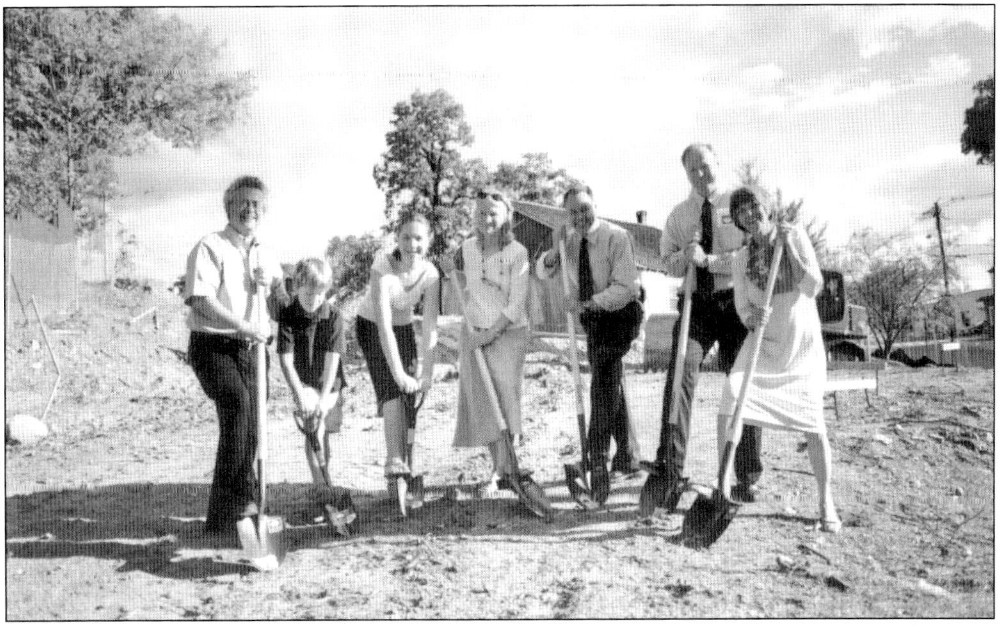

A groundbreaking ceremony was held for the more recent addition to the Elting Memorial Library on September 18, 2005. Participating in the ceremony were, from left to right, Town Supervisor Don Wilen, John Garvin, Kelsey Logan, Mary Ottaway, library director John Giralico, Jeff Wood, and library board president Sally Rhoads. The renovated library, with its 4,500 square-foot addition, opened in August 2006. (Photograph by Ron Turner.)

Consistent with our mission to preserve history on a local level, this book was printed in South Carolina on American-made paper and manufactured entirely in the United States. Products carrying the accredited Forest Stewardship Council (FSC) label are printed on 100 percent FSC-certified paper.